Armstrong's Handbook of Reward Management Practice

Also available by Michael Armstrong

FIFTH EDITION

Armstrong's Handbook of Reward Management Practice

An evidence-based guide to improving performance through reward

Michael Armstrong

KoganPage

LONDON PHILADELPHIA NEW DELHI

First published in 2005 as *A Handbook of Employee Reward Management Practice* by Kogan Page
  Limited
Second edition, 2007
Third edition published in 2010 as *Armstrong's Handbook of Reward Management Practice*
Fourth edition, 2012
Fifth edition, 2015

2nd Floor, 45 Gee Street	1518 Walnut Street, Suite 1100	4737/23 Ansari Road
London EC1V 3RS	Philadelphia PA 19102	Daryaganj
United Kingdom	USA	New Delhi 110002
www.koganpage.com		India

© Michael Armstrong, 2005, 2007, 2010, 2012, 2015

ISBN   978 0 7494 7389 1
E-ISBN   978 0 7494 7390 7

British Library Cataloguing-in-Publication Data

A CIP record for this book is available from the British Library.

Library of Congress Control Number

2015024582

Typeset by Graphicraft Limited, Hong Kong
Printed and bound in India by Replika Press Pvt Ltd

CONTENTS

PART THREE Rewarding and recognizing performance
and merit   205

17   Merit pay   207

18   Bonus schemes   223

19   Team pay   233

Introduction

This handbook provides guidance on how to use reward processes to improve organizational, team and individual performance while catering for the needs of employees. Reward is defined as the recognition of the contribution or achievement of individuals or groups by a financial payment or the provision of some form of non-financial recognition or benefit.

The book is primarily concerned with formal reward systems that provide the framework and processes required to manage reward effectively and consistently. But it should be noted that many businesses, especially smaller ones and those which operate flexibly, do without such systems – nearly half the respondents to the Chartered Institute of Personnel and Development (CIPD) 2013 reward survey did not have a formal pay structure. However, even informal systems need to be managed to ensure that the organization gets value for money from its expenditure on reward and much of the contents of this book deals with basic principles of reward management which are valid for both formal and informal systems. The management of unstructured pay systems is covered in Chapter 15.

The book is evidence-based in that it makes use of the practical lessons learned from academic research projects but also refers to the considerable number of surveys and case studies conducted or produced by organizations such as e-reward and the CIPD.

The theme of the book is that reward delivers performance. It is in line with the main message of the performance and reward professional map produced by the CIPD. This spells out that those involved in reward management are there to build a high-performance culture by delivering programmes that recognize and reward critical skills, capabilities, experience and performance, and ensure that reward systems are market-based, equitable and cost-effective.

American and some British companies refer to compensation or compensation and benefits rather than reward. The objection to 'compensation' is that it implies that people need to be recompensed for the unpalatable necessity of having to work for a living. The term is not therefore used in this book.

Plan of the book

The book consists of the following parts:

Part One   An overview of reward management
This part is designed to give a general introduction to reward and performance management. In it, reward and performance management systems are described, an analysis is made of how reward impacts on performance, the

elements of total rewards – financial and non-financial rewards – are considered, as are the special features of international reward policy and practice. Importantly, a new chapter deals with the ethical approach to reward and performance management and the part is completed with a review of the contribution of strategic reward, which takes account of each aspect of reward considered earlier.

Part Two   Base pay management

This part covers the fundamental process of base pay management, which involves deciding on pay levels, fixing rates of pay and developing and operating grade and pay structures. The first chapter in the part examines amongst other things the factors that affect pay levels. Subsequent chapters are concerned with job evaluation, market rate analysis and the features and design of grade and pay structures. The part ends with a chapter dealing with the important subject of equal pay.

Part Three   Rewarding and recognizing performance and merit

In this part individual merit pay and bonus schemes are described. The part also covers rewards based on team or organizational performance and recognition schemes.

Part Four   Rewarding special groups

Consideration is given in this part to the reward requirements of the special groups of people who are employed in organizations – executives and directors, sales and customer service staff, knowledge workers and manual workers. Reward practices may differ between these groups and the result may be a degree of segmentation in the reward system.

Part Five   Employee benefits

This part focuses on policies and practices in the provision of pensions and benefits and the flexible benefit schemes that allow an element of choice to employees.

Part Six   The practice of reward management

The practice of reward management as described in this part covers the use of an evidence-based approach to the review and evaluation of reward systems, the development and management of reward systems, managing reward risk, and the allocation of responsibility for reward.

PART ONE
An overview of reward management

01
Fundamentals of reward management

KEY CONCEPTS AND TERMS

- Guiding principles
- Reward management
- Reward philosophy
- Reward system

LEARNING OUTCOMES

On completing this chapter you should understand and be able to define these key concepts:

- reward management
- aims of reward management
- reward philosophy
- reward management guiding principles

Reward management defined

Reward management deals with the strategies, policies and processes required to ensure that the value of people and the contribution they make to achieving organizational, departmental and team goals are recognized and rewarded. It is about the design, implementation and maintenance of reward systems (interrelated reward processes, practices and procedures covering how jobs and people should be valued, the design and management of grade and pay structures, rewarding and recognizing achievements and performance, providing employee benefits and managing the system). Reward systems aim to satisfy the needs of both the organization and its stakeholders and to operate fairly, equitably and consistently. These needs will particularly include the improvement of performance (reward and performance issues are examined in Chapter 8).

But it should be emphasized that reward management is not just about pay and employee benefits. It is equally concerned with non-financial rewards such as recognition, learning and development opportunities, and increased job responsibility.

The aims of reward management are set out below. As discussed later, reward management processes are based on a philosophy, which may be expressed in the form of guiding principles. They function through a reward system, as described in the next chapter, within the context of the organization.

Aims of reward management

Reward management provides answers to two fundamental questions: (1) How do we value people? and (2) How are we going to reward them according to their value?
The aims of reward management are to:

- support the achievement of business goals by developing a performance culture and stimulating high performance;
- define what is important in terms of behaviours and outcomes;
- align reward practices with employee needs;
- reward people according to the value they create;
- attract and retain the high-quality people the organization needs;
- motivate and win the engagement of employees;
- add value through the introduction of effective but affordable reward practices.

But Ghoshal and Bartlett (1995) reminded us that reward management is essentially about adding value to people. It is not just about attaching value to them.

Reward philosophy

Reward philosophy consists of the set of values and beliefs that influence reward strategy and the design and operation of the reward system. An organization's reward philosophy may be defined and set out in the form of guiding principles. But it may be implicit – all organizations have a reward philosophy which governs reward practice, even if they do not articulate it. And it may be just a crude understanding of what should be done such as offering competitive rates of pay or paying for performance.

Reward philosophies are concerned with the ways in which people are paid, the levels of payment, the extent to which pay should be related to performance, the scale of employee benefits and the adoption of total reward policies which provide for both financial and non-financial rewards. They also cover the degree to which reward practices are ethical in the sense that they are fair, equitable and transparent. The following is an example of a reward philosophy produced by Colt Telecom:

> Colt believes that talented and motivated people make a difference; talented people put us ahead of the competition and deliver the results on which the success of Colt is built. Colt seeks to offer a compensation and benefits package that rewards people for their contribution to the success of the company and ensures that external market competitiveness and internal relativities are taken into account.

Guiding principles

Guiding principles specify the approach an organization intends to use in managing reward. Reward guiding principles may be concerned with such matters as:

- developing reward policies and practices which support the achievement of business goals;
- providing rewards which help to develop a high-performance culture and attract, retain and motivate staff;
- maintaining competitive rates of pay;
- rewarding people according to their contribution;
- recognizing the value of all staff who are making an effective contribution, not just the exceptional performers;
- allowing a reasonable degree of flexibility in the operation of reward processes and in the choice of benefits by employees;
- devolving more responsibility for reward decisions to line managers.

Guiding principles are often agreed by top management with advice from company reward specialists or external consultants. But they will be more acceptable if members of the organization are involved in their definition. Guiding principles can then be communicated generally to increase understanding of what underpins reward policies and practices. However, employees will suspend their judgement of the principles until they experience how they are applied. What matters to them is not the principles themselves but the pay practices emanating from them and the messages about the employment 'deal' that they get as a consequence. It is the reality that is important, not the rhetoric.

The following are some examples of guiding principles.

BT

- business linkage;
- clarity and transparency;
- market competitiveness;
- performance differentiation;
- choice and flexibility;
- equal pay.

Civil Service

1 Meet business needs and be affordable:
- business, operational and workforce needs are the drivers for a reward strategy;
- business cases outline benefits, risks and costs and justify investment;
- reward arguments need to be sustainable.

2 Reflect nature of work:
- recognize and reflect workforce groups identified by function and skills utilized (eg operational, corporate or policy decisions);
- organizations employing similar workforce groups in similar markets are encouraged to consider similar reward arrangements.

3 Recognize performance:
- reward reflects the continuing value and the sustained contribution of an employee and their performance in a given position;
- value and performance rewarded reflect how jobholders contribute to their organization, impact delivery and meet Professional Skills for Government (PSG) requirements.

4 Manage total reward:
- reward includes all aspects of the 'employee deal'; tangible and intangible elements of what is offered;
- total reward is tailored and promoted to attract, engage and retain the right talent as well as providing personal choice and flexibility;
- employers/employees need to develop a full understanding and appreciation of the value of the total reward package.

5 Manage all cash:
- total cash comprises base pay and variable pay;
- base pay reflects job challenge and individuals competence in the job;
- variable pay reflects performance delivered against agreed objectives.

6 Face the market:
- reward levels, generally and for specific skills, aligned with agreed market positioning to attract, motivate and retain the right talent;
- reward competitiveness covers each element of total reward (eg base pay, pensions, leave) and the overall deal.

7 Support equal pay:
- eliminate direct and indirect reward discrimination and reduce any unjustified gender pay gaps;
- operate reward systems that are perceived by staff to be reasonable and transparent;
- reward systems and structures evaluated and kept up to date to ensure that they continue to meet the requirements of legislation.

Diageo

- *Performance*: rewards are developed that reflect team and individual achievements.
- *Market*: rewards reflect the market in which an employee is based, whether that be geographical or functional, and compare favourably with those of competitors.
- *Communication*: Diageo aims to explain to 'everyone the components and value of their reward package, the criteria that affect it, and how they can influence it'.
- *Effectiveness*: the company seeks 'best practice' and ensures its benefits programmes 'remain effective for the business and our employees'.

Tesco

- We will provide an innovative reward package that is valued by our staff and communicated brilliantly to reinforce the benefits of working for Tesco.
- Reward investment will be linked to company performance so that staff share in the success they create and, by going the extra mile, receive above-average reward compared to local competitors.
- All parts of the total reward investment will add value to the business and reinforce our core purpose, goals and values.

Reference

Ghoshal, S and Bartlett, C A (1995) Changing the role of top management: Beyond structure to process, *Harvard Business Review*, 73 (1), pp 86–96

02
Reward systems

LEARNING OUTCOMES

On completing this chapter you should be able to define these concepts and understand the nature and elements of formal reward systems and the methods of developing such systems.

Reward systems defined

Reward systems consist of the methods used by organizations to pay their employees and provide them with other types of reward. They can be formal with defined grade and pay structures and ways of progressing pay. Or they can be informal, especially in smaller organizations, doing without any formal methods of valuing jobs, using individual rates (spot rates) rather than pay structures and involving ad hoc decisions on pay progression. This chapter focuses on formal reward systems.

The six elements of reward systems are:

1 base pay management;
2 contingent pay;
3 employee benefits;
4 non-financial rewards;
5 performance management;
6 total rewards.

In a formal reward system these elements are interconnected and contain various sub-elements as set out in Figure 2.1. They flow from the business and reward strategies as influenced by the organization's context and combine to achieve performance and reward objectives.

Description of the main elements of a formal reward system

Business strategy

The starting point of the reward system is the business strategy of the organization. This identifies the business drivers and sets out the business goals. The drivers are unique to any organization but will often include items such as high performance, profitability, productivity, innovation, customer service, quality, price/cost leadership and the need to satisfy stakeholders – shareholders and employees.

Reward strategy

The reward strategy flows from an analysis of the business drivers. The question is: 'How can these be supported by reward in order to achieve the goals of the business?' The strategy will define longer-term intentions in such areas as pay structures, merit pay and other forms of contingent pay, employee benefits, steps to increase engagement and commitment, and adopting a total rewards approach. The strategy will be influenced by the reward philosophy of the organization and by the context within which the organization operates – its internal culture, structure, operations and size, and the external economic and competitive environment.

Reward policy

Reward policy deals with levels of pay and benefits, achieving equal pay, the use of job evaluation and market surveys, how pay should progress covering the use of merit pay and other forms of contingent pay, transparency (the extent to which details of the reward system and how it affects people are released) and the adoption of an ethical approach to rewards management.

FIGURE 2.1 The reward system

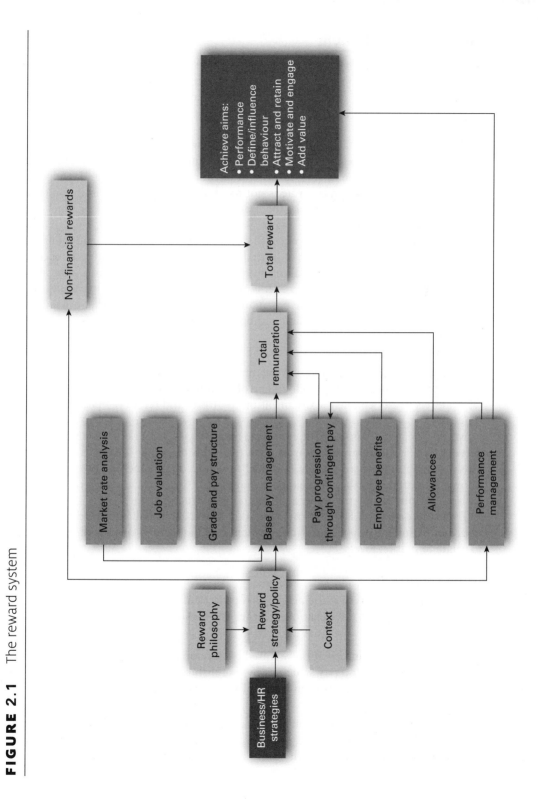

Base pay management

Base pay is the rate for the job. It may be a fixed rate (often called a spot rate), which is attached to a job. People on such rates are said to be getting job-based pay. This form of base pay can be called a time rate with wages for manual or casual workers expressed as an hourly rate while staff salaries are paid on a weekly, monthly or, most commonly, annual basis.

Alternatively, a job may be placed in a grade to which a range of pay is attached. In this case, the base rate can be defined as the minimum of the range or, sometimes, as a target rate within the range – the rate of pay for a fully qualified and competent holder of the job. However, this rate is not fixed; pay can progress within the range according to the perceived merit of the individual (person-based pay) or time spent in the job (service-related pay).

Base pay management is the process of deciding on base pay levels and managing base pay with or without the help of formal grade and pay structures. It is concerned with deciding on levels of pay taking into account the various factors that affect those levels as described in Chapter 5. It is also concerned with achieving equity, fairness and equal pay. The three base pay management activities of market pricing, job evaluation, and pay structure design and operation are described below.

Market pricing

Market pricing is the process of analysing market rates to establish external relativities and provide a guide to the development of a competitive pay structure, ie one in which levels of pay enable the organization to attract and retain the talented people it needs.

Market pricing is based on the collection and analysis of market rate data through surveys that produce information data on the levels of pay and benefits for similar jobs in comparable organizations. It is the basis either for the method of valuing jobs known as extreme market pricing (see Chapter 14) or for deciding on rates of pay for specific jobs or pay ranges in a grade and pay structure.

Decisions on levels of pay following market rate analysis will be guided by the pay policy of the organization or its 'market stance' – that is, how it wants its pay levels to relate to market levels.

Job evaluation

Job evaluation is the systematic and formal process of defining the relative worth or size of jobs within an organization in order to establish internal relativities. It has three aims:

1 To generate the information required to develop and maintain an internally equitable grade and pay structure by establishing the relative value of roles or jobs within the organization (internal relativities) based on fair, sound and consistent judgements.

2 To provide the data required and ensure that pay levels in the organization are externally competitive by making valid market comparisons with jobs or roles of equivalent complexity and size, preferably in similar organizations.

3 To ensure transparency so that the basis upon which grades are defined, jobs graded and rates of pay determined is clear to all concerned.

Grade and pay structure design and operation

Where grade and pay structures exist (many organizations do without them) they provide a framework for managing base pay. In a formal structure jobs are grouped into grades, bands or levels to which are attached pay ranges, brackets or scales. They define the rates of pay for jobs by reference to external and internal relativities established through market pricing and job evaluation. As described in Chapter 15, there are several types of structures with varying numbers of grades or levels or different methods of pay progression or grouping jobs. Managing a formal structure involves deciding on methods of pay progression through merit pay or time-related increments and controlling the implementation of the structure. In the typical graded structure this may be done through mid-point management techniques in which compa-ratios (the relationship in a graded pay structure between actual and policy rates of pay expressed as a percentage) are used to control the extent to which the way the pay structure is being managed in accordance with policy guidelines.

Pay progression

Pay progression is the process through which pay increases within a reward system. It may take place in a formal structure by variable increments related to performance or merit. Pay progression in a graded pay structure is typically planned to decelerate through the grade for two reasons. First, it is argued in line with learning curve theory that pay increases should be higher during the earlier period in a job when learning is at its highest rate. Second, it may be assumed that the central or reference point in a grade represents the market value of fully competent people. Depending on the pay policy of the organization, this may be at or higher than the median. Especially in the latter case, it may be believed that employees should progress quite quickly to that level but, because beyond it they are already being paid well, their pay need not increase so rapidly. This notion is reasonable but it can be difficult to explain to people why they get smaller percentage increases when they are performing well at the upper end of their scale. An alternative arrangement, restricted mainly to the public and voluntary sectors, is to provide fixed increments linked to service.

In an informal structure the spot rate for persons in a job may be increased either to recognize the value of individuals to the organization and thus help to motivate and retain them, or in response to perceived increases in the 'market worth' of the job. Market worth is the value of an individual person in the marketplace expressed in terms of level of pay. It is taken into account by employers when deciding on what someone should be paid in order to maintain a competitive rate of pay for that person and thus attract them to the organization or help to retain them. Pay can also progress through promotion or upgradings. Research by IDS (2014) established that pay progression is almost always based on more than one criterion, eg increases in market rates or the cost of living as well as merit.

Contingent pay

Contingent pay is related to individual merit or length of service or team or business performance. It takes the following forms:

Merit pay, which is linked to the performance, competence, contribution or skill of individuals and results in consolidated increases to base pay.

Service-related pay, which provides for consolidated fixed increments on a pay scale or pay spine related to time in the job. It is a typical feature of the pay systems in most public or voluntary sector organizations. It is supported by unions because it is perceived to be fair and not subject to the individual and possibly biased judgement of managers. It is easier to manage than merit pay; in fact, it does not need to be managed at all. But it fails to recognize differences in performance and can be described as the gift that goes on giving.

Individual cash bonuses, which are paid to recognize performance as an alternative or in addition to a merit or service-related increment. They are not consolidated into base pay.

Team pay, which gives team members a non-consolidated cash sum, related to team performance.

Pay related to business performance, which takes the form of cash bonuses, profit sharing or company shares or share options.

Employee benefits

Employee benefits such as pensions, sick pay, insurance cover, company cars and a number of other 'perks' comprise elements of remuneration additional to the various forms of cash pay and also include provisions for employees that are not strictly remuneration, such as annual holidays. 'Flexible' benefit schemes allow employees to decide on the make-up of their benefits package within certain limits.

Allowances

Allowances are paid in addition to basic pay for special circumstances (eg living in London) or features of employment (working unsocial hours). They may be determined unilaterally by the organization but they are often the subject of negotiation if trade unions are recognized. The main types of allowances are location allowances, overtime payments, shift payments, working conditions allowances and stand-by or call-out allowances (made to those who have to be available to come in to work when required).

Performance management

Performance management processes define individual performance and contribution expectations, assess performance against those expectations, provide for regular constructive feedback, and result in agreed plans for performance improvement, learning and personal development. They are a means of providing non-financial motivation and may also inform contingent pay decisions.

Non-financial rewards

Non-financial rewards do not involve any direct payments and often arise from the work itself. They comprise recognition, achievement, autonomy, scope to use and develop skills and training and career development opportunities.

Total remuneration

Total remuneration is the value of all cash payments (base pay, contingent pay and allowances, ie total earnings) plus the pensions and benefits received by employees.

Total rewards

Total rewards are the combination of financial and non-financial rewards available to employees.

Reward systems in action

Aegon UK

- The career-family structure contains four career families.
- Target rates are defined which support three performance zones providing guidance on the pay range for different roles within the band.
- Pensionable, lump-sum bonus payments are awarded on a non-consolidated basis. An incentive scheme enables line managers to recognize and reward outstanding contribution by individuals or teams outside the annual pay cycle.
- A variety of financial and non-financial awards is available to recognize personal development and ongoing contribution which employees make towards the overall effectiveness and efficiency of the company.

B&Q

- The 20,000 customer advisers are paid on one of six different spot rates in the upper quartile of similar jobs.
- Pay progression is based on the acquisition – and application on the shop floor – of skills and knowledge. There are four additional spot rates beyond the established rate designed to reward 'excellence in the role'.
- There is a store team bonus, based on sales, shrinkage (resulting from losses such as theft and stocktaking errors) and customer service measures set at store level, and a formal recognition scheme.

BT

- Pay structure of 250-plus roles in 18 different job families representing major work functions.
- Broad pay ranges attached to each role are determined by reference to market data.
- All roles are benchmarked against equivalent roles and salary ranges in the external market in order to gather competitive reward data.
- Published salary ranges are attached to each generic role.
- Hierarchical promotion from grade to grade is replaced by role change.
- Simplified benefits package and target bonus percentage defined for each role.
- Based on benchmarking in external market.
- Each role assigned to one of three benefit levels.
- Three levels of bonus achievement linked to balanced scorecard.
- Salary progression within a role range is predominantly via annual reviews based on individual performance, position in range and affordability.
- Other principal type of salary progression results from role change – a move between job families or within a job family.

Friends Provident

- Five broad career bands for non-management staff. Three additional bands cover everyone below executive director.
- Eighteen job families with a small number of generic role profiles, based on key skills and competency levels, in each of the five career bands.
- Job-family salary ranges for each career band.
- An annual salary review, with individual reviews analysed by a range of criteria, such as gender, to help ensure fairness and equity across the company.
- Regional salary ranges, to reflect the influence of regional pay where appropriate.
- Performance management.
- A discretionary non-consolidated performance bonus.

GlaxoSmithKline (GSK)

- The pay structure has five bands. Each band is divided into a number of zones. The combination of band and zone produces the grade, and there are 29 grades in total. The grades determine bonus entitlement. The pay for each grade ranges approximately 25 per cent either side of the range mid-point.
- The main method of paying for performance each year is through the bonus scheme, but individuals are also able to progress through their grade range on the basis of performance, their 'behaviours', relativities with peers and their market value.

- There is a two-way performance and development planning process whereby individuals agree their objectives with their manager and identify development needs for the forthcoming year.
- The financial recognition scheme rewards effort above normal job requirements. There are four different levels of award.

Kent County Council

- Jobs allocated to one of 35 generic job profiles organized into seven job families.
- Jobs evaluated using the Hay system and placed into one of six pay grades.
- Summary band descriptions of the grades enable staff to understand why their job falls in a particular grade.
- The analytical points factor system ensures that staff are all evaluated on a fair and equal basis.
- Regular equal pay reviews are conducted.
- Total Contribution Pay (TCP) rewards the 'how' of someone's performance, as well as the results that they deliver.
- Managers can recognize the contribution of their staff on an ongoing basis with cash and non-cash awards.
- A total award approach is adopted.

Developing formal reward systems

The critical and most demanding task that anyone concerned with reward will have to undertake is that of developing and implementing new or revised reward systems concerned with total rewards, job evaluation, grade and pay structure design, contingent pay and employee benefits. It is critical because of the fast-moving nature of the reward scene. Regular reviews of the system are required to ensure that it is meeting business needs and this frequently means innovating new or fundamentally revised processes. Business and HR strategies change and the reward strategy must change accordingly. Job evaluation schemes decay in use and do not fit new organizational arrangements, pay structures are no longer appropriate, merit pay schemes do not deliver what was expected from them and pension and benefit schemes have to be changed to meet new legal and fiscal requirements, to cater for different employee needs or to make them more affordable. This is an exacting process of change management.

It is necessary not only to know what to do but also to know how to do it, and even more importantly, to ensure that it has been done as it was supposed to have been done. This means being absolutely clear about the objectives of the change, planning the change on the basis of an analysis of the situation (evidence-based reward management) and a diagnosis of the causes of any problems, involving people – managers and staff alike – in the change process, and communicating to them about what is happening and why. It also means ensuring that everyone acquires the skills needed to manage the new processes and play a part in them. Finally it involves planning the implementation, managing the implementation process effectively, and monitoring and evaluating outcomes to ensure that the objectives of the exercise have been achieved.

The task starts with objective setting and continues with processes of analysis, diagnosis, evaluation of alternatives and selection of the most appropriate one, design or development, implementation and evaluation.

Objective setting

It is important at an early stage to be clear about the objectives of any initiative, to clarify what is to be achieved and, after implementation, serve as a basis for evaluation. Broad objectives may be formed at the beginning of the exercise but these are likely to be modified during the project as more information on requirements is obtained and processed. The following are some examples of reward development project objectives.

BT

At BT their objectives were expressed as follows:

> Use the full range of rewards (salary, bonus, benefits and recognition) to recruit and retain the best people, and to encourage and reward achievement where actions and behaviours are consistent with the BT values.

Diageo

The objectives at Diageo were to:

- support and enable the talent agenda;
- provide clear principles to enable reward decision making in the business;
- align the reward approach with Diageo's business strategy;
- enable every employee to understand why they get paid what they get paid;
- have a customer service ethic that results in great execution.

A finance sector company

The objectives for their 'fresh approach to reward' produced by a finance sector company were:

> Change the emphasis from measuring the job and its accountabilities to recognizing the person and the contribution they make to the business; reflect the way the organization is changing by encouraging us to be more responsive to customers; improve reward for excellent performance by freeing up salary ranges.

Friends Provident

The objectives at Friends Provident were to:

- match salaries directly to the market;
- give line managers greater accountability for staff salaries and career progression;

- increase the flexibility of pay arrangements at business unit level;
- facilitate a real and fundamental top-down change in corporate culture;
- reward the best performers by paying salaries above the market rate;
- manage salary costs;
- encourage greater accountability by staff for development of their own competencies.

Tesco

At Tesco the objectives of introducing a broad-banded structure were to:

- achieve more flexibility in determining pay;
- develop a flatter, more flexible organization;
- reward staff for their contribution;
- link remuneration to responsibility and contribution;
- simplify career planning and job classification.

The process of development and implementation

No initiative should be planned without making a business case for it. The extent to which it will add value rather than create work should be assessed. A value-added approach means that processes and schemes will not be introduced or updated without assessing the effect they are expected to have on the engagement and performance of people, on the ability of the organization to recruit and keep the right sort of employees and, ultimately, on the results achieved by the organization.

Bearing this in mind, and against the background of a preliminary statement of objectives, the approach to the development and implementation of reward systems should be evidence-based, realistic about costs and what can be achieved, focused on how it will be put into effect, and positive about involving stakeholders and communicating information to them on proposals and plans and how they will be affected by them. In addition the risks involved should be identified and managed as described in Chapter 31.

Evidence-based development

The development of a reward system should be evidence-based. This means considering what needs to be done by reference to an analysis of the internal and external context and the strengths and weaknesses of the present reward arrangements, benchmarking good practice elsewhere and consulting relevant research. The following questions should be answered:

- What are the aims of our reward practices? What do we want to achieve with them?
- What would successful reward practices look like? How would we know? What criteria and measures can we use to assess their effectiveness?
- What evidence do we have to assess the current level of effectiveness and to highlight the strongest and weakest aspects of the current rewards package?

- What information can we gather to inform that review and how do we relate financial and non-financial information in making any assessment?
- What should we do in response to these findings?
- What level and type of change are appropriate?
- What are the objectives of the change in such terms as higher levels of engagement, and how will we know they have been achieved?
- How do we pilot, test and implement any changes to maximize their chances of success?
- How do we ensure continuing success in the future, and how should rewards respond to further internal and external changes and developments?

Costs

A new or substantially revised reward system is an investment. But the costs of that investment need to be assessed to answer the question, 'Is it affordable?' Thus a basis is provided for deciding whether or not the investment is worthwhile and indicating what can be done to contain costs and how costs will be controlled during the project.

A reality check

Any proposals or plans should be subjected to a reality check:

- Is it worth doing? What return will we get on our investment? What's the business case in terms of added value? What contribution will it make to supporting the achievement of the organization's strategic goals?
- Can it be done?
- Who does it?
- Have we the resources to do it?
- How do we manage the change?

Planning for implementation

It is normally assumed that the processes of development and implementation are sequential: you develop something and then you implement it. This is a mistake. If constant thought is not given during and throughout the development of a reward system on how it will work and how it will be made to work, then the implementation will fail. The two go together. Implementation plans have to take account of the barriers to reward changes reported by respondents to the survey conducted by Brown and Purcell (2007) as shown in Figure 2.2, especially those concerned with the attitudes of line managers and staff, communications and line managers' skills.

FIGURE 2.2 Barriers to the implementation of reward changes

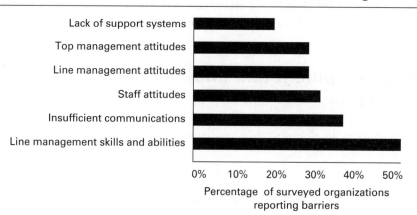

SOURCE: Brown, D and Purcell, J (2007) Reward management: on the line, *Compensation and Benefits Review*, **39**, pp 28–34.

The plan for implementation should cover:

- the use of pilot tests to identify any operational problems;
- the possibility of phasing the introduction of the changed system so that each step is manageable in the time available;
- setting up a project team with an experienced project manager;
- developing an involvement strategy – deciding who should be involved in the development programme and how they should be involved;
- preparing a detailed project plan setting out objectives, timings and cost budgets for each phase and indicating how the project will be controlled;
- formulating a communications strategy;
- preparing a plan for briefing and training line managers.

Involvement

Involve stakeholders from the word go – bottom up as well as top down. It is vital to get the contribution of line managers, staff and employee representatives as well as senior management at all stages of the project. Use attitude surveys, focus groups and workshops to obtain views, explore issues and exchange ideas. The aim is to achieve ownership and acceptance of the outcome of the project.

Communication

Effective communications are important because reward systems can be complex and difficult to understand and therefore need to be explained carefully. Rewards are an emotive issue. So many personal needs are tied up in them – for security, recognition, status and so on – that changes to them almost inevitably generate emotional and often hostile responses from at least some employees. People can be suspicious about the reasons for change and feel that it will affect them adversely. It may be difficult to overcome these fears but a sustained attempt must be made to do so.

The development and implementation programme

The stages of a development and implementation programme are illustrated in Figure 2.3.

Implement and review – the BT approach

The BT approach to development is as follows:

Business sponsorship and ownership are key. Secure 'sponsorship and ownership' amongst senior people – a feeling that the change is something that they are happy to live with because they have been involved in its planning and introduction – it has become their change.

Don't underestimate resistance. The level of resistance that may arise when reorganizing reward systems should never be underestimated, hence the importance of sponsorship, communication and training.

Project management skills are critical. The project must be carefully planned and managed under a skilled project manager.

Engage. Ownership and acceptance are much more likely if the maximum degree of engagement of all concerned is built into the entire change programme.

Clear, consistent communications. It is imperative to communicate clearly and consistently to staff at every stage of the process.

Centrica

Centrica's nine success criteria for developing reward systems are:

1 partnership;
2 preparation;
3 business engagement;
4 employee engagement;
5 union engagement;
6 financial modelling;
7 communications;
8 project administration;
9 business-as-usual administration.

FIGURE 2.3 Development and implementation of a reward system

Set objectives	→ Define what the programme is intended to achieve (modify as necessary later)
Analysis of strengths and weaknesses	• *Present arrangements* – strategy, policy, job evaluation, pay structure and levels, equal pay, contingent pay, performance management, benefits and pensions, procedures and administration • *Problems* – attraction and retention, motivation and performance, pay inequities, uncompetitive pay, grade drift, value for money not obtained from contingent pay and benefits expenditure, employee dissatisfaction
Diagnosis of cause of problems	Examples: • reward strategy unclear or unaligned to business/HR strategy • incoherent approach to total reward • policy guidelines inappropriate or unclear • pay levels uncompetitive • equal pay not provided for • decayed job evaluation scheme • too many grades • contribution not rewarded properly • performance management processes not working • inflexible pay and benefits arrangement • poor communications to staff • lack of staff involvement • capability and commitment of line managers inadequate • professional expertise and quality of support provided by HR inadequate • poor cost control
• Evaluate alternatives • Decide course of action • Cost proposals • Prepare and execute development plan	Examples of possible developments: • revise reward strategy and policy • introduce total rewards • replace/revise job evaluation • conduct market rate analysis • design new grade and pay structure • conduct equal pay review • introduce contribution pay or revise existing arrangements • revise performance management processes • introduce flexible benefits • improve communications to staff • involve staff more in development process • improve budgeting and control procedures • train managers • improve quality of specialist HR advice
Implement	• Pilot test and phase as necessary • Brief and train • Action • Monitor • Evaluate

Involve and communicate

GlaxoSmithKline

Don't expect people to change overnight and don't try to force change. It is better to reinforce desirable behaviour than to attempt to enforce a particular way of doing things.

(Paul Craven, compensation director, R&D)

Developing reward systems: six tips

The following tips on developing reward systems were made by the reward practitioners responding to e-reward surveys in 2009 and 2014.

- Be clear on what has to be achieved and why.

- Ensure that what you do fits the strategy, culture and circumstances of the organization.

- Don't follow fashion – do your own thing.

- Keep it simple – over-complexity is a common reason for failure.

- Don't rush – it takes longer than you think.

- Communicate, involve and train.

References

Brown, D and Purcell, J (2007) Reward management: on the line, *Compensation and Benefits Review*, **39** (28), pp 28–34

e-reward (2003–2009) Research reports, e-reward.co.uk [accessed 21 July 2015]

IDS (2014) incomesdata.co.uk [accessed 21 July 2015]

03
Strategic reward

LEARNING OUTCOMES

On completing this you should be able to define these key concepts. You should also know about:

- The nature of strategic reward
- Strategic reward – characteristics and critical evaluation
- Reward strategy
- Reward philosophy
- Formulating reward strategy
- Implementing reward strategy

Introduction

Strategic reward is the overall approach adopted by an organization to the development of policies and practices which make an impact on organizational performance by helping to attract and retain talented people, providing for their motivation and engagement and ensuring that they feel valued. This approach is put into practice through the development and implementation of specific reward strategies.

The chapter starts with a definition of strategic reward, a description of its characteristics and a critical evaluation of it as a concept and in practice. The rest of the chapter is devoted to a detailed examination of reward strategy – what it means, its problematic nature and how it can be implemented.

Strategic reward

Strategic reward is concerned with the development and implementation of reward strategies, which ensures that they are integrated with and support the business strategy and other HR strategies and that specific reward strategies cohere. It takes account of individual as well as business needs.

In the words of Duncan Brown (2001), strategic reward 'is ultimately a way of thinking that you can apply to any reward issue arising in your organization, to see how you can create value from it'. Jonathan Trevor (2011) observed that strategic pay 'is positioned as a means of enhancing company performance and securing competitive advantage through the alignment of pay strategies, systems, practices and processes to the organizational strategy'. He noted that this is achieved 'by attracting and retaining valued labour, driving effort and performance and encouraging desired behaviours among the broad-based workforce'.

The characteristics of strategic reward

Strategic reward can be regarded as an attitude of mind rather than a set of prescribed techniques. It is based on a belief in the need to integrate reward and business strategy and to be forward looking – to plan ahead and make the plans happen. It is visionary in the sense that it is concerned with creating and conceptualizing ideas of where the reward policies and processes of the organization should be going. But it also leads to empirical management decisions on how in practice it is going to get there.

Strategic reward is based upon a philosophy expressed in the form of guiding principles. It is systematic in the sense that it is based on evidence – analyses of the organization's internal and internal environment, its business needs and the needs of its stakeholders. It is goal orientated – the desired ends and the means of attaining them are clearly defined. It takes account of the business strategy and what can be done by reward to further its achievement. Importantly, it is a key instrument in achieving an integrated approach to reward management, one in which the various aspects of the reward system are linked together and associated with other HR practices so that they are mutually supportive. It focuses on implementation – it is about getting things done rather than just thinking about what needs to be done.

Critical evaluation of the concept of strategic reward

The problem with the concept of strategic reward is that it can promise more than it delivers. This contradicts the main message delivered by US writers such as Lawler (1990) in his *Strategic Pay* and Schuster and Zingheim (1992) in their *The New Pay*, which was that it provides a powerful lever for improving business performance. But as Thompson (1998) commented: 'The most that companies can hope to do in their approach to reward is to make sure that it does not distort the relationship [between management and employees]. Managing reward is thus a job of damage limitation and perhaps not the "strategic lever for organizational transformation" that appears so seductive in the writing of American commentators.'

This comment was followed up by Armstrong and Brown (2006) with an analysis of the limitations of conventional assumptions about strategic reward.

> When mostly North American concepts of strategic HRM and reward first entered into management thinking and practice in the UK we were both some of their most ardent advocates, writing and advising individual employers on the benefits of aligning their reward systems so as to drive business performance. We helped to articulate strategic plans and visions, and to design the pay and reward changes that would secure better alignment and performance.
>
> Some twenty years later, we are a little older and a little wiser as a result of these experiences. We remain passionate proponents of a strategic approach to reward management. But in conducting and observing this work we have seen some of the risks as well as the opportunities in pursuing the reward strategy path: of an over-focus on planning at the expense of process and practice: on design rather than delivery; on the boardroom and the HR function rather than on first and front-line managers and employees; and on concept rather than communications.
>
> At times there has been a tendency to over-ambition and optimism in terms of what could and couldn't be achieved by changing pay and reward arrangements, and how quickly real change could be delivered and business results secured. At times the focus on internal business fit led to narrow-minded reward determinism, and a lack of attention to the increasingly important external influences and constraints on reward, from the shifting tax and wider legislative, economic and social environment. And sometimes the focus on designs and desires meant that the requirements and skills of line and reward managers were insufficiently diagnosed and developed.

Jonathan Trevor (2011) posed the question: To what extent can pay be strategic? He claimed that rationalism is limited and pointed out that pay systems tend to be selected for their legitimacy (best practice as advocated by institutions such as the CIPD and by management consultants) rather than for purely economic reasons. His research into the pay policies and practice of seven large consumer goods companies led to the following conclusions:

> All firms encounter significant difficulties when attempting to implement strategic pay systems with the result that in the majority of cases, what is realized operationally as pay practice is neither what was desired nor intended strategically. As a result of the gap between intended policy and achieved practice, between the espoused and the realized, pay within a number of the case companies does not fulfil the strategic objectives of motivating managerial, professional and technical employees to work harder. It does not engender commitment or loyalty as outcomes, nor does it equip management with the behavioural 'lever' promised by standard theory. Despite the best efforts of leading

companies, and the rhetoric of their espoused pay practice, pay practice is operationally non-strategic.

This problem is not unique to pay. Wright and Nishii (2004) commented that HR strategies are not always implemented and if they are, may be implemented in ways that differ from the original intention. Dreaming up a strategy is fairly easy; getting it to work is hard. Rosabeth Moss Kanter (1984) noted that: 'Many companies, even very sophisticated ones, are much better at generating impressive plans on paper than they are at getting "ownership" of the plans so that they actually guide operational decisions.' There are limitations to the logical model of management, which underpins the concept of strategic human resource management. Mabey *et al* (1998) commented that: 'The reality is... that strategies may not always be easy to discern, that the processes of decision making may be implicit, incremental, negotiated and compromised.' And the integration and matching of HR and business strategies was acknowledged to be problematic by Karen Legge (1995).

In spite of these difficulties it is possible to believe, as does Jonathan Trevor (2011) that: 'In principle, strategic pay remains a laudable ambition.' But a realistic approach is necessary. It is good to have aspirations as long as they are put into practice and work. This is a matter of carefully planned and executed implementation. It is necessary to be realistic about what can be achieved on the basis of an evidence-based analysis of limitations and an assessment of potential unintended consequences and risks. Implementation issues are discussed in more detail later in this chapter. Risk management is considered in Chapter 31.

Reward strategy

Reward strategy aims to provide answers to two basic questions:

1 What do we need to do about our reward practices to ensure that they are fit for purpose?

2 How do we intend to do it?

Reward strategy defined

Reward strategy is a declaration of intent, which defines what the organization wants to do in the future to develop and implement reward policies, practices, and processes which will further the achievement of its business goals and meet the needs of its stakeholders. The aim is to provide a sense of purpose and direction and a basis for developing reward policies, practices and processes. It is based on an understanding of the needs of the organization and its employees and how they can best be satisfied.

Reward strategy is sometimes seen as merely a process of defining broad plans for the future. But there is more to it than that. Reward strategy is also concerned with the design and implementation of the reward system.

Reward strategy should be underpinned by a reward philosophy, which represents the views of the organization on how people should be valued. This can be articulated as a set of guiding principles, which act as a framework for reward system design and operation and can be communicated to employees so that they understand the background to the reward policies and practices that affect them.

The content of reward strategy

As Armstrong and Murlis (2007) stated: 'Reward strategy will be characterized by diversity and conditioned both by the legacy of the past and the realities of the future.' All reward strategies are different just as all organizations are different. Of course, similar aspects of reward will be covered in the strategies of different organizations but they will be treated differently in accordance with variations between organizations in their contexts, business strategies and cultures. But the reality of reward strategy is that it is not such a clear-cut process as some believe. It evolves, it changes and it has sometimes to be reactive rather than proactive.

Reward strategy often has to be a balancing act because of potentially conflicting goals. For example, it may be necessary to reconcile the competing claims of being externally competitive and internally equitable – paying a specialist more money to reflect market rate pressures may disrupt internal relativities. Or the belief that a universally applicable reward system is required may conflict with the perceived need to adopt a policy of segmentation (varying the reward package for different jobs, occupations or people to reflect particular knowledge and skills and the types and levels of contribution they make).

Reward strategy may be a broad-brush affair, simply indicating the general direction in which it is thought reward management should go, which might include adopting a total rewards approach. Additionally or alternatively, reward strategy may set out a list of specific intentions dealing with particular aspects of reward management; for example:

- the development of a total rewards approach;
- the introduction of performance pay;
- replacement of an existing merit pay or bonus scheme;
- the introduction of a new grade and pay structure;
- the replacement of an existing decayed job evaluation scheme;
- the introduction of a formal recognition scheme;
- the development of a flexible benefits system;
- the conduct of an equal pay review.

Examples of key themes in reward strategies

Airbus: Introduce performance pay for all employees, ensure that its rates are competitive with the external market and deal with anomalies caused by previous rigidities, such as grade drift brought about by people having to be promoted to a higher grade to receive additional pay.

AstraZeneca: Promote a culture that values, recognizes and rewards outstanding performance.

Centrica: Establish a link between pay and performance and align pay with the market.

The Children's Society: Develop flexible and fair reward systems, which will support its mission and corporate objectives by recognizing contribution, accountability, team working and innovation, and are market sensitive but not market led.

Diageo: Release the potential of every employee to deliver Diageo's performance goals.

Kent County Council: Pay people a fair rate for the job and give additional reward for excellent contribution.

National Union of Teachers: Develop a new broad-graded pay structure and introduce a new job evaluation scheme as a basis for the structure.

Tesco: Reward staff for their contribution in a way that enables them to benefit directly from the success they help to create.

Why have a reward strategy?

The basic arguments for having a reward strategy are that it will:

- provide a sense of purpose and direction;
- support the business strategy;
- align reward processes to business needs;
- integrate reward and HR policies and processes;
- provide guidance for reward system design and implementation;
- articulate the reward values of the organization.

In addition, because it can be argued that there is a positive relationship between rewards and performance, steps should be taken to strengthen that link. The problem with the belief that there is a positive relationship is that the existence of a clear and universal link between reward and organizational performance is uncertain. The reward value chain used to support the contention looks like this:

Reward strategy >> Reward practice, eg performance pay >> Improved
individual performance >> Improved organizational performance

But there are doubts about each link in this chain. The reward strategy might state 'Let there be performance pay' but there is no guarantee that it will be implemented as intended. As Trevor (2011) put it, 'What is desired (approach), and what is intended (design), may not be reflected in what is achieved (operation).' Even if, as in this example, performance pay were implemented, there is no guarantee that it would improve individual performance (there is little evidence that it does that). Even if performance pay improves individual performance it may not significantly affect organizational performance (there are so many other factors at work).

However, the other arguments in favour of reward strategy are persuasive and a sense of purpose and direction is clearly a good thing. The problem is how to do this realistically bearing in mind that putting pay into practice is non-strategic. To deal with this the focus should not be limited to the development of an overarching strategy but extended to include the design and operation of the pay system so that any ideas produced at the formulation stage can be translated into operationally effective designs. On the basis of his research, Trevor (2011) suggested that it is necessary to regard the management of pay practice as taking place at three levels:

1 The pay approach, which reflects the implicit or espoused values, principles and aspirations that underpin pay strategy and practice.
2 The pay design, which reflects the technical content of the intended pay policy.
3 The pay operation, which reflects what is achieved operationally as pay practice.

He also noted in 2012 that: 'Strategic reward systems are often extremely difficult to manage because of their complexity. Indeed, for many organizations, research indicates that attempts to use reward strategically can prove to be more of a liability than a benefit, producing conflict rather than unity.'

The pay approach

The pay approach is expressed in reward philosophy and guiding principles as described in Chapter 1. The research conducted by Jonathan Trevor (2011) in seven companies established that in all cases senior management decided on the pay approach. They:

- agreed guiding principles;
- provided broad guidelines in the form of expected outcomes;
- reviewed options for action;
- settled the course of action.

Pay design

The pay approach is the basis for the design stage, which is determined largely by benchmarking best practice and internal concerns over relativity, equity (fairness), governance and performance. The following reward strategy questions need to be answered at the design stage:

- How will it add value?
- How is it going to be put into effect?
- What supporting processes will be needed and can they be made available?
- Who is going to be involved in implementation?
- How are we going to make sure that those involved know what they have to do, know why they are expected to do it, believe that it is worthwhile and have the skills to do it?

- Are people likely to react negatively to the proposed strategy and if so, how do we deal with their concerns?
- How much time will be needed; how much time have we got?
- Will any additional resources be required and can they be made available?
- Are there any likely implementation problems and how will they be dealt with?

Pay operation

The aim is to make the reward strategy an operating reality by building the capacity of the organization to put into practice the proposals worked out in the design stage. Armstrong and Brown (2006) stressed that: 'It is always essential to design with implementation in mind.' Particular attention has to be paid to issues arising from process factors (how the strategy will work), involving people and communicating with them, and the part played by line managers.

Difficulties with implementation can arise because of over-engineered reward systems, misalignment and acting precipitately as discussed below.

Over-engineering

The temptation presented to reward specialists (both practitioners and consultants) is to design highly complicated processes which are hard to explain and justify and even harder to operate. Nicki Demby, when Performance and Reward Director at Diageo, explained to the e-reward researcher:

> It is essential to assess the extent to which changes will add value rather than create work. Reward processes and schemes should not be introduced or updated without assessing whether there is a good reason for doing so. Does it give energy or take it away? For example, is the reward plan so complicated that by the time you have waded through it you wish you hadn't? If so, you are taking away an effective management tool. So how does Diageo take complexity out of the reward system? Our mantra is 'Keep it simple, but simple isn't easy!' It's just as hard as making something complicated, but in terms of effectiveness, well-thought-through simplicity can pay huge dividends.

Misalignment

Implementation problems can be created if alignment with the business and HR strategies is not achieved when formulating reward strategy. Lack of vertical alignment with the business strategy – which is difficult – means that there is a risk of reward policies becoming isolated or irrelevant. Line managers will be less willing to implement them and their impact will be reduced. Failure to achieve a measure of horizontal alignment with associated reward and HR strategies will diminish the impact of reward practices by reducing the amount of mutual enhancement and support that can be achieved through 'bundling' HR policies.

Precipitate implementation

Those involved in developing reward strategy naturally want to get results, and this particularly applies to top managers who often tend to put project managers and their teams under pressure to deliver. The risk of taking precipitate action is that new policies and practices will not have been tested properly to identify any problems that might be met in their implementation, through inappropriate or poor design, or the absence of adequate supporting processes such as performance management. This has been a major reason for the failure of many new reward schemes to live up to expectations.

It is essential to allow time in the project plan to reflect on the implications of proposals and identify potential problems and areas where particular care has to be taken in avoiding them. These problems may include the capacity of line managers and employees to understand what they have to do and to acquire the skills to do it, the snags that inevitably occur and are difficult to deal with over a short timescale, and the failure of existing processes such as performance management to provide adequate support.

Dealing with the problems – developing reward strategy

There are two ways of dealing with these problems. First, wherever possible, the new or significantly altered reward process should be pilot tested in a division or department or with a selected sample of employees. This applies particularly to merit pay schemes (performance, competency- or contribution-related pay). It also applies to performance management systems. The tests should be designed to establish the extent to which front-line managers can and will carry out their responsibility, the support that HR will need to provide, any inadequacies in existing processes, the approach that should be adopted to informing employees generally and individuals in particular on how they will be affected by the strategy and the need to involve people in further discussions on the proposals. The outcome of the tests could be the amendment of the proposed practice or existing processes and the improvement of involvement, communication and training processes, as well as a better understanding of what problems may arise and how they can be solved.

The second approach, which can be used where there is more than one component of the reward strategy, is to phase the introduction of the different parts. An incremental approach means that people are given the time to absorb and adjust to the new practice and the resources such as HR support required to deliver the strategy are not overstretched. For example, the Corporation of London phased the implementation of a comprehensive reward strategy initiative, which included a major cultural shift from service-related increments to contribution-related pay. First they developed and introduced a new job evaluation scheme. Then they amended the grade and pay structure by reference to job evaluation scores and a market rate survey, retaining the existing incremental system. Next they introduced a measure of contribution pay by making increments dependent on achieving satisfactory levels of competence. Finally they implemented a full contribution-related pay scheme, rewarding people both for their outputs (results) and their inputs (competence).

The principles of procedural and distributive justice apply. People must feel that the procedures used to determine their grades, pay level and pay progression are fair, equitable, applied consistently and transparent. They must also feel that the awards distributed to them are just in terms of their contribution and value to the organization.

Case studies

Integrated approach to reward at AEGON UK

Like many companies, AEGON UK (a large insurance company) had pay systems and supporting processes such as job evaluation and performance appraisal, which used to stand alone, apart from other HR processes. The company adopted a more holistic approach to the development of its new reward system – which it calls the Human Resources Integrated Approach – so that from whatever angle staff now look at the elements of pay management, performance, career development and reward, they are consistent and linked.

The stated objective of this programme is 'to develop a set of HR processes which are integrated with each other and with the business objectives'. In other words, AEGON UK aims to ensure that the processes of recruiting, retaining and motivating people, as well as measuring their performance, are in line with what the business is trying to achieve.

The Human Resources Integrated Approach is underpinned by a competency framework. The established competencies form the basis of the revised HR processes:

Recruitment: competency based with multi-assessment processes as the basic approach.

Reward: market driven with overall performance dictating rate of progress of salaries within broad bands rather than existing grades.

Performance management: not linked to pay, concentrated on personal development, objective setting and competency development.

Training and development: targeted on key competencies and emphasizing self-development.

Reward strategy at BT

Reward strategy at BT is a fairly broad-brush affair simply indicating the general direction in which it is thought reward management for the 90,000 staff at BT should go, with an emphasis on adopting a more holistic, total reward approach. It is summarized as follows:

> Use the full range of rewards (salary, bonus, benefits and recognition) to recruit and retain the best people, and to encourage and reward achievement where actions and behaviours are consistent with the BT values.

Guiding principles

BT's reward strategy is underpinned by a set of guiding principles defining the approach the organization takes to dealing with reward. These guiding principles are the basis for reward policies and provide guidelines for the actions contained in the reward strategy. They express the reward philosophy of the organization – its values and beliefs about how people should be rewarded. The six guiding principles governing the design of the reward system at BT are as follows:

1 business linkage;
2 clarity and transparency;
3 market competitiveness;
4 performance differentiation;
5 choice and flexibility;
6 equal pay.

Broadly speaking, the three principal elements driving individual reward are:

- The individual's performance and contribution in the role – what does it mean to have high individual performance?
- The competitiveness of the individual's existing salary, together with the actual (and anticipated) salary movement in relevant local markets – how does salary align to the external market?
- The company's business results and ability to pay – can the company afford to invest money in terms of additional reward?

Underpinning these pillars are the principles of clarity (a 'focus on roles'), equal pay and choice.

DSG International: aligning reward with the business plan

In a difficult economic environment, DSG simplified their complex mix of reward arrangements to establish a close alignment between rewards and the five components of a new business turnaround plan, primarily through the redesign of executive incentive plans. The change was designed to enhance the perception of line of sight between individual performance, group performance and reward. It illustrates the vital role of communications to explain the 'why' of reward change, what it means for the business and how each component of reward links to a business plan.

Total cash strategy at GlaxoSmithKline (GSK)

The basic element of TotalReward at GSK is total cash. This consists of base salary and bonus. The philosophy behind this is that superior performance deserves superior reward. This, says the company, is 'performance with a sense of urgency and integrity, performance that enables our patients and consumers to do more, feel better and live longer, and performance that will enable GSK to achieve its strategic goals'.

Total cash has been designed to reinforce the achievement of business objectives – when GSK and the business unit do well, the individual employee will do well too. The key features of total cash are:

- 'pay for performance' is a key principle;
- GSK performance and business unit performance drive bonus plans;
- it is aligned with the achievement of business objectives;

- it reflects competitive leading market practices;
- it rewards team and individual contributions;
- it is aligned with roles and responsibilities.

References

Armstrong, M and Brown, D (2006) *Strategic Reward*, Kogan Page, London

Armstrong, M and Murlis, H (2007) *Reward Management*, revised 5th edn, Kogan Page, London

Brown, D (2001) *Reward Strategies*, CIPD, London

Kanter, R M (1984) *The Change Masters*, Allen & Unwin, London

Lawler, E E (1990) *Strategic Pay*, Jossey-Bass, San Francisco, CA

Legge, K (1995) *Human Resource Management*, Macmillan, London

Mabey, C, Salaman, G and Storey, J (1998) *Human Resource Management*, Blackwell, Oxford

Schuster, J R and Zingheim, P K (1992) *The New Pay*, Lexington Books, New York, NY

Thompson, M (1998) Trust and reward, in (eds) Stephen Perkins and St John Sandringham, *Trust, Motivation and Commitment*, Strategic Remuneration, Faringdon, Research Centre

Trevor, J (2011) *Can Pay be Strategic?* Palgrave Macmillan, Basingstoke

Trevor, J (2012) A rewarding crisis for HR? *People Management*, January 2012, pp 40–44

Wright, P M and Nishii, L H (2004) Strategic HRM and Organizational Behaviour: Integrating multiple levels of analysis, *Digital Commons @ ILR* [online] http://digitalcommons.ilr.cornell.edu/cgi/viewcontent.cgi?article=1404&context=cahrswp [accessed 21 July 2015]

04
Reward policies

LEARNING OUTCOMES

On completing this chapter you should be able to define these concepts and understand the nature of reward policy and its key elements.

Reward policies defined

Reward policies set specific guidelines for decision making and action and therefore provide the framework for managing a reward system. They indicate what the organization and its management are expected to do about managing reward and how they will behave in given circumstances when dealing with reward issues. They can be distinguished from guiding principles, which usually express a more generalized philosophy and from reward strategies which indicate intentions on how the reward system should be developed but do not describe in detail how it will be operated.

Reward policy areas

Level of rewards

The policy on the level of rewards indicates whether the company is a high payer, is content to pay median or average rates of pay or even, exceptionally, accepts that it has to pay below the average. Pay policy, which is sometimes referred to as the pay stance or pay posture of a company, will depend on a number of factors. These include the extent to which the company demands high levels of performance from its employees, the degree to which there is competition for good-quality people, the traditional stance of the company, the organization culture, and whether or not it can or should afford to be a high payer. A firm may say, 'We will pay upper quartile salaries because we want our staff to be upper quartile performers.'

Policies on pay levels will also refer to differentials and the number of steps or grades that should exist in the pay hierarchy. This will be influenced by the structure of the company. In today's flatter organizations an extended or complex pay hierarchy may not be required on the grounds that it does not reflect the way in which work is organized and will constrain flexibility.

Policies on the level of rewards also cover employee benefits – pensions, sick pay, health care, holidays and perks such as company cars.

External competitiveness versus internal equity

A policy needs to be formulated on the extent to which rewards are market driven rather than equitable. This policy will be influenced by the culture and reward philosophies of the organization and the pressures on the business to obtain and keep high-quality staff. Any organizations that have to attract and retain staff who are much in demand and where market rates are therefore high, may, to a degree, have to sacrifice their ideals (if they have them) of internal equity to the realism of the marketplace. They will provide market pay; in other words, they will be market driven.

The pay management process must cope as best it can when the irresistible force of market pressures meets the immovable object of internal equity. There will always be some degree of tension in these circumstances, and while no solution will ever be simple or entirely satisfactory, there is one basic principle that can enhance the likelihood of success. That principle is to make explicit and fully identifiable the compromises with internal equity that are made and have to be made in response to market pressures.

The policy may indicate that market considerations will drive levels of pay in the organization. It may, however, allow for the use of market supplements – a payment that reflects market rates in addition to the rate for a job as determined by internal equity. The policy may lay down that these payments should be reviewed regularly and no longer offered if they are unnecessary. Market supplements for those who have them may not be withdrawn (the people concerned would not lose pay), but adjustments may be made to pay progression to bring their rates more into line with those for comparable jobs. Market pay and market supplements can lead to gender inequalities if, as is often the case, men in comparable jobs are paid more generously or men rather than women tend to get market supplements. Equal pay case law has ruled that market pay and market supplements should be objectively justified, and the requirement to do this should be included in the pay policy.

The 2007 e-reward survey of grade and pay structures revealed that respondents with market supplements adopted the following policies when such supplements were no longer required:

- remove immediately – 33 per cent;
- retain until upgraded – 30 per cent;
- reduce progressively – 19 per cent;
- protect in line with policy – 18 per cent.

Segmentation

Segmentation involves varying the reward package for different jobs or to reflect the types and levels of contribution people make, or providing rewards that are tailored to meet individual needs.

A policy on segmentation will recognize that parts of the workforce and individuals in the successive stages of their career may be motivated by different combinations of rewards. A total rewards package can be tailored to meet these needs. Rewards may be segmented to take account of key employee differences. This could mean individual merit pay for some, team reward for others, and various forms of pay progression and recognition rather than incentives for a third group. This is a flexible approach to reward management although it should be flexibility within a framework, the framework being provided by guiding principles that apply to all aspects of reward.

Assimilation policies

The introduction of a new or considerably revised pay structure means that policies have to be developed on how existing employees should be assimilated into it. These policies cover where people should be placed in their new grades and what happens to them if their new grade and pay range means that their existing rate is above or below the new scale for their job.

When the introduction of a new pay structure results in some people being over-graded and therefore overpaid, a decision has to be made about how to deal with them. The usual practice is that they should not suffer an immediate loss of pay. In these circumstances they may be required to 'mark time', ie remain at the same rate until other people catch up. They are then said to be 'red-circled'. A protection policy as described below may be required to safeguard their existing rate of pay.

If staff are paid less than the minimum for their new grade they should ideally have their pay increased to that minimum. But this can be expensive and organizations sometimes reduce the immediate cost by phasing the increase over a reasonably limited period of time. Employees in this situation are referred to as being 'green-circled'.

Protection policies

Protection or safeguarding policies define the general rule that no one should suffer an immediate reduction in their present rate of pay following the introduction of a new pay structure. Beyond this, the issues are what exactly is to be protected and whether or not the protection should be for a limited period, and if so, for how long.

Employees are usually entitled to receive any generally available across-the-board (cost of living) increases awarded during the protection period, if it is limited, or for as long as they remain in their present job if there is no limit (in the latter case they are on what is sometimes called a 'personal to job holder' scale). If the period is limited, they will no longer be entitled to general increases after the limit has been reached until their rate of pay falls within the new scale for their job. They will then be entitled to the same increases as any other staff in their grade. When the individual concerned leaves the job, the scale of pay for the job reverts to the standard range as set up following job evaluation.

The argument for limiting the protection period is that, unless this is done, equal pay problems may arise because an inequitable differential will have been perpetuated. The Equality and Human Rights Commission (2011) in its Code of Practice stated that 'it may be difficult to prove that protecting the men's higher pay for any length of time is a proportionate means of achieving the aim where the reason for the original pay disparity is sex discrimination'.

The respondents to the 2007 e-reward survey of grade and pay structures adopted the following protection periods:

- unlimited – 53 per cent;
- one year – 12 per cent;
- two years – 10 per cent;
- three years – 6 per cent;
- four years – 15 per cent;
- five to ten years – 4 per cent.

If employees are paid by means of a time-related incremental system, the usual approach is to allow them to continue to earn any increments to which they are entitled under existing arrangements up to the maximum of their present scale.

The role of line managers

The extent to which the responsibility for rewards should be devolved to line managers is a policy decision. The aim may be to devolve it as far as possible, bearing in mind the need to ensure that other reward policy guidelines are followed and that consistent decisions are made by managers across the organization. The policy may cover the level of decisions managers can make, the guidance that should be made available to them and how consistency will be achieved.

Transparency

Traditionally, organizations in the private sector have kept information about pay policies secret. This is no longer a tenable position. Without transparency, people will believe that the organization has something to hide, often with reason. There is no chance of building a satisfactory psychological contract unless the organization spells out its reward policies and practices. Transparency is achieved through involvement and communication.

Reward policies: six tips

1 Assess the need to develop new policies or revise existing ones by reference to internal requirements and external legislation and regulations.

2 Check with managers, starting from the top, on their views about how policies could be improved.

3 Consult with employees on proposals for new or amended policies.

4 Ensure that the policies are realistic and can be readily implemented.

5 Communicate details of the new or revised policies to managers and employees generally.

6 Provide guidance and help as required to managers in implementing the policies.

References

Equality and Human Rights Commission (2011) Equal pay: Statutory code of practice, *Equality and Human Rights Commission* [online] www.equalityhumanrights.com/uploaded_files/EqualityAct/equalpaycode.pdf

e-reward (2007) The e-reward grade and pay structure survey 2007, *e-reward* [online] www.e-reward.co.uk/research/surveys/the-e-reward-grade-and-pay-structure-survey-2007 [accessed 22 July 2015] Registration is required to access this survey.

05
Factors affecting reward

KEY CONCEPTS AND TERMS

- Agency theory
- Bureaucratic organization
- Classical economic theory
- Efficiency wage theory

- The effort bargain
- Human capital theory
- The labour theory of value
- Tournament theory

LEARNING OUTCOMES

On completing this chapter you should understand and be able to define these concepts and terms. You will also know about how the internal and external contexts of the organization affect reward policies and practice and appreciate the many factors that affect pay levels.

Introduction

Reward strategies and policies and the design and operation of reward systems are contingent on the internal and external environment. There are also a number of contextual or environmental factors that affect the level of pay within an organization.

Internal context

The characteristic features of the internal context are as follows.

The organization's culture

Organizational culture consists of shared values, norms and assumptions which influence the way people act and the way things get done. In reward management, the most important aspects of culture that need to be taken into account are the core values of the organization which express beliefs about what sort of behaviour is desirable. Reward practices should fit in with and support the culture and they can help to reshape it.

Organization type

The degree to which the organization is bureaucratic will affect reward practice. As defined by Trevor (2011), the differences between a bureaucratic organization and a 'post-bureaucratic' one are shown in Table 5.1.

TABLE 5.1   Bureaucratic and post-bureaucratic organization

Bureaucratic	Post-bureaucratic
• Vertically integrated	• Horizontal integration
• Hierarchical	• Network not hierarchy
• Rational design	• Informal system
• Control and order (compliance)	• Focus on individual capabilities
• Policies, rules and procedures	• Common task

Tendencies in reward practice in a bureaucratic or a post-bureaucratic organization are illustrated in Table 5.2.

TABLE 5.2   Tendencies in reward practice in a bureaucratic or a post-bureaucratic organization

Bureaucratic	Post-bureaucratic
• Multi-graded pay structure or pay spine	• Broad-graded structure or spot rates
• Job content determines grading and pay	• Grading and pay strongly related to personal skills and competencies
• Pay progression strictly governed by performance ratings or service criteria	• Flexible approach to pay progression
• Fixed range of benefits	• Flexible benefits
• Tight centralized control of pay decisions	• Maximum devolution of pay decisions to line managers

The organization's business or sector

The business or sector of the organization – for example manufacturing, financial services, retail services, transport, media, public sector services, not-for-profit services or education – will govern its ethos and therefore core values. It will influence the type of people it employs and the degree to which it is subject to turbulence and change. All these factors affect reward strategy and practice.

The work environment

The ways in which work is managed and carried out will influence pay structure and the use of contingent pay. The introduction of new technology may result in considerable changes to systems and processes. Different skills are required, new methods of working and therefore reward are developed. The result may be an extension of the skills base of the organization and its employees, including multiskilling. A teamworking environment may encourage the introduction of team pay. Traditional piecework pay systems in the manufacturing industry may be replaced by higher fixed pay and rewards focused on quality and employee teamwork.

People

People's occupations may affect their wants and needs. Bankers, entrepreneurial directors and sales representatives are more likely to be interested in financial incentives than, possibly, people engaged in charitable work. Reward strategies and policies should take account of the different needs of people and this may mean segmenting rewards to meet those needs.

Business strategy

Where the business is going – the business strategy – determines where reward should go. Integrating reward and business strategies ensures that they work together to achieve the mission or purpose of the organization.

Political and social climate

Organizational politics and social factors such as the way people interact will affect how the organization functions and therefore what approach to reward management it adopts.

External context

The following aspects of the external context may affect reward management policies.

Globalization

Globalization requires organizations to move people, ideas, products and information around the world to meet local needs. Traditionally, discussions of international reward strategies and practices have tended to focus on an elite of expatriate workers, sourced from headquarters locations and rewarded in isolation from local country staff. A more diverse and complex pattern is now emerging, requiring a more strategic approach as described in Chapter 26.

Rates of pay in the marketplace

The external environment exerts considerable influence on rates of pay and pay reviews within organizations. Market or going rate levels and movements have to be taken into account by organizations if they want their pay to be competitive. Some organizations are affected by national agreements with trade unions.

The economy

The economy, whether it is in a boom or bust mode, will inevitably affect reward policy and practice. A recession increases the attention organizations pay to getting value for money and reduces the amounts that can be distributed in the form of base and contingent pay and the scale of benefits provision.

Societal factors

Views about reward held in society at large may affect internal reward policies. For example, the opprobrium recently levelled at 'fat cats' in boardrooms and the bonus culture in the City may possibly have some influence on members of remuneration committees. Again, it may not.

UK employment legislation

The following pieces of UK legislation directly or indirectly affect pay policies and practices:

- The Equality Act 2010 provides that pay differences are allowable only if the reason for them is not related to the sex of the job holder. Equal pay legislation is described in Chapter 16.
- The National Minimum Wage Act 1998 provides workers in the UK with a level of pay below which their wages must not fall – regardless of where they live or work or the sector or size of company in which they work. It is not a going rate. The government prescribes by regulation the minimum wage.
- The Working Time Regulations 1998 provide, inter alia, for a limit of 48 hours on average weekly working time which an individual worker may voluntarily

agree to exceed and a minimum of four weeks' paid annual leave subject to a 13-week qualifying period.

- The Data Protection Act 1998 provides, inter alia, that employees are entitled to make a formal request to access information on the personal data held on them and the uses to which this will be put.

- The Transfer of Undertakings (Protection of Employment) Regulations 1981 (TUPE) provide that when a business or part of a business is transferred the workers in that business automatically transfer into the employment of the transferee together with their existing terms and conditions of employment (except for pensions) intact and with their accrued periods of continuous service.

- The Financial Services Act 1986 places restrictions on the provision of financial advice to employees. Only those who are directly authorized by one of the regulatory organizations or professional bodies are permitted to give detailed financial advice on investments.

The trade unions

Trade unions, especially in the public sector, influence reward practices at national level through national pay negotiations, pronouncements on such issues as the pay of top executives, and exerting pressure to achieve equal pay. They produce policies and advice for their members on job evaluation (they are in favour of analytical schemes while emphasizing the need for involvement in their design), pay structures (they tend to be against broad-banded structures) and performance-related pay (they are generally hostile to it).

Factors affecting levels of pay

The factors that influence pay levels and affect pay decisions are:

- the nature of the external and internal labour market;
- classical economic theory (the economic 'laws' of supply and demand);
- the labour theory of value;
- human capital theory;
- efficiency wage theory;
- agency theory;
- the effort bargain;
- tournament theory.

The labour market

Markets consist of buyers and sellers. The efforts of the buyers and sellers of labour constitute a labour market. An external market may be local, national or international.

It may be related to specific occupations, sectors or industries in any of these areas. It is within these markets that the economic determinants of pay levels operate which include supply and demand factors as described later and the impact of inflationary pressures. Market rate analysis is used to obtain information about the external market.

In any sizeable organization there is also an internal labour market. This is the market which exists when firms fill their vacancies from the ranks of existing employees. Pay levels and relativities in the internal market may differ significantly between firms in spite of general external market pressures. These arise particularly when long-term employment takes place, although this is becoming less common. Pay in the internal market will be affected by views on the intrinsic value of jobs and what individuals are worth on the basis of their expertise and contribution irrespective of the market rate for their job. Pay progression related to length of service and an annuity approach to pay increments (ie pay which goes up but does not come down, what economists call the sticky wage) may lead to higher internal rates. But the relationship between internal and external rates will also depend on policy decisions within the firm on its levels of pay generally compared with the going rate in the external market.

Classical economic theory

The first theory of wages was advanced by Adam Smith (1776) when he wrote: 'The whole of the advantages and disadvantages of different employments and stock must, in the same neighbourhood, be either perfectly equal or continually tending to equality.' He suggested that workers seek to maximize total utility, not just wages, with total utility (and thus job choice) being a function of the total net advantage of various jobs. Besides pay this includes the agreeableness or disagreeableness of work, difficulty and expense of learning it, job security, responsibility and the possibility of success or failure. A higher wage or 'compensating wage differential' was required for jobs without some or all of these characteristics. Conversely, jobs with them could be paid less and still offer the same net advantages as those that pay more but lack the other advantages. Workers seek to maximize this net advantage or total utility, not just wages. The theory of total net advantage underpins the concept of total rewards.

Later classical and neo-classical theory in the 19th century treated wages as the price of labour and therefore subject to the laws of supply and demand. This meant adopting the questionable assumption that all non-pecuniary aspects of jobs are equal. The theory focused on the external labour market. Classical wages theory states that if the supply of labour exceeds the demand, pay levels go down; if there is a scarcity of labour and demand exceeds the supply, pay goes up. Pay stabilizes when demand equals supply at the 'market clearing' or 'market equilibrium' wage. This is sometimes known as the theory of equalizing differences. According to the classical labour economists, the price of labour is the rate of pay required to attract and retain people in organizations.

As Elliott (1991) noted:

> Competitive theory predicts that the forces of supply in the market as a whole will determine the rates of pay within each firm. The relative pay of any two occupations in a single firm will be the mirror image of the relative pay of the same two occupations in the market as a whole.

However, classical economic theory is based on the premises that 'other things are equal' and that a 'perfect market' for labour exists. In the real world, of course, other things are never equal and there is no such thing as a universally perfect market, that is, one in which everyone knows what the going rate is, there is free movement of labour within the market and there are no monopolistic or other forces interfering with the normal processes of supply and demand. Imperfections in the market exist because of poor information, lack of opportunity and immobility. They also arise when employers or trade unions exert pressures on pay levels or when governments intervene in normal pay determination processes.

Human capital theory as discussed later also explains why individual rates of pay may be influenced by other forces besides supply and demand.

The labour theory of value

In 1867 Karl Marx wrote in *Das Kapital* that the value of goods and services is determined by the amount of labour that goes into them. It is not the marketplace that sets prices. Thus the content of labour determines the price of labour. Mainstream economists have never accepted this theory and assert the primacy of supply and demand in the marketplace in setting prices of goods and services. However, as pointed out by Nielsen (2002), conventional job evaluation schemes are based on the labour theory of value in that they are only concerned with job content and ignore market rate pressures. They make no attempt to price jobs directly.

Human capital theory

Levels of pay are influenced by the value of human capital in terms of the skills and expertise people possess. Workers invest in education and training to increase their value as human capital and so enhance their future earnings. As explained in more detail by Ehrenberg and Smith (1994) human capital theory

> ... conceptualizes workers as embodying a set of skills which can be 'rented out' to employers. The knowledge and skills a worker has – which come from education and training, including the training that experience brings – generate a certain stock of productive capital.

For the employee, the expected returns on human capital investments are a higher level of earnings, greater job satisfaction and, at one time, but less so now, a belief that security in employment is assured. For the employer, the return on investment in human capital is expected to be improvements in performance, productivity, flexibility and the capacity to innovate, which should result from enlarging the skill base and increasing levels of competence.

Efficiency wage theory

Efficiency wage theory proposes that firms will pay more than the market rate because they believe that high levels of pay will contribute to increases in productivity. This can happen in two ways: an incentive effect (generating higher amounts of effort among current employees) and a sorting effect (attracting higher quality employees in the first place). This theory is also known as 'the economy of high wages'. Organizations are using efficiency wage theory (although they will not call it that) when they formulate pay policies which place them as market leaders or at least above the average.

Resource dependence theory (Pfeffer and Davis-Blake, 1987) is associated with efficiency wage theory but focuses on the idea of paying more to attract and retain high-quality employees in critical positions.

Agency theory

Agency theory, also known as principal agent theory, states that in most firms there is a separation between the owners (the principals) and the agents (the managers). Because the principals may not have complete control over their agents the latter may act in ways which may not be in accordance with the wishes of those principals and are not revealed to them. This generates what economists call agency costs. These consist of the extent to which the amount earned for the company by the managers as agents to the owners or principals is more than might have been earned if the principals had been the managers.

Agency theory as described above can be extended to the concept of the employment relationship which may be regarded as a contract between a principal (the employer) and an agent (the employee). The payment aspect of the contract is the method used by the principal to motivate the agent to perform work to the satisfaction of the employer. But according to this theory, the problem of ensuring that agents do what they are told remains. It is necessary to clear up ambiguities by setting targets and monitoring performance to ensure that those objectives are achieved.

Agency theory also indicates that it is desirable to operate a system of incentives to motivate and reward acceptable behaviour. This process of incentive alignment consists of paying for measurable results, which are deemed to be in the best interests of the owners. Incentive systems track outcomes in the shape of quantifiable indices of the firm's performance such as earnings per share rather than being concerned with the behaviour that led up to them. Agency theory is used to justify executive bonuses in accordance with the belief that if incentives schemes are designed properly, top managers will out of self-interest closely monitor performance throughout the organization.

Agency theory was criticized by Bruce et al (2005) who suggested that it cannot be used to explain executive pay because some researchers adopting an agency theory perspective have failed to find a strong empirical link between executive pay and firm performance. A riposte to this from Gomez-Mejia et al (2005) claimed that agency theory does not make any reference to pay performance sensitivity, and that the failure of this research can be attributable to a variety of problems with the methodologies used.

The basic proposition of the theory is that the only way in which principals can get loyalty from their agents is by paying them more. As Perkins and Hendry (2005) commented: 'Agency theory takes an essentially negative view of the relationship between principal and agents.'

The effort bargain

The notion of the effort bargain is referred to less frequently nowadays but it has its uses as a further means of describing the employment relationship. The concept states that the task of management is to assess what level and type of inducements it has to offer in return for the contribution it requires from its workforce.

The aim of workers is to strike a bargain about the relationship between what they regard as a reasonable contribution and what their employer is prepared to offer to elicit that contribution. This is termed the effort bargain and is, in effect, an agreement which lays down the amount of work to be done for a rate of pay or wage rate, not just the hours to be worked. Explicitly or implicitly, all employees are in a bargaining situation with regard to pay. A system will not be accepted as effective and workable until it is recognized as fair and equitable by both parties and unless it is applied consistently.

Tournament theory

Tournament theory (Lazear and Rosen, 1981) explains the basis of pay dispersion. The tournament model, as its name suggests, describes a process of increasing the motivation of high-quality staff by offering lucrative prizes (ie pay) for a small number of people who are promoted to higher-level jobs, with the highest prize of all given to the person who wins the tournament by getting the top job. Pay growth is larger at higher levels because the scope for further promotions is lower. The relationship between pay level and organizational level is therefore convex.

The theory indicates that this arrangement will encourage managers to outperform other managers and thereby gain the prize of advancing up the pay structure. Winners stay on to compete again for even larger pay increases. Losers, however, are eliminated from further competitions and are expected to leave their organization, since their only alternative is to accept inferior pay and limited career expectations. Thus, according to the theory, dispersed pay structures help to retain the star managers in a firm and encourage poor-quality managers to leave. And people at the highest levels do not need to be worth the amount of the prize for the scheme to be efficient because efficiency is a result of the incentive effects that these larger prizes have on people lower down in the hierarchy. Resource dependence theory as mentioned earlier focuses on the level of pay required to attract and retain staff in critical positions rather than the differentials between those at the higher levels.

Research on management pay hierarchies by Conyon *et al* (2001), using data on 500 executives from the top three levels of 100 UK firms, found not only the predicted convex relationship between executive pay and organizational level but also that higher chief executive differentials were associated with larger numbers of executives in the levels just below the top. For each added executive in the next two levels below the chief executive, the difference between the latter's pay and that of the rest of the executive team increased by 3.5 per cent.

Other research has questioned some of the claimed beneficial effects of the tournament model. The results of a study by Bloom (1999) indicated that greater dispersion in pay within an organization is associated with lower individual and group performance, at least where work interdependencies are important. Research by Bloom and Michel (2002) established that organizations with greater dispersion in their pay structures had managers with lower tenures and higher probabilities of turnover.

Pay determination within organizations

The process of determining pay levels and the rates of pay for individual jobs within organizations are influenced by all the factors described above. Levels of pay are affected by an implicit belief in efficiency wage theory – that higher rates of pay attract good candidates (the sorting effect), enhance performance (the incentive effect) and help to retain employees. There will be policies and practices on the range or dispersion of pay between different levels in the organization. The organization will have a defined or implicit 'pay stance' policy, ie the relationship desired between the levels of pay within the organization and market rates.

The other factors affecting rates of pay are beliefs about the value of the job and the person, internal relativities, financial considerations (the ability to pay), the influence of trade unions and the minimum wage.

Value of the job

The intrinsic value of a job is a measure of what a job (not a person) is worth in terms of what it contributes to achieving the purpose of the organization. An intrinsic value is attached to jobs because of the impact they make on organizational results and by reference to the levels of responsibility and skill required to perform them. Increases in impact and these levels lead to higher rates of pay. This concept is in line with the labour theory of value and provides the theoretical base for job evaluation. However, as an explanation of the value attached to jobs it is limited because it ignores external relativities.

Value of the person

Individuals are valued by organizations for three main reasons: (1) the contribution they make to organizational success; (2) their competencies and skills; (3) the experience they bring to their jobs. People also have their own value in the marketplace – their market worth – which has to be taken into account by employers in setting their rates of pay.

Internal relativities

It can be argued that the value of anything, including jobs, is always relative to something else, that is, other jobs. Views on job values within organizations are based on perceptions of the worth of one job compared with others. This may be a matter of opinion but attempts can be made to measure relative worth through job evaluation, which is essentially a comparative process. The aim is to achieve internal equity, which occurs when people are rewarded appropriately in relation to others according to the value of their contribution. The case for equal pay for work of equal value is based on the imperative to achieve internal equity.

Financial circumstances of the organization

Affordability is an important concept in reward management. The aim is to ensure that pay systems do not cost more than the organization can afford and this will influence the level of pay that can be offered to employees. Extra expenditure on pay, eg bonus payments, should add value in the sense that the benefits resulting from improved performance outweigh the cost.

Trade union influence

Pay levels may be determined through collective bargaining with trade unions. They will want their members' pay to keep ahead of inflation, to match market rates and to reflect any increases in the prosperity of the business. The amount of pressure they can exert on pay levels will depend on the relative bargaining strengths of the employer and the union.

The minimum wage

Minimum wage legislation in the UK sets minimum rates of pay. The amount is increased from time to time.

Example of pay policy

An example of a policy on pay levels is provided by AEGON UK, where the reward system is designed to recognize three core factors that affect the level of pay. The policy states that individuals should be rewarded for their 'personal commitment and consistent contribution within their roles'. The core factors are:

- Internal job value – the bigger the job, the higher the reward.
- External job value – the level of reward will be influenced by external market rates and the degree to which market forces affect the salaries required to attract and retain quality staff.
- Value of the person – individual employees may be rewarded at a higher level because they are making a greater contribution, are performing better,

meeting objectives and have achieved a higher level of skill or competence than their colleagues (measured through the performance management process).

As an internal policy statement explains: 'Whilst the first two factors are the primary responsibility of the compensation and benefits in group personnel, line managers are best placed to manage the third factor for all staff within their reporting teams.'

Summary of factors affecting pay levels

The factors affecting individual pay levels are summarized in Figure 5.1.

FIGURE 5.1   Factors affecting pay levels

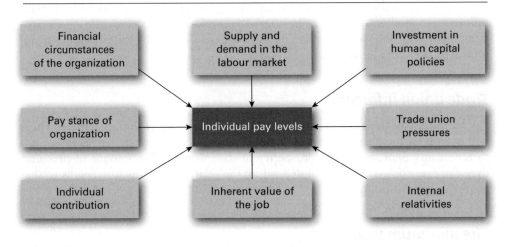

References

Bloom, M (1999) The performance effects of pay dispersion on individuals and organizations, *Academy of Management Journal*, **42** (1), pp 25–40

Bloom, M and Michel, J G (2002) The relationships among organizational context, pay dispersion, and managerial turnover, *Academy of Management Journal*, **45** (1), pp 33–47

Bruce, A, Buck, T and Main, B G (2005) Top executive remuneration: a view from Europe, *Journal of Management Studies*, **42** (7), pp 1493–506

Conyon, M J, Beck, S I and Sadler, G V (2001) Corporate tournaments and executive compensation: evidence from the UK, *Strategic Management Journal*, **22** (8), pp 805–15

Ehrenberg, R G and Smith, R S (1994) *Modern Labor Economics*, Harper Collins, New York, NY

Elliott, R F (1991) *Labour Economics*, McGraw-Hill, Maidenhead

Gomez-Mejia, L, Wiseman, R M and Dykes, B J (2005) Agency problems in diverse contexts: a global perspective, *Journal of Management Studies*, **42** (7), pp 1507–17

Lazear, E P and Rosen, S (1981) Rank order tournaments as an optimum labor contract, *Journal of Political Economy*, **89**, pp 841–64

Marx, K (1867, translated in 1976) *Capital*, Penguin, Harmondsworth

Nielsen, N H (2002) Job content evaluation techniques based on Marxian economics, *WorldatWork Journal*, **11** (2), pp 52–62

Perkins, S J and Hendry, C (2005) Ordering top pay: interpreting the signals, *Journal of Management Studies*, **42** (7), pp 1443–68

Pfeffer, J and Davis-Blake, A (1987) Understanding organizational wages structures: a resource dependence approach, *Academy of Management Journal*, **30**, pp 437–55

Smith, Adam (1776) *The Wealth of Nations*, published by Penguin Books, Harmondsworth, 1986

Trevor, J (2011) *Can Pay be Strategic?* Palgrave Macmillan, Basingstoke

06
Motivation and reward

KEY CONCEPTS AND TERMS

- Discretionary effort
- Extrinsic motivation
- Intrinsic motivation
- Line of sight
- Motivation
- Self-efficacy

LEARNING OUTCOMES

On completing this chapter you should be able to define these key concepts. You should also know about:

- The process of motivation
- Types of motivation
- Instrumentality theory
- Reinforcement theory
- Content (needs) theory
- Process theory
- Expectancy theory
- Goal theory
- Equity theory
- Cognitive evaluation theory
- How motivation theories affect reward management

Introduction

High performance is achieved by well-motivated people who are prepared to exercise discretionary effort (the choice people can make about the amount of effort they exert and the productive behaviour they display in their jobs). Hunter *et al* (1990) found that even in fairly basic roles the difference in value-added discretionary performance between 'superior' and 'standard' performers was 19 per cent. For highly complex jobs it was 48 per cent.

It is often said that one of the three main aims of reward management is to motivate (the other two are to attract and retain people). It is therefore important when managing reward to understand how motivation takes place and what part reward management plays in it. This provides the basis for the analysis of financial and non-financial rewards as covered in Chapters 9 and 10.

The process of motivation

A motive is a reason for doing something. Motivation is concerned with the strength and direction of behaviour and the factors that influence people to behave in certain ways. People are motivated when they expect that a course of action is likely to lead to the attainment of a goal and a valued reward – one which satisfies their needs and wants.

The term motivation can refer variously to the goals individuals have, the ways in which individuals choose their goals and the ways in which others try to change their behaviour. As described by Arnold *et al* (1991), the three components of motivation are:

1 direction – what a person is trying to do;

2 effort – how hard a person is trying;

3 persistence – how long a person keeps on trying.

Well-motivated people engage in discretionary behaviour – in the majority of roles there is scope for individuals to decide how much effort to exert. Such people may be self-motivated, and as long as this means they are going in the right direction to attain what they are there to achieve, then this is the best form of motivation. But additional motivation provided by the work itself, the quality of leadership and various forms of recognition and reward builds on self-motivation and helps people to make the best use of their abilities and perform well.

There are two types of motivation and a number of theories explaining how it works as discussed below.

Types of motivation

The two types of motivation are intrinsic motivation and extrinsic motivation.

Intrinsic motivation

Intrinsic motivation can arise from the self-generated factors, which influence people's behaviour. It is not created by external incentives. It can take the form of motivation by the work itself when individuals feel that their work is important, interesting and challenging and provides them with a reasonable degree of autonomy (freedom to act), opportunities to achieve and advance, and scope to use and develop their skills and abilities. Deci and Ryan (1985) suggested that intrinsic motivation is based on the needs to be competent and self-determining (that is, to have a choice).

Intrinsic motivation can be enhanced by job or role design. An early writer on the significance of the motivational impact of job design (Katz, 1964) wrote: 'The job itself must provide sufficient variety, sufficient complexity, sufficient challenge and sufficient skill to engage the abilities of the worker.' In their job characteristics model, Hackman and Oldham (1974) emphasized the importance as motivators of the core job dimensions, namely: skill variety, task identity, task significance, autonomy and feedback.

Extrinsic motivation

Extrinsic motivation occurs when things are done to or for people to motivate them. These include rewards, such as incentives, increased pay, praise, or promotion; and punishments, such as disciplinary action, withholding pay, or criticism.

Extrinsic motivators can have an immediate and powerful effect, but this will not necessarily last long. The intrinsic motivators, which are concerned with the 'quality of working life' (a phrase and movement which emerged from this concept), are likely to have a deeper and longer-term effect because they are inherent in individuals and the work they do and are not imposed from outside in such forms as incentive pay.

The motivation theories summarized below (instrumentality, reinforcement, content and process) attempt to explain the ways in which intrinsic and extrinsic motivation take place.

Instrumentality theory

Instrumentality is the belief that if we do one thing it will lead to another. In its crudest form, instrumentality theory states that people only work for money.

The theory emerged in the second half of the 19th century, with its emphasis on the need to rationalize work and on economic outcomes. It assumes that people will be motivated to work if rewards and penalties are tied directly to their performance; thus the awards are contingent upon effective performance. Instrumentality theory has its roots in the scientific management methods of Taylor (1911), who wrote: 'It is impossible, through any long period of time, to get workmen to work much harder than the average men around them unless they are assured a large and permanent increase in their pay.'

Motivation using this approach has been and still is widely adopted and can be successful in some circumstances such as piecework, when payment is directly related to output. But it is based exclusively on a system of external controls and fails to recognize a number of other human needs. It also fails to appreciate the fact that the formal control system can be seriously affected by the informal relationship existing between workers. Instrumentality theory is associated with reinforcement theory.

Reinforcement theory

Reinforcement theory as developed by Hull (1951) suggests that successes in achieving goals and rewards act as positive incentives and reinforce the successful behaviour, which is repeated the next time a similar need emerges. The more powerful, obvious and frequent the reinforcement, the more likely it is that the behaviour will be repeated until, eventually, it can become a more or less unconscious reaction to an event. Conversely, failures or punishments provide negative reinforcement, suggesting that it is necessary to seek alternative means of achieving goals. This process has been called the law of effect.

But motivational theories based on the principle of reinforcement pay insufficient attention to the influence of expectations, and no indication is given of any means of distinguishing in advance the class of outcomes, which would strengthen responses, and those which would weaken them. They are limited because they imply, in Allport's (1954) vivid phrase, a 'hedonism of the past'. They assume that the explanation of the present choices of individuals is to be found in an examination of the consequences of their past choices. They ignore the present context in which choices are made.

Content (needs) theory

Content theory focuses on the content of motivation in the shape of needs and proposes that all behaviour is motivated by unsatisfied needs. Its basis is the belief that an unsatisfied need creates tension and a state of disequilibrium. To restore the balance a goal is identified which will satisfy the need, and a behaviour pathway is selected which will lead to the achievement of the goal and the satisfaction of the need, but new needs may emerge and have to be satisfied. This process is modelled in Figure 6.1. This illustrates a process of motivation, which involves setting goals that are likely to meet individual needs and encouraging the behaviour required to achieve those goals.

But it is necessary to remember two fundamental truths about motivation. First, there is a multiplicity of needs, goals and actions, which depend on the person and the situation. It is unwise to assume that any one approach to motivation will appeal to all affected by it. Motivation policies and practices must recognize that people are different. Second, while we can observe how people behave – the actions they take – we cannot be certain about what has motivated them to behave that way, ie what the needs and goals are that have affected their actions. These factors mean that

FIGURE 6.1   The process of motivation according to content theory

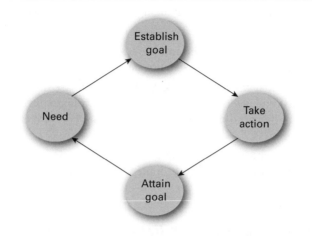

simplistic methods of increasing motivation such as merit pay rarely work as well as intended.

Needs theory has been developed by Maslow, Alderfer, McClelland and Herzberg as described below.

Maslow's hierarchy of needs

The best-known classification of needs is the one formulated by Maslow (1954). He suggested that there are five major need categories which apply to people in general, starting from the fundamental physiological needs and leading through a hierarchy of safety, social and esteem needs to the need for self-fulfilment, the highest need of all. When a lower need is satisfied the next highest becomes dominant and the individual's attention is turned to satisfying this higher need. The need for self-fulfilment, however, can never be satisfied. 'Man is a wanting animal': only an un-satisfied need can motivate behaviour, and the dominant need is the prime motivator of behaviour. Psychological development takes place as people move up the hierarchy of needs, but this is not necessarily a straightforward progression. The lower needs still exist, even if temporarily dormant as motivators, and individuals constantly return to previously satisfied needs.

Maslow's needs hierarchy has an intuitive appeal and has been very popular. But it has not been verified by empirical research such as that conducted by Wahba and Bridwell (1979). It has been criticized for its apparent rigidity – different people may have different priorities – and the underpinning assumption that everyone has the same needs is invalid. It is difficult to accept that needs progress steadily up the hierarchy and Maslow himself expressed doubts about the validity of a strictly ordered hierarchy. But he did emphasize that the higher-order needs are more significant.

ERG theory (Alderfer)

Alderfer (1972) produced a more convincing and simpler theory, which postulated three primary categories of needs:

1 Existence needs such as hunger and thirst – pay, fringe benefits and working conditions are other types of existence needs.

2 Relatedness needs, which acknowledge that people are not self-contained units but must engage in transactions with their human environment – acceptance, understanding, confirmation and influence are elements of the relatedness process.

3 Growth needs, which involve people in finding the opportunities 'to be what they are most fully and to become what they can'. This is the most significant need.

McClelland's achievement–affiliation–power needs

An alternative way of classifying needs was developed by McClelland (1961), who based it mainly on studies of managers. He identified three needs, of which the need for achievement was most important:

1 The need for achievement, defined as the need for competitive success measured against a personal standard of excellence.

2 The need for affiliation, defined as the need for warm, friendly, compassionate relationships with others.

3 The need for power, defined as the need to control or influence others.

Herzberg's two-factor model

The two-factor model of motivation developed by Herzberg (1966, 1987) was based on an investigation into the sources of job satisfaction and dissatisfaction of accountants and engineers who were asked what made them feel exceptionally good or exceptionally bad about their jobs. According to Herzberg, this research established that the factors that affected positive feelings were quite different from those that affected negative feelings. He called these respectively the motivating factors and the hygiene factors. Motivating factors or 'satisfiers' relate to the job content and consist of the need for achievement, the interest of the work, responsibility and opportunities for advancement. They are the intrinsic motivators. He summed this up in the phrase 'motivation by the work itself'.

The hygiene factors relate to the job context including such things as pay and working conditions. 'Hygiene' is used in the medical use of the term, meaning preventative and environmental. In themselves hygiene factors neither satisfy nor motivate and they serve primarily to prevent job dissatisfaction, while having little effect on positive job attitudes. Pay is not a satisfier but if it is inadequate or inequitable it can cause dissatisfaction. However, its provision does not provide lasting satisfaction.

Herzberg's theory has been widely criticized by academics as being unsupported by his evidence. Denise Rousseau (2006) summed up these views as follows: 'Herzberg's long-discredited two-factor theory is typically included in the motivation section of management textbooks, despite the fact that it was discredited as an artefact of method bias over 30 years ago.'

In spite of these objections the Herzberg two-factor theory continues to thrive; partly because it is easy to understand and seems to be based on real life rather than academic abstractions, and partly because it convincingly emphasizes the positive value of the intrinsic motivating factors and highlights the need to consider both financial and non-financial factors when developing reward systems. It is also in accord with a fundamental belief in the dignity of labour and the Protestant ethic that work is good in itself. Herzberg's strength as a proselytizer rather than a researcher meant that he had considerable influence on the job enrichment movement, which sought to design jobs in a way that would maximize the opportunities to obtain intrinsic satisfaction from work and thus improve the quality of working life. As Herzberg famously remarked: 'If you want people to do a good job give them a good job to do' (quoted by Dowling, 1971).

Comment on needs theory

Shields (2007) observed that needs theories share some common shortcomings. He wrote:

> They assume the existence of a universally applicable set of human needs. They tend to treat the workplace as the primary site of human need fulfilment. They underestimate the motivational potency of extrinsic rewards, including financial rewards. They assume that needs conform to a simple ordered hierarchy of need importance, when in reality, needs seem to operate in a more flexible, less ordered and predictable way. Most importantly, however, they assume that the link between needs and behaviours is direct and automatic, rather than mediated by human consciousness, values and choice. Even if we all have the same needs to satisfy, we may each prioritize them differently and choose different priorities to satisfy them.

Process theory

In process theory, the emphasis is on the psychological processes or forces that affect motivation, as well as on basic needs. It is also known as cognitive theory because it is concerned with people's perceptions of their working environment and the ways in which they interpret and understand it. According to Guest (1992), process theory provides a much more relevant approach to motivation that replaces the theories of Maslow and Herzberg which, he claims, have been shown by extensive research to be wrong.

Process or cognitive theory can certainly be more useful to managers than needs theory because it provides more practical guidance on motivation techniques and the design of reward systems. The main processes are expectations, goal achievement, feelings about equity and cognitive evaluation.

Expectancy theory

Expectancy theory states that motivation will be high when people know what they have to do to get a reward, expect that they will be able to get the reward and expect that the reward will be worthwhile.

The concept of expectancy was originally contained in the valency–instrumentality–expectancy (VIE) theory, which was formulated by Vroom (1964). Valency stands for value, instrumentality is the belief that if we do one thing it will lead to another, and expectancy is the probability that action or effort will lead to an outcome.

The strength of expectations may be based on past experiences (reinforcement), but individuals are frequently presented with new situations – a change in job, payment system, or working conditions imposed by management – where past experience is an inadequate guide to the implications of the change. In these circumstances, motivation may be reduced.

Motivation is only likely when a clearly perceived and usable relationship exists between performance and outcome, and the outcome is seen as a means of satisfying needs. This explains why extrinsic financial motivation – for example, an incentive or bonus scheme – works only if the link (line of sight) between effort and reward is clear and the value of the reward is worth the effort. It also explains why intrinsic motivation arising from the work itself can be more powerful than extrinsic motivation: intrinsic motivation outcomes are more under the control of individuals, who can place greater reliance on their past experiences to indicate the extent to which positive and advantageous results are likely to be obtained by their behaviour.

This theory was developed by Porter and Lawler (1968) into a model which follows Vroom's ideas by suggesting that there are two factors determining the effort people put into their jobs: first, the value of the rewards to individuals in so far as they satisfy their needs for security, social esteem, autonomy, and self-actualization; and second, the probability that rewards depend on effort, as perceived by individuals – in other words, their expectations about the relationships between effort and reward. Thus the greater the value of a set of awards and the higher the probability that receiving each of these rewards depends upon effort, the greater the effort that will be put forth in a given situation.

But, as Porter and Lawler emphasized, mere effort is not enough. It has to be effective effort if it is to produce the desired performance. The two variables additional to effort which affect task achievement are (1) ability – individual characteristics such as intelligence, knowledge and skills, and (2) role perceptions – what individuals want to do or think they are required to do. These are good from the viewpoint of the organization if they correspond with what it thinks the individual ought to be doing. They are poor if the views of the individual and the organization do not coincide. A model of the theory is shown in Figure 6.2.

FIGURE 6.2   Expectancy motivation model (Porter and Lawler)

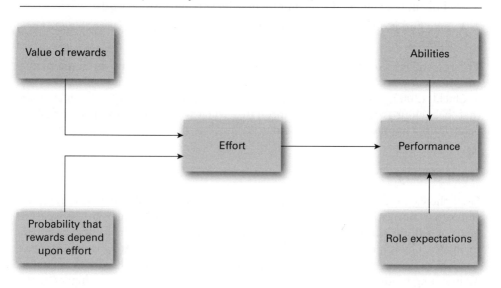

Alongside goal theory (see below), expectancy theory has become the most influential theory affecting reward management and performance. But reservations have been expressed about it. House *et al* (1974) commented that 'Evidence for the validity of the theory is very mixed.' They also established that there were a number of variables affecting expectations, which make it difficult to predict how they function. These are:

- leadership behaviour – the function of the leader in clarifying expectations, guiding, supporting and rewarding subordinates;
- individual characteristics – the subject's perception of their ability to perform the required task;
- nature of the task – whether accomplishing the task provides the necessary reinforcements and rewards;
- the practices of the organization – its reward and control systems and how the organization functions.

Research conducted by Behling and Starke (1973) established that individuals:

- make crucial personal decisions without clearly understanding the consequences;
- do not in practice consistently evaluate their order of preference for alternative actions;
- have to assign two values when making a decision: its desirability and its achievability; but they tend to be influenced mainly by desirability: they let their tastes influence their beliefs;

- may be able to evaluate the extrinsic rewards they expect but may find it difficult to evaluate the possibility of achieving intrinsic rewards;
- may find it difficult to distinguish the benefits of one possible outcome from another.

The researchers concluded that: 'Expectancy theory can account for some of the variations in work effort but far less than normally attributed to it.'

Shields (2007) commented that a problem with expectancy theory is that it assumes that 'behaviour is rational and premeditated when we know that much workplace behaviour is impulsive and emotional'.

Goal theory

Goal theory as developed by Latham and Locke (1979) following their research states that motivation and performance are higher when individuals are set specific goals, when goals are demanding but accepted, and when there is feedback on performance. Goals must be clearly defined. Participation in goal setting is important as a means of getting agreement to the setting of demanding goals. Feedback is vital in maintaining motivation, particularly towards the achievement of even higher goals. This theory has had a significant effect on the concept of performance management as described in Chapter 8.

However, the universality of goal theory has been questioned. For example, Pintrich (2000) noted that people have different goals in different circumstances and that it is hard to justify the assumption that goals are always accessible and conscious. And Harackiewicz *et al* (2002) warned that goals are only effective when they are consistent with and match the general context in which they are pursued. But support for goal theory was provided by Bandura and Cervone (1983), who emphasized the importance of self-evaluation and self-efficacy (a belief in one's ability to accomplish goals).

Equity theory

Equity theory, as defined by Adams (1965), is concerned with the perceptions people have about how they are being treated compared with others. He proposed that employees assess the fairness or otherwise of their rewards (outcomes) in relation to their effort or qualifications (inputs) and that they do this by comparing their own input/output ratio against that of other individuals. If the input/output ratio is perceived to be unfavourable, they will feel that there is reward inequity.

It explains only one aspect of the processes of motivation and job satisfaction, although it may be significant in terms of morale and, possibly, of performance.

Cognitive evaluation theory

Cognitive evaluation theory contends that the use of extrinsic rewards may destroy the intrinsic motivation that flows from inherent job interest. It was formulated by Deci and Ryan (1985). On the basis of their research, they stated: 'Rewards, like feedback, when used to convey to people a sense of appreciation for work well done, will tend to be experienced informationally and will maintain or enhance intrinsic motivation. But when they are used to motivate people, they will be experienced controllingly and will undermine intrinsic motivation.'

Deci *et al* (1999) followed up this research by carrying out a meta-analysis of 128 experiments on rewards and intrinsic motivation to establish the extent to which intrinsic motivation was undermined by rewards. The results of the study indicated that for high-interest tasks, rewards had significant negative effects on what the researchers called free-choice measures, which included the time spent on the task after the reward was removed.

But as noted by Gerhart and Rynes (2003): 'The vast majority of research on this theory has been performed in school rather than work settings, often with elementary school-aged children.' But that did not stop other commentators assuming that the results were equally significant for working adults. It is interesting to note that research in industry conducted by Ryan *et al* (1983), while finding that financial incentives did decrease intrinsic motivation in high-control organizational cultures, also established that in organizations with the opposite high-involvement culture, intrinsic and extrinsic motivation were both increased by monetary incentives. Context is all-important. Moreover, a meta-analysis of 145 studies conducted by Cameron *et al* (2001) led to the conclusion that: 'What is clear at this time is that rewards do not inevitably have pervasive negative effects on intrinsic motivation.'

Conclusions on motivation theory

Instrumentality and reinforcement theories provide a simplistic explanation of how motivation works. Needs and content theories are more sophisticated but have their limitations. As Gerhart and Rynes (2003) commented:

> Although the ideas developed by Maslow, Herzberg and Deci have had considerable appeal to many people, the prevailing view in the academic literature is that the specific predictions of these theories are not supported by empirical evidence. On the other hand it would be a mistake to underestimate the influence that these theories have had on research and practice. Pfeffer, Kohn and others continue to base their argument regarding the ineffectiveness of money as a motivator on such theories.

And Steers (2001) contended that: 'Motivation theories that were discredited long ago still permeate current textbooks.' He was referring mainly to Maslow and Herzberg.

But, bearing in mind the reservations set out earlier, needs theory still offers an indication of the factors that motivate people and content theory provides some useful explanations of how motivation takes place. And while instrumentality and reinforcement theories may be simplistic they still explain some aspects of how rewards affect motivation and performance and they continue to exert subliminal influence on the beliefs of some managers about the power of incentives to motivate people. The effect of motivation theories on reward management is summarized below and the ways in which money motivates are considered in more detail in Chapter 9, which deals with financial rewards.

How motivation theories affect reward management

Instrumentality theory provides the traditional rationale for incentive schemes, ie that financial rewards are the prime motivators. The existence of other non-financial or intrinsic motivators is ignored. Instrumentality theory influenced the philosophy underpinning the 'new pay' movement of the 1990s (Schuster and Zingheim, 1992), which focused on the use of variable pay as a means of improving performance.

Reinforcement theory suggests that the results expected from employees and the reward they get if they achieve the results should be clearly defined and follow the achievement closely. But reinforcement theory takes, as Shields (2007) put it, a 'depressingly mechanistic view of the human condition'. He suggests that it may possibly only be applicable to simple and routine jobs.

Content (needs) theory indicates that rewards should focus on satisfying individual needs, especially the higher-order needs. Bearing in mind the complexity and variability of needs, it is necessary to understand what needs may be relevant and how they vary. It is also necessary to avoid crude approaches to meeting them. Motivation policies and reward practices must recognize that people are different.

Herzberg's two-factor theory emphasizes the significance of the intrinsic motivating factors when considering reward policies. It provides the rationale for striking a balance between financial and non-financial rewards as reflected in the concept of total rewards.

Cognitive evaluation theory also focuses on the need to consider intrinsic motivating factors when managing reward and performance.

Expectancy theory provides a powerful conceptual basis for designing pay for performance or contribution schemes. It stresses the needs (1) to have a clear link or 'line of sight' between performance and reward which clarifies what has to be done to obtain the reward and what level of reward can be expected; (2) to provide rewards which people feel are worthwhile; and (3) to ensure that people believe that the level of performance required to achieve the reward is attainable. It also indicates that employees should be given information on what is expected of them through the performance management system and advice and support in achieving those expectations.

Goal theory impacts primarily on performance management by indicating the effect on performance made when performance goals are agreed which are specific, challenging but attainable. But it is also an important factor in reward management because it reveals the importance of relating performance payments to agreed objectives.

Equity theory focuses on the need to achieve fairness in base pay management, the use of contingent pay schemes and the provision of employee benefits.

References

Adams, J S (1965) Injustice in Social Exchange, in *Advances in Experimental Psychology*, ed L Berkowitz, Academic Press, New York, NY

Alderfer, C (1972) *Existence, Relatedness and Growth*, The Free Press, New York, NY

Allport, G (1954) The Historical Background of Modern Social Psychology, in *Theoretical Models and Personality*, ed G Lindze, Addison-Wesley, Cambridge, MA

Arnold, J, Robertson, I T and Cooper, C L (1991) *Work Psychology*, Pitman, London

Bandura, A and Cervone, D (1983) Self-Evaluation and Self-Efficacy Mechanisms Governing the Motivational Effects of Goal Systems, *Journal of Personality and Social Psychology*, **45** (5), pp 1017–28

Behling, O and Starke, F A (1973) The Postulates of Expectancy Theory, *Academy of Management Journal*, **16** (3), pp 375–88

Cameron, J, Banko, K M and Pierce, W D (2001) Pervasive Negative Effects of Rewards on Intrinsic Motivation: The myth continues, *The Behavior Analyst*, **24** (1), pp 1–44

Deci, E L and Ryan, R M (1985) *Intrinsic Motivation and Self-determination in Human Behaviour*, Plenum, New York, NY

Deci, E L, Koestner, R and Ryan, R M (1999) A Meta-Analytic Review of Experiments Examining the Effects of Extrinsic Rewards on Intrinsic Motivation, *Psychological Bulletin*, **25**, pp 627–68

Dowling, W E (1971) An Interview with Frederick Herzberg, *Management Review*, **60**, pp 2–15

Gerhart, B and Rynes, S L (2003*) Compensation: Theory, evidence and strategic implications*, Sage, Thousand Oaks, CA

Guest, D E (1992) *Motivation after Herzberg*, Unpublished paper delivered at the Compensation Forum, London

Hackman, J R and Oldham, G R (1974) Motivation Through the Design of Work: Test of a theory, *Organizational Behaviour and Human Performance*, **16** (2), pp 250–79

Harackiewicz, J M, Barron, P R, Pintrich, P R, Elliot, A J and Thrash, T M (2002) Revision of Goal Theory: Necessary and illuminating, *Journal of Educational Psychology*, **94** (3), pp 638–45

Herzberg, F (1966) *Work and the Nature of Man*, Staple Press, New York, NY

Herzberg, F (1987) One More Time: How do you motivate employees? *Harvard Business Review*, January–February, pp 109–20 (first published 1967)

House, R J, Shapiro, H J and Wahba, M A (1974) Expectancy Theory as a Predictor of Work Behaviour and Attitude: A re-evaluation of empirical evidence, *Decision Science*, **5** (3), pp 481–506

Hull, C (1951) *Essentials of Behaviour*, Yale University Press, New Haven, CT

Hunter, J E, Judiesch, M K and Schmidt, F L (1990) Individual Differences in Output Variability as a Function of Job Complexity, *Journal of Applied Psychology*, **75** (1), pp 28–42

Katz, D (1964) The Motivational Basis of Organizational Behaviour, *Behavioural Science*, **9**, pp 131–36

Latham, G and Locke, E A (1979) Goal Setting: A motivational technique that works, *Organizational Dynamics*, Autumn, pp 68–80

Maslow, A (1954) *Motivation and Personality*, Harper & Row, New York, NY

McClelland, D C (1961) *The Achieving Society*, Van Nostrand, New York, NY

Pintrich, P R (2000) An Achievement Goal Perspective on Issues in Motivation Technology, Theory and Research, *Contemporary Educational Psychology*, **25**, pp 92–104

Porter, L W and Lawler, E E (1968) *Managerial Attitudes and Performance*, Irwin-Dorsey, Homewood, IL

Rousseau, D M (2006) Is There Such a Thing as Evidence-Based Management? *Academy of Management Review*, 31 (2), pp 256–69

Ryan, R M, Mims, V and Koestner, R (1983) Relation of Reward Contingency and Interpersonal Context to Intrinsic Motivation: A review and test using cognitive evaluation theory, *Journal of Personality and Social Psychology*, 45, pp 736–50

Schuster, J R and Zingheim, P K (1992) *The New Pay*, Lexington Books, New York, NY

Shields, J (2007) *Managing Employee Performance and Reward*, Cambridge University Press, Port Melbourne, Victoria

Steers, R M (2001) Call For Papers: The future of work motivation theory, *Academy of Management Review*, 26 (4), pp 686–87

Taylor, F W (1911) *Principles of Scientific Management*, Harper, New York, NY

Vroom, V (1964) *Work and Motivation*, Wiley, New York, NY

Wahba, M A and Bridwell, L G (1979) Maslow Reconsidered: A review of research on the need hierarchy theory, in *Motivation and Work Behaviour*, ed R M Steers and L W Porter, McGraw Hill, New York, NY

07
Engagement and reward

LEARNING OUTCOMES

On completing this chapter you should be able to define these key concepts. You should also know about:

- The meaning of employee engagement
- Why engagement is important
- The factors that affect engagement
- The role of reward in enhancing engagement
- Developing engagement policies through reward
- Steps to enhance engagement
- Enabling employees

Introduction

The concept of engagement has become very popular. The term is sometimes used loosely as a powerful notion that embraces pretty well everything the organization is seeking with regard to the contribution and behaviour of its employees in terms of levels of job performance, willingness to do that much more through discretionary effort, motivation, commitment and identification with the organization. It is also used in a more specific way to describe what takes place when people are interested in and positive, even excited, about their jobs and motivated to achieve high levels of performance. This specific idea of job engagement is distinguished from organizational commitment or engagement, which focuses on attachment to the organization as a whole rather than to a job.

Reilly and Brown (2008) noted that the terms 'job satisfaction', 'motivation' and 'commitment' are generally being replaced now in business by 'engagement' because it appears to have more descriptive force and face validity. As Emmott (2006) commented: 'Employee engagement has become a new management mantra – and it's not difficult to see why. Engaged employees – those who feel positive about their jobs – perform better for their employers and can promote their organization as "an employer of choice".'

In this chapter consideration is given to the meaning of employee engagement (there are different definitions) and the relationship between reward and employee engagement.

Engagement defined

One of the earliest writers to consider engagement (Kahn, 1990) regarded it as a psychological state experienced by employees in relation to their work, together with associated behaviours. A definition based on research by Maslach *et al* (2001) referred to engagement as 'a positive, fulfilling, work-related state of mind that is characterized by vigour, dedication, and absorption'. In their study of employee engagement, MacLeod and Clarke (2009) concluded: 'The way employee engagement operates can take many forms.' So can descriptions of what it means.

Macey *et al* (2009) produced the following working definition:

> Engagement is an individual's purpose and focused energy, evident to others in the display of personal initiative, adaptability, effort and persistence directed towards organizational goals.

Engagement can take two forms: job engagement and organizational engagement.

Job engagement

The term engagement can be used in a specific job-related way to describe what takes place when people are enthusiastic about their work, exercise discretionary behaviour and are determined to achieve high levels of performance. Ericksen (2007) described the job as the key antecedent of the state of engagement. Truss *et al* (2006) stated: 'Put simply, engagement means feeling positive about your job.' They went on to explain that 'The engaged employee is the passionate employee, the employee who is totally immersed in his or her work, energetic, committed and completely dedicated.' Gallup, as quoted by Balain and Sparrow (2009), defined engagement as 'The individual's involvement and satisfaction with as well as enthusiasm for work'.

Organizational engagement

Organizational engagement focuses on attachment to or identification with the organization as a whole. The Conference Board (2006) defined employee engagement as the heightened connection that employees feel for their organization. Robinson *et al* (2004) emphasized the organizational aspect of engagement when they referred to it as 'a positive attitude held by the employee towards the organization and its values'.

Why engagement is important

However it is defined, employee engagement is important to employers because a considerable amount of research indicates that high levels of engagement result in behaviours such as taking initiatives, wanting to develop and aligning actions with organizational needs. This delivers a range of organizational benefits, for example:

- higher productivity/performance: engaged employees perform 20 per cent better than the average (Conference Board, 2006);
- lower staff turnover: engaged employees are 87 per cent less likely to leave (Corporate Leadership Council, 2004);
- better attendance: engaged employees have lower sick-leave levels (CIPD, 2007);
- improved safety (Vance, 2006).

Truss *et al* (2013) suggested that 'engagement may constitute the mechanism through which HRM practitioners impact individual and organizational performance'.

Developing engagement through reward

Reilly and Brown (2008) contended that appropriate reward practices and processes, both financial and non-financial and managed in combination, can help to build and improve employee engagement, while badly designed or executed rewards can hinder it. Their model based on research into how reward policies influence performance through engagement is shown in Figure 7.1.

FIGURE 7.1   How reward policies influence performance through engagement

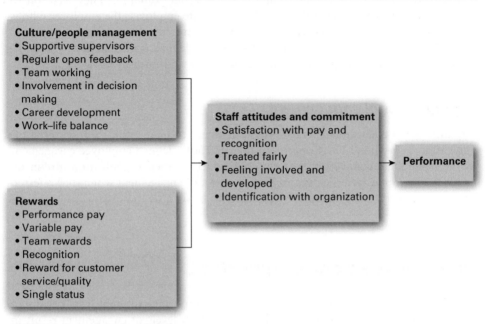

Culture/people management
- Supportive supervisors
- Regular open feedback
- Team working
- Involvement in decision making
- Career development
- Work–life balance

Rewards
- Performance pay
- Variable pay
- Team rewards
- Recognition
- Reward for customer service/quality
- Single status

Staff attitudes and commitment
- Satisfaction with pay and recognition
- Treated fairly
- Feeling involved and developed
- Identification with organization

Performance

SOURCE: Reilly, P and Brown, D (2008)

Research conducted by WorldatWork (Scott *et al*, 2010) led to the finding that intangible rewards generally have a much higher impact on employee engagement than tangible rewards. The most important intangible rewards are the nature of the job, the work environment, career development opportunities and work–life balance. Short-term incentives are the tangible rewards that have the most impact on engagement, followed by employee benefits and base salary levels and increases. They reached the following conclusions on the reward priorities for engagement:

- Go beyond compensation and benefits to a total rewards mindset.
- Include employees and managers in rewards design and launch. To balance the needs and wants of the organization it is necessary to know what employees value in rewards.
- Tailor total rewards to workforce segmentation. Recognize that different employee groups value different rewards and base the design of the total rewards toolkit on this understanding.
- Use engagement metrics in performance criteria in order to monitor rewards trends in achieving engagement levels.
- Communicate the value of what you have. Clarify and focus on communicating a few core rewards messages.

Reilly and Brown (2008) offered the following six tips on enhancing engagement through reward:

1 Analyse the existing performance culture of the organization and develop an engagement model which describes what brings people to work, what keeps them with the organization and what motivates them to perform whilst there.

2 Define the drivers of engagement (and disengagement) for different categories of employees.

3 Assess and define the reward elements that affect engagement for the different groups of employees and develop reward programmes which will enhance these different aspects of engagement.

4 Introduce a total rewards approach which brings together all the reward elements (pay and non-pay) that engage staff.

5 Segment total reward to take account of key employee differences.

6 Implement the total rewards approach and measure and evaluate its impact and success.

Conclusion

The following cautionary remarks were made by Shiraki *et al* (2011) on the basis of research by the Hay Group:

> Employee engagement is critical, but the research shows that it's not enough to sustain high performance over time. People must also have systems and work environments that help them to be effective on both a personal and an organizational level. Motivated employees must also be able to channel their enthusiasm into productive action.

References

Balain, S and Sparrow, P (2009) *Engaged to Perform: A new perspective on employee engagement*, Lancaster University Management School, Lancaster

Chartered Institute of Personnel and Development (2007) *Working Life: Employee attitudes and engagement*, CIPD, London

Conference Board (2006) *Employee Engagement: A review of current research and its implications*, Conference Board, New York, NY

Corporate Leadership Council (2004) *Driving Performance and Retention through Employee Engagement*, Corporate Executive Board, Washington DC

Emmott, M (2006) Hear Me Now, *People Management*, 23 November, pp 38–40

Ericksen, J (2007) High Performance Work Systems: Dynamic workforce alignment and firm performance, *Academy of Management Proceedings*, pp 1–6

Kahn, W A (1990) Psychological Conditions of Personal Engagement and Disengagement at Work, *Academy of Management Journal*, 33 (4), pp 692–724

Macey, W H, Schneider, B, Barbera, K M and Young, S A (2009) *Employee Engagement*, Wiley-Blackwell, Malden, MA

MacLeod, D and Clarke, N (2009) *Engaging for Success: Enhancing performance through employee engagement*, Department for Business Innovation and Skills, London

Maslach, C, Schaufeli, W B and Leiter, M P (2001) Job Burnout, *Annual Review of Psychology*, **52**, pp 397–422

Reilly, P and Brown, D (2008) Employee Engagement: Future focus or fashionable fad for reward management? *Worldat Work Journal*, **17** (4), pp 37–49

Robinson, D, Perryman, S and Hayday, S (2004) *The Drivers of Employee Engagement*, Institute for Employment Studies, Brighton

Scott, D, McMullen, T and Royal, M (2010) The Role of Rewards in Building Employee Engagement, *Worldat Work Journal*, Fourth Quarter, pp 29–40

Shiraki, J, Stark, M and Royal, M (2011) How to Sustain Performance Like a World's Most Admired Company, *Worldat Work Journal*, Fourth Quarter, pp 6–14

Truss, C, Schantz, A, Soane, E, Alfes, K and Delbridge, R, (2013) Employee Engagement, Organizational Performance and Individual Well-Being: Exploring the evidence, developing the theory, *International Journal of Human Resource Management*, **24** (14), pp 2657–69

Truss, C, Soane, E, Edwards, C, Wisdom, K, Croll, A, and Burnett, J (2006) *Working Life: Employee attitudes and engagement*, CIPD, London

Vance, R J (2006) *Effective Practice Guidelines: Employee engagement and commitment*, SHRM Foundation, Alexandria, VA

08
Performance and reward

LEARNING OUTCOMES

On completing this chapter you should be able to define these key concepts. You should also know about:

- The meaning of performance
- The impact of reward on performance
- How reward impacts on performance
- The role of a performance management system in providing rewards and improving performance

Introduction

The CIPD's HR Profession Map (2009) defines what an HR professional needs to do and know about performance and reward as follows:

> Builds a high-performance culture by delivering programmes that recognize and reward critical skills, capabilities, experience and performance.

This chapter explains how this is done by defining the concept of performance and examining how reward and performance management systems combine to make that impact.

The meaning of performance

The *Oxford English Dictionary* defines performance as: 'The accomplishment, execution, carrying out, working out of anything ordered or undertaken'. This refers to outputs/outcomes (accomplishment) but also states that performance is about doing the work as well as being about the results achieved.

Brumbach (1988) developed this definition as follows:

> Performance means both behaviours and results. Behaviours emanate from the performer and transform performance from abstraction to action. Not just the instruments for results, behaviours are also outcomes in their own right – the product of mental and physical effort applied to tasks – and can be judged apart from results.

This concept of performance leads to the conclusion that when managing individual performance both inputs (behaviour/competencies) and outputs (results) have to be considered.

Impact of reward on organizational performance

The assumption is that improvements in organizational performance will follow improvements in individual performance. This sounds reasonable but it is difficult to prove, although some US research projects have attempted to do this.

The findings of the research conducted by Allen and Helms (2001) were that reward practices were significant predictors of performance and explained nearly 41 per cent of the variance in organizational performance. A relatively small number of reward practices explained the bulk of variability in organizational performance. These were: employee share option plans (ESOPs), individual-based performance systems, regular expressions of appreciation, and customer satisfaction monitoring tied to rewards. Team-based pay, flexible benefits and increased job autonomy were not significant predictors of firm performance.

A study by Brown *et al* (2003) explored the relationship between pay policy as indicated by pay levels and pay structure on organizational performance in 333 general hospitals in the State of California. The findings were:

- pay level practices and pay structures interact to affect resource efficiency, patient care outcomes and financial performance;
- higher pay levels are associated with greater efficiency;
- there are diminishing returns for pay's effects on employee performance;
- no single theory can fully explain how compensation relates to organizational performance, but the results show support for efficiency

theory (the belief that high levels of pay will contribute to increases in productivity);

- higher wages can compensate for the negative effects of inequitable pay systems.

Data on pay satisfaction and organizational level outcomes was collected by Curral *et al* (2005) from 6,394 public school teachers and 117 public school districts. The findings were that pay satisfaction was positively related to school district level academic performance and negatively related to intention to quit.

Research carried out by McAdams and Hawk (1994) supported the premise that performance reward plans are instrumental in performance improvements, often with calculable returns. Just under half the companies in the study were able to attach a financial value to their plans. For these organizations, the value of the performance improvement translated into a 134 per cent net return on what was paid out to employees (excluding the costs associated with training, communications and consulting).

How does reward impact on performance?

Reward generally influences performance by providing the means to recognize achievement, competence and merit. Specifically, rewards make an impact on performance by motivating people and by enhancing engagement. However, extrinsic rewards (ie those provided by the organization, especially financial rewards) are not necessarily effective as motivators and the links between reward and engagement are not always precise.

But there are two other important ways in which reward can make an impact. First, as discussed below, reward can make a major contribution to the creation and maintenance of a high-performance culture; second, reward can exert considerable influence over the attraction and retention of talented people as part of a talent management programme.

High-performance culture

Reward makes an overall positive impact on performance by helping to develop and implement a high-performance culture, one in which the values, norms and HR practices of an organization combine to create a climate in which the achievement of high levels of performance is a way of life. Such a culture can be manifested in a high-performance work system. Within the high-performance culture and work system reward impacts on individual and organizational performance by:

- focusing attention on the values of the organization for high performance and the behaviours required to achieve it;
- ensuring that performance expectations are defined and understood;
- providing the means to encourage and recognize high performance.

Reward and talent management

Talent management programmes are concerned with:

- the identification of talent;
- ensuring that talented people are attracted to the organization and stay with it;
- enhancing the engagement of talent;
- defining and providing career opportunities for talented people;
- developing levels of talent throughout the organization.

Reward and performance management provide a combined force, which strikes at the very heart of talent management. The contribution they make is to develop and maintain a compelling employee value proposition. Essentially, this consists of what an organization has to offer which prospective or existing employees value and which persuades them to join or remain with the business.

What employees value will, of course, vary immensely between individuals. But research conducted by Watson Wyatt quoted by Hathaway (2008) showed that, in general, the key factors affecting attraction for top performers, in order, were job security, base pay, nature of the work (including work–life balance) and career development opportunities. The key factors affecting retention were base pay, stress levels, promotion opportunity, incentive pay opportunity and career development opportunities. As explained below, with the exception of job security, every one of these factors can be affected by reward and performance management operating as associated activities.

The role of performance management

Performance management, if carried out properly, can reward people by recognition through feedback, the provision of opportunities to achieve, the scope to develop skills, and guidance on career paths. All these are non-financial rewards, which can encourage job and organizational engagement and make a longer-lasting and more powerful impact on performance than financial rewards such as performance-related pay. A detailed description of what performance management can contribute was provided by Jones *et al* (1995) as follows:

- communicate a shared vision throughout the organization to help to establish and support appropriate leadership and management styles;
- define individual requirements and expectation of all employees in terms of the inputs and outputs expected from them thus reducing confusion and ambiguity;
- provide a framework and environment for teams to develop and succeed;
- provide the climate and systems which support reward and communicate how people and the organization can achieve improved performance;
- help people manage ambiguity.

Performance management is also associated with pay by generating the information required to decide on pay increases or bonuses related to performance, competence or contribution. In some organizations this is its main purpose, but performance management is, or should be, much more about developing people and rewarding them in the broadest sense.

This section starts with a definition of performance management and continues with an analysis of the characteristics of a performance management system. But it is easier to describe performance management than to get it to work well. Consideration is therefore given to the problems of operating performance management and how they can be overcome.

Performance management defined

Performance management is the continuous process of improving performance by setting individual and team goals which are aligned to the strategic goals of the organization, planning performance to achieve the goals, reviewing and assessing progress, and developing the knowledge, skills and abilities of people.

Performance management systems

A performance management system as modelled in Figure 8.1 is a set of interrelated activities and processes. These are treated as integrated and key components of an organization's approach to managing performance through people and developing the skills and capabilities of its human capital. The system flows from the organization's goals and then operates as a continuous and self-renewing cycle.

Figure 8.2 shows how performance management activities take place over the year.

Performance management issues

The many-faceted nature of performance was commented on as follows by Cascio (2010): 'It is an exercise in observation and judgement, it is a feedback process, it is an organizational intervention. It is a measurement process as well as an intensely emotional process. Above all, it is an inexact, human process.'

As a human process, performance management can promise more than it achieves. Coens and Jenkins (2002) delivered the following judgement:

> Throughout our work lives, most of us have struggled with performance appraisal. No matter how many times we redesign it, retrain the supervisors, or give it a new name, it never comes out right. Again and again, we see supervisors procrastinate or just go through the motions, with little taken to heart. And the supervisors who do take it to heart and give it their best mostly meet disappointment.

Shields (2007) argued that 'Ill-chosen, badly designed or poorly implemented performance management schemes can communicate entirely the wrong messages as to what the organization expects from its employees.'

FIGURE 8.1   The performance management cycle

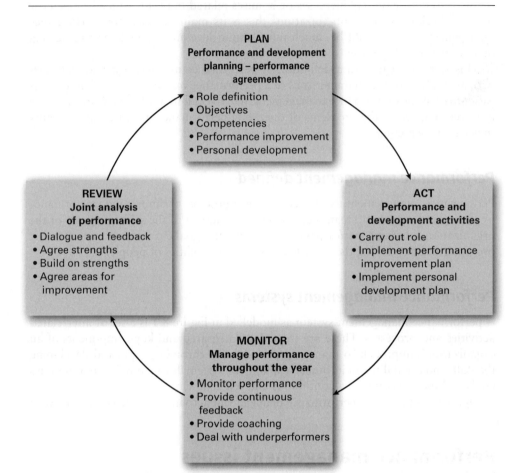

The belief that staff were more demotivated than motivated by performance management was expressed by 23 per cent of the respondents to the 2104 e-reward performance management survey – a disturbingly high proportion.

Duncan Brown (2010) remarked that:

> The problems [of performance management] are... not of ambition or intent, but rather practice and delivery. Low rates of coverage and even more frequently low-quality conversations and non-existent follow-up are commonplace, in the wake of uncommitted directors, incompetent line managers, uncomprehending employees and hectoring HR with their still complex and bureaucratic HR processes.

FIGURE 8.2   Summary of performance management activities over the year

Start of year	*Performance agreement*	• Define role profiles, updating as necessary • Ensure that role profiles set out updated key result areas and competency requirements • Define goals and standards of performance • Identify and define key performance indicators • Draw up performance development plans • Draw up personal development plans
Continuing dialogue	*Ongoing performance management*	• Monitor progress and review evidence of achievement • Provide informal feedback as required • Provide coaching as required • Update role profiles and objectives as necessary
End of year	*Performance review*	• Prepare for performance review by analyzing achievements (work and learning) against objectives • Identify specific strengths and weaknesses on the basis of evidence • Assess overall performance • Provide feedback • Use conclusions of performance review as the basis for next year's performance and development agreement

According to Pulakos *et al* (2008) the main problems with performance management in the United States are:

- performance management is regarded as an administrative burden to be minimized rather than an effective strategy to obtain business results;
- managers and employees are reluctant to engage in candid performance discussions;
- judgement and time factors impede accurate performance assessments.

A survey by WorldatWork and Sibson (2010) established that the top three performance management challenges reported by respondents were (1) managers lack courage to have difficult performance discussions (63 per cent); (2) performance management is viewed as an 'HR process' instead of as a 'business critical process' (47 per cent); and (3) that they experienced poor goal setting (36 per cent). They also noted that 'Too much attention has been placed on the design of a [performance management] system and not enough on how it works when implemented.'

To deal with these issues respondents to the e-reward (2014) survey on performance management emphasized the importance of doing the following:

- Train, communicate, evaluate performance management through employee engagement surveys, have HR business partners work with line managers, organize round tables (calibration), provide details of expected competency levels per job type/level, clarify that good is acceptable (not everyone can be a star), encourage ongoing performance management; it's more than just an annual administrative hoop – it's a powerful management tool.

- Keep it very, very simple, be able to translate strategy to individual goals and give people a clear line of sight, ensure all people managers are capable to deliver performance management, ie have a performance dialogue (this is the key!) at any time and not just at the annual review.

- Focus on the positives, create a culture of continual performance management rather than restricting it to an annual appraisal (to avoid surprises when it comes to ratings and encourage individuals to focus on performance throughout the year). Make a performance management system open and available all year round (rather than releasing an appraisal at certain set times of the year). Analyse the data on performance ratings, to see trends, highlight areas for improvement and ensure no discriminatory bias. Train.

- Ensure the paperwork (hardcopy or e-) does not drive the process. The appraisal should be clearly aligned to the organization's strategic objectives and values. It is the conversation between the manager and employee that is most important. Managers need to be given the skills to manage difficult conversations and all staff need to know how to give and receive feedback.

- Ensure the system isn't hampered by bureaucracy and tedious paperwork. Make it easy for all to actively engage with the system and put the focus on having quality open conversation between reviewer and reviewee.

- Consistency – one scheme for all, make it about good conversations, not just a process.

- Clear line of sight between objective setting, performance review and business goals. Regularly review and update in accordance with any changes in business needs.

- Acknowledge any link to remuneration – if you don't, people will create their own links.

References

Allen, R S and Helms, M H (2001) Reward Practices and Organizational Performance, *Compensation & Benefits Review*, July/August, pp 74–80

Brown, D (2010) Performance Management: Can we practice what we preach? *rewardblog* [online] www.cipd.co.uk/blogs/cipdbloggers/b/reward_blog/archive/2011/02/05/performance-management-can-we-practice-what-we-preach-by-duncan-brown.aspx [accessed 11 May 2015]

Brown, M P, Sturman, M C and Simmering, M J (2003) Compensation Policy and Organizational Performance: The efficiency, operational and financial implications of pay levels and pay structure, *Academy of Management Journal*, **46** (6), pp 752–82

Brumbach, G B (1988) Some Ideas, Issues and Predictions About Performance Management, *Public Personnel Management*, Winter, pp 387–402

Cascio, W F (2010) *Managing Human Resources: Productivity, quality of work life, profits*, 8th edition, McGraw-Hill Irwin, New York, NY

Chartered Institute of Personnel and Development (2009) Profession Map, *CIPD* [online] www.cipd.co.uk/cipd-hr-profession/profession-map/ [accessed 24 February 2012]

Coens, T and Jenkins, M (2002) *Abolishing Performance Appraisals: Why they backfire and what to do instead*, Berrett-Koehler, San Francisco, CA

Curral, S C, Towler, A J, Judge, T A and Kohn, L (2005) Pay Satisfaction and Organizational Outcomes, *Personnel Psychology*, **58** (3), pp 613–40

e-reward (2014) Performance Management: Part 2 – survey, *e-reward* [online] www.e-reward.co.uk/research/surveys/performance-management-part-2-survey [accessed 22 July 2015] Registration is required to access this survey.

Hathaway, C (2008) *Integrated Reward and Talent Management*, Unpublished presentation at e-reward annual update, November

Jones, P, Palmer, J, Whitehead, D and Needham, P (1995) Prisms of Performance, *The Ashridge Journal*. April, pp 10–14

McAdams, J and Hawk, E J (1994) *Organizational Performance and Rewards*, American Compensation Association, Scottsdale, AZ

Pulakos, E D, Mueller-Hanson, R A and O'Leary, R S (2008) Performance Management in the United States, in *Performance Management Systems: A global perspective*, eds, AVarma, A, Budhwar, P S and DeNisi, A, Routledge, London

Shields, J (2007) *Managing Employee Performance and Reward*, Cambridge University Press, Port Melbourne

WorldatWork and Sibson (2010) *Study on the State of Performance Management*, WorldatWork, Scottsdale AZ

09
Financial rewards

KEY CONCEPTS AND TERMS

- Cognitive evaluation theory
- Contingent pay
- Distributive justice
- Extrinsic motivation
- Extrinsic rewards
- Felt-fair principle
- Financial rewards
- Hierarchy of human needs
- High-involvement culture
- Hygiene factor
- Incentives
- Incentive effect

- Intrinsic motivation
- Intrinsic rewards
- Job enrichment
- Job satisfaction
- Merit pay
- Meta-analysis
- Moral hazard
- Motivation
- Motivation-hygiene theory
- Procedural justice
- Rewards
- Sorting effect

LEARNING OUTCOMES

On completing this chapter you should be able to define these key concepts. You should also know about:

- The difference between incentives and rewards
- The theories that underpin beliefs about financial rewards
- The role of money
- Factors affecting satisfaction with pay
- The link between job satisfaction and performance
- Key research projects on financial rewards
- The arguments for and against financial rewards

Introduction

Financial rewards comprise all rewards that have a monetary value and add up to total remuneration – base pay, merit pay (pay related to performance, competency or contribution), skill-based pay, incentives, service-related pay, bonuses, financial recognition schemes, and benefits such as pensions, sick pay and health insurance. They are the core elements in total rewards as explained in Chapter 11.

The management of a reward system requires decisions on levels of pay, how jobs should be valued, the design and operation of grade and pay structures and the choice of benefits. Such decisions can be complex and difficult, but the problems pale by comparison with the issues surrounding the use of financial rewards, especially merit pay and bonuses.

The aim of this chapter is to present the evidence on the role and effectiveness of financial rewards in order to inform decisions on what can usefully be done about them by means of merit pay as described in Chapter 17 or the other financial reward schemes examined in Part Three. In the first section of the chapter an important distinction is made between the natures of rewards and incentives. The chapter continues with a review of the motivation theories that have influenced views about how incentives work or don't work. This is followed by an examination of the role of money in motivating people and the factors that affect satisfaction with pay, which leads to a summary of the associated research on financial rewards.

A vociferous chorus of disapproval has been heard on the incentive effect of rewards by writers like Alfie Kohn, Jeffrey Pfeffer and Daniel Pink and these are examined in the next section of the chapter prior to a final section summarizing the advantages and disadvantages of financial rewards, which takes into account the outcomes of research and the views of reward commentators.

Incentives and rewards

There is a strong body of opinion that financial rewards are bad – because they don't work and indeed are harmful – while non-financial rewards are good, at least when they provide intrinsic motivation. But the critics referred to later in this chapter are mainly referring to financial incentives. They do not appear to recognize that incentives are not the same as rewards. The two can be distinguished as follows:

- *Rewards* offer tangible recognition after the event to people for their achievements. Financial rewards consist of base pay related to the value of the job, and person-based pay, which provides rewards in the shape of merit pay or bonuses that recognize the individual's contribution or competence. Rewards can also be non-financial, for example recognition. If rewards are worth having and attainable and people know how they can attain them, rewards can act as motivators.

- *Incentives* are intended to encourage people before the event to work harder and achieve more. Incentives are supposed to provide direct motivation: 'Do this and we will make it worth your while.' Incentives are generally financial but they can take the form of non-financial rewards such as promotion or a particularly interesting assignment.

If this distinction is not made it may be assumed that financial rewards only exist to provide an incentive. They may do this or, as the nay-sayers contend, they may not. But financial rewards in the form of person-based pay may be justified because they are a form of tangible recognition – they are a means of informing people that they have done well, and accord with the reasonable belief that people who do better should be valued more and rewarded accordingly. As Deci and Ryan (1985) stated, 'Rewards, like feedback, when used to convey to people a sense of appreciation for work well done, will tend to be experienced informationally and will maintain or enhance intrinsic motivation.'

Labour economists distinguish between the incentive effect of financial rewards (generating more engagement and effort) and the sorting effect (attracting better-quality employees). The issue which has concerned many commentators as discussed later in this chapter is the extent to which financial rewards provide an incentive effect. The sorting effect is important but creates less controversy, perhaps because it is more difficult to pin down.

The theoretical framework

The theoretical framework is largely based on the concepts of extrinsic and intrinsic motivation as described in Chapter 4. To summarize, extrinsic motivation arises when something is done to or for people to motivate them. Extrinsic rewards include pay, praise and promotion. Intrinsic motivation is provided by the self-generated factors that influence people to behave in a particular way or to move in a particular direction. Intrinsic rewards arise from the work people do, their opportunity to achieve and the scope to enhance their skills.

Financial rewards are, of course, extrinsic rewards and the doubts about them expressed by commentators are mainly based on the three motivation theories discussed in Chapter 6: Maslow's (1954) hierarchy of human needs, Herzberg's (1966, 1987) two-factor motivation-hygiene theory, and Deci and Ryan's (1985) cognitive evaluation theory (CET). All these theories downgrade the role of money or extrinsic rewards as motivators. They have been very influential, especially Maslow and Herzberg, but for some people like Kohn, Pfeffer and Pink the contribution of Deci and Ryan appears to have had the most powerful effect.

Cognitive evaluation theory

Cognitive evaluation theory emphasizes the importance of intrinsic motivation. According to this theory, extrinsic rewards have a negative effect on intrinsic rewards and therefore performance because they are perceived as controlling. But, as pointed out by Rynes *et al* (2005) there is 'a general concern about the generalizability of CET-inspired research, which is that the vast majority of this research has been conducted in the laboratory under conditions that differ substantially from real work settings'.

Research to test the theory in work settings was conducted by Fang and Gerhart (2012). Their findings were that higher levels of perceived autonomy, competence and intrinsic interest accompanied performance pay. They thought it was possible that even if intrinsic motivation were affected by performance pay, increases in extrinsic motivation might more than offset such negative effects. They concluded that:

> Conventional wisdom and widely held beliefs regarding the detrimental effect of PFIP [pay for individual performance]... should be revisited. Although successful design and implementation of a PFIP program certainly carries its share of challenges and risks, our study provides both conceptual logic and empirical evidence for why such a detrimental effect on performance through decreased intrinsic interest and motivation is unlikely to be one of those risks.

This theoretical framework provides the background to the following discussion on the role of money in motivating people and in enhancing job satisfaction.

The role of money

It is reasonable to assume that people need money and therefore want money but the question is: How well does it perform as a motivator? It has been suggested by Wallace and Szilagyi (1982) that money can serve the following reward functions:

- it can act as a goal that people generally strive for, although to different degrees;
- it can act as an instrument that provides valued outcomes;
- it can be a symbol that indicates the recipient's value to the organization;
- it can act as a general reinforcer because it is associated with valued rewards and therefore takes on reward value itself.

Money can motivate because it is linked directly or indirectly with the satisfaction of many needs. It satisfies the basic need for survival and security, if income is regular. It can also satisfy the need for self-esteem (it is a visible mark of appreciation). Money can satisfy the less desirable but nevertheless prevalent drives of acquisitiveness and cupidity – it can set people in a grade apart from their fellows and can buy them things the others cannot afford. Money may in itself have no intrinsic meaning, but it acquires motivating power because it comes to symbolize so many intangible goals. It acts as a symbol in different ways for different people, and for the same person at different times. Pay is often a dominant factor in the choice of employer and is an important consideration when people are deciding whether or not to stay with an organization.

Money can motivate but it is not the only motivator. As Gerhart and Rynes (2003) comment: 'Although we see little evidence to support the notion that money is of secondary importance as a motivator, there is nevertheless ample evidence that money is not the only reward that motivates.' In their job characteristics model, Hackman and Oldham (1974) emphasized the importance as motivators of the core job dimensions, namely: skill variety, task identity, task significance, autonomy and feedback.

However, according to Herzberg (1966) money does not result in lasting satisfaction. People may feel good when they get an increase as, apart from the extra money, it is a way of making others aware that they are valued. But the feeling of euphoria can die away and it must be re-emphasized that different people have different needs. Some will be much more motivated by money than others. What cannot be assumed is that money motivates everyone in the same way and to the same extent.

To believe that financial incentives will always motivate people to perform better is as naive as to assume, like Kohn, Pfeffer and Pink, that they never motivate people to perform better. Some people will be more motivated by money than others and, if handled properly, an incentive scheme in the right context can encourage them to perform more effectively as long as they can link their effort to the reward and the reward is worth having. But others may be less interested in money and will respond more to intrinsic or non-financial rewards. It can be argued in accordance with total rewards philosophy (see Chapter 11) that most people are likely to react positively to a judicious mix of both financial and non-financial rewards.

What is clear is that assumptions about the power of money to motivate can lead organizations into developing simplistic performance-related pay schemes or other forms of incentives. And we can be sure that a multiplicity of interdependent factors are involved in motivating people. Money is only one of those factors that may work for some people in some circumstances, but may not work for other people in other circumstances.

It should also be remembered that while an increase in pay arising from a merit pay or bonus scheme may motivate people who get it, for a limited period perhaps, it may well demotivate those who don't get it or feel that they are not getting enough compared with other people. The number of people demotivated in this way could be larger than the number who have been motivated. Paradoxically, therefore, such schemes are in danger of increasing the amount of demotivation existing in the organization rather than enhancing motivation.

Views about the importance of money

Commentators who question the usefulness of financial rewards often contend that money is much less important than many people think. As Pfeffer (1998) wrote: 'People do work for money – but they work even more for meaning in their lives. In fact, they work to have fun. Companies that ignore this fact are essentially bribing their employees and will pay the price in a lack of loyalty and commitment.' Furnham (2006) stated that: 'Money is not everything. Many would be happy with more time off, or more job security, than more money. People are prepared to trade-off things for money once they have enough or grow weary of the game.'

Many surveys have been carried out to assess the relative importance of pay in relation to other factors affecting motivation. Typically, pay is somewhere down the list after job interest, achievement, recognition and development opportunities. As Kohn (1998) stated: 'Numerous studies have shown that when people are asked what is most important to them about work, money ranks well behind such factors as interesting work or good people to work with.' For example, 1,355 managers and other professionals surveyed by Ritchie and Martin (1999) placed money and tangible rewards ninth in a list of 12 motivational drivers.

In an earlier study, Jurgensen (1978) assessed the relative importance of job characteristics (including pay) to 50,000 job applicants over a 30-year period. Pay was the fifth most important characteristic to men and the seventh most important to women. However, when asked to rate the importance of the same ten attributes to 'someone just like yourself – same age, education, gender and so on', pay jumped to being the most important factor among both men and women. In other words, people seemed to believe that pay was the main motivator to everyone except themselves.

Slovic and Lichtenstein (1971) commented that people tend to give lower ratings to factors that are regarded as socially less acceptable than others. They overrate the socially desirable importance of job challenge and opportunities for learning, and underrate the importance of 'low-level motivators such as pay'. Such ranking exercises, as Lawler (1971) pointed out, produce results that vary according to the methodology used and can therefore be misleading. They do not prove that pay is perceived to be relatively unimportant. Studies such as those conducted by McDougall (1973) and Blackburn and Mann (1979) have indicated that the opposite is the case.

However, although pay may be important, its effectiveness will be affected by the degree to which people are satisfied with their pay and the extent to which, if they are satisfied, this improves their performance.

Factors affecting satisfaction with pay

As Lawler (1990) observed, people's feelings about the adequacy of their pay are based upon comparisons they make between their own and others'. External market comparisons are the most critical because they are the ones that strongly influence whether individuals want to stay with the organization. Many people, however, are unlikely to leave for pay reasons alone unless the increase they expect from a move is substantial, say 10 per cent.

Lawler also commented: 'Sometimes it seems that individuals are never satisfied with their pay.' One of the reasons suggested by Lawler for low pay satisfaction seems to be that individuals seek out unfavourable comparisons. First they look externally: if comparisons there are favourable, they then focus on internal comparisons. Only if these are favourable as well are they likely to be satisfied. He states that 'A finding that employees are dissatisfied with pay is, in effect, a non-finding. It is to be expected. The key thing that the organization needs to focus on is whether its employees are more dissatisfied with their pay than are employees in other organizations.'

Reactions to reward policies and practices will depend largely on the values and needs of individuals and on their employment conditions. It is therefore dangerous to generalize about the causes of satisfaction or dissatisfaction. However, it seems reasonable to believe that, as mentioned above, feelings about external and internal equity (the felt-fair principle as defined by Jaques, 1961) will strongly influence most people. Research by Porter and Lawler (1968) has also shown that higher-paid employees are likely to be more satisfied with their rewards but the satisfaction resulting from a large pay increase may be short-lived. People tend to want more of the same. In this respect, at least, the views of Maslow and Herzberg have been supported by research.

Other factors that may affect satisfaction or dissatisfaction with pay include the degree to which individuals feel their rate of pay or increase has been determined fairly (the principle of procedural justice):

- Rewards are commensurate with the perceptions of individuals about their ability, contribution and value to the organization founded on information or beliefs about what other people, inside and outside the organization, are paid (the principle of distributive justice).

- Individuals are satisfied with other aspects of their employment – for example, the quality of working life, work–life balance, their status, promotion prospects, opportunity to use and develop skills, and relations with their managers and colleagues.

Job satisfaction and performance

Pay may arguably increase job satisfaction but does job satisfaction improve performance? It is a commonly held and seemingly reasonable belief that it does. But research has not established any strongly positive connection between satisfaction and performance. A review of the extensive literature on this subject by Brayfield and Crockett (1955) concluded that there was little evidence of any simple or appreciable relationship between employee satisfaction and performance. An updated review of their analysis by Vroom (1964) covered 20 studies, in each of which one or more measures of job satisfaction or employee attitudes was correlated with one or more criteria of performance. The median correlation of all these studies was 0.14, which is not high enough to suggest a marked relationship between satisfaction and performance.

It is possible that it is not job satisfaction that produces high performance but high performance that produces job satisfaction. A satisfied worker is not necessarily a productive worker and a high producer is not necessarily a satisfied worker. People are motivated to achieve certain goals and will be satisfied if they achieve these goals through improved performance. They may be even more satisfied if they are then rewarded by extrinsic recognition or an intrinsic sense of achievement. It can also be argued that some people may be complacently satisfied with their job or at least reconciled to it and will not be inspired to work harder or better. They may find other ways to satisfy their needs.

Research on the effectiveness of financial rewards

The theory as described below has been much influenced by the research that has been conducted on the effectiveness of financial rewards in terms of their impact on people and performance. A number of UK projects in the early 1990s produced negative results on the impact of performance-related pay (PRP) on people, and these have influenced views about PRP ever since. But these were early days for PRP, especially in the public sector, and four more recent studies in the UK and many studies in the United States over the years have established a positive relationship between incentive pay and performance. A selection of these negative and positive projects is summarized below.

Research projects producing mainly negative results

Kessler and Purcell (1992)

Research into individual performance-related pay (PRP) was conducted over a three-year period in nine private and public sector organizations of varying sizes and operating in different product and labour markets. Material was also gained from interviews with over 60 senior and management figures.

The main findings and conclusions were that:

- PRP was seen as a means of targeting pay to those who most deserve it and thus provides better value for money than inflexible, less discriminatory increases related to cost of living or service.
- Managements often experienced difficulties in operating the scheme because of the lack of formal supporting systems, absence of prior management training and the highly subjective nature of assessments.
- The potential for distorting the system is perhaps at its greatest at the assessment stage.
- PRP depends on 'sending messages' to individual members of staff but this entails the risk of sending the wrong messages.

It was also concluded by the researchers that at the crudest of levels, PRP schemes are informed by the view that employees will be motivated if they perceive a direct relationship between effort and reward. It was asserted that such a view is simplistic for a number of reasons. First, as a means of explaining employee behaviour it clearly has limited value, with a whole body of research stressing the importance of employee expectations and need in understanding motivation. Second, it is highly questionable whether employee expectations of the performance-reward link underlying this motivational approach can remain undistorted by ongoing social, political and economic workplace pressures influencing the operation of the pay system. Third, it misses the point because many senior managers are sceptical of such a link themselves.

In addition, it was noted that:

- The amount of money available may be too small to make any impact.
- The sophisticated procedures and systems needed and their application by managers present a range of difficulties to the achievement of recruitment, retention and motivation.
- 'There are major difficulties in finding measures of PRP effectiveness. The bottom-line measure of effectiveness for any payment system is an improvement in overall organizational performance, assumed to flow from improved employee performance. It is, however, clear that the complex range

of factors interacting to determine organizational performance make it difficult to isolate the impact of a payment system alone.'

Thompson (1992a)

Marc Thompson, then with the IMS (now the Institute for Employment Studies), investigated the employer's experience of individual performance-related pay (IPRP) in 20 organizations in the public and private sectors. He found that:

- Employers did not know if their scheme was effective in raising productivity for the simple reason that they did not monitor schemes on this basis.
- Many companies did not think through the introduction of IPRP in a coherent manner.
- There was some indication that line managers were neither totally aware nor convinced of the appropriateness of IPRP – it was this issue that led to some of the most difficult problems in practice.
- There are two main problems with the operation of IPRP schemes:
  1) the values of employers may conflict with the values of employees, and
  2) tensions may arise from employers' beliefs about employee motivation and behaviour.
- One employer commented: 'It's an act of faith really... we think things would be worse if we weren't using it.'
- One of the few employers who had conducted a survey on perceptions of IPRP found that when it was first introduced, less than 20 per cent felt it motivated them; changes in the scheme's administration had seen this rise to over 60 per cent (just over 80 per cent felt that they were rated fairly).
- One of the most consistent problems encountered in studying the effects of performance pay is that of causality – attributing increases or decreases in productivity to the payment system rather than to other factors such as technology, changes in working practices or changes in the product market.
- The theoretical framework most used to support IPRP is expectancy theory, but this is based exclusively on the motivating effects of extrinsic rewards and ignores intrinsic rewards – it implies that 'money is the central incentive in terms of human motivation'.
- There is no best approach to the introduction of IPRP and employers are advised to tread carefully when considering its implementation.

Thompson (1992b)

A survey was conducted of nearly 1,000 employees in three organizations to obtain their views about performance-related pay. The findings were as follows:

- There was little evidence that PRP had served to motivate employees.
- 'It is possible that performance pay may be more successful in demotivating the very employees it needs to stimulate most – the average performers – and may, in practice, contribute to a downward spiral of motivation among such employees.'

- In only one of the three cases was PRP associated with the retention of high performers.
- Poor performers were as likely to stay as high performers.
- The relationship between the subordinate and the line manager was the most important in influencing employee perceptions about PRP.
- Achieving distributive and procedural justice was important.
- 'Informing staff, training them in appraisal and involving them in the design of the scheme from the outset is key to gaining employee trust in and winning commitment to PRP.'
- 'Unfortunately none of the three organizations undertook all these interventions and very few had either informed or trained their staff.' Their absence 'may explain the widespread distrust of the fairness and equity of the schemes'.
- 'Across the three case study organizations there was a surprising consensus in the perceived poor management of the appraisal and merit pay process by line managers.'
- 'Given that performance management is a policy intervention to be owned by the line there is a need to equip managers to take on this responsibility.'
- 'There is evidence that participative processes may be important in ensuring the greater success of PRP among employees.'

Marsden and Richardson (1994)

The results of a survey of 2,000 Inland Revenue staff indicated that the performance pay system had only a small positive motivational effect on staff. The researchers concluded that 'If motivation was not improved at all significantly, or had deteriorated, it is hard to see why performance should have been changed for the better. Why should performance pay have had so little general effect on motivation when 57 per cent of the staff reported being in favour of the principle of PRP? First, and most importantly, it was widely judged to be unfair in its operation.'

Implications

A recurring theme in these negative UK studies was that the problems arose because of the ways in which schemes were introduced and operated within particular contexts rather than because of the principles upon which they were based. An example was the incorrect assumption that schemes that worked well in the private sector would work equally well in the public sector.

This was confirmed in research conducted for the Department of Employment by Bowey and Thorpe (1982). This showed that performance pay design bore no correlation with successful outcomes, which were more dependent on the effectiveness of communication and support systems. The quality and communication of scheme objectives linked to business strategy and goals were found to be a key differentiator between successful and unsuccessful performance. It was noted that the essential requirement is to tailor pay schemes to suit the particular organization and environment.

Research projects producing mainly positive results

Evidence is available from a number of academic studies that indicate that performance pay improves performance:

- Abowd (1990) showed that bonus payments based on economic or market measures could contribute to a strong economic return.
- Booth and Frank (1999) found through their analysis of UK data provided by the British Household Panel Survey that jobs with performance-related pay attracted workers of higher ability and induced workers to provide greater effort.
- Gupta and Shaw (1998) conducted a meta-analysis of 39 rigorously designed studies examining the effects of financial incentives on performance. A strong positive effect was found on performance quantity. But only six studies examined performance quality separately and a consistent relationship between incentives and quality was not found.
- Guzzo et al (1985) found through a meta-analysis that, when applied in the right way and in the right situations, incentives can have strongly positive effects on productivity.
- Heneman (1992) reviewed five studies that established a positive link between a merit-pay system and performance.
- Jenkins et al (1998) said of their study that it 'underscores the generalizable positive relationship between financial incentives and performance'.
- Lazear (1999) found that the productivity of operatives in a factory increased by 44 per cent following the introduction of a piece-rate incentive plan.
- Locke et al (1980) reviewed 44 studies on the adoption of incentive systems that showed in almost all cases a substantial improvement in performance.
- Marsden (2004) conducted a series of surveys across a range of UK public services on employee and line manager judgements on the effects of performance pay. Performance pay was the instrument of a major renegotiation of performance norms, and this rather than motivation was the principal dynamic. Goal setting and appraisal by line managers played a key role in this process.
- Prendergast (1999) reviewed the effect of incentives in both private and public sectors, leading to the conclusion that workers do respond to them.
- Prentice et al (2007) found that research indicated strong evidence that UK civil servants do respond to financial incentives.
- Stajkovic and Luthans (2001) showed that routine pay for performance increased performance over its baseline level by 11 per cent, while a systematic approach to performance pay increased performance by 31.7 per cent.
- Sturman et al (2003) used utility analysis techniques to assess the costs and benefits of a performance pay strategy. The conclusion was that the four-year benefit of linking pay to performance was substantial.

- Thompson (1998) in a study of 400 companies in the British aerospace industry established that the high-value-added and low-value-added companies were clearly differentiated in terms of their pay practices, with virtually double the number of high-value-added companies applying individual performance-related pay schemes to more than two-thirds of their staff.

- West *et al* (2005) conducted research in 15 customer service organizations into methods of rewarding customer service, and found that in the five organizations superior to others in terms of customer service, 60 per cent had performance pay while in the other 10 only 29 per cent had performance pay.

Opponents of financial rewards

The opponents of financial rewards say that there are better ways of recognizing people than throwing money at them. They emphasize the power of intrinsic rewards and assert that extrinsic rewards erode intrinsic interest.

One of the earliest voices was that of Alfie Kohn (1993) who stated in the *Harvard Business Review* that 'bribes in the workplace simply can't work'. He asserted that 'Rewards, like punishment, may actually undermine the intrinsic motivation that results in optimal performance. The more a manager stresses what an employee can earn for good work, the less interested that employee will be in the work itself.' He also claimed that 'At least two dozen studies over the last three decades have conclusively shown that people who expect to receive a reward for completing a task or for doing that task successfully simply do not perform as well as those who expect no reward at all.' He did not identify these studies although some of them were referred to by Deci *et al* (1999). Kohn returned to the fray in 1998 when he wrote that 'Offering workers the equivalent of a doggie biscuit for whatever we demand is never going to be successful in any meaningful sense.'

Jeffrey Pfeffer (1998) concluded in his influential *Harvard Business Review* article 'Six dangerous myths about pay' that 'Most merit-pay systems share two attributes: they absorb vast amounts of management time and make everybody unhappy.' Adrian Furnham (2006) asserted that 'The idea that better-paid people are more productive and happy is naive and essentially evidence-free.'

A more recent and much quoted opponent of financial rewards is Daniel Pink (2009). He listed the following 'seven deadly sins' of 'carrots and sticks' as follows:

1 they can extinguish intrinsic motivation;
2 they can diminish performance;
3 they can crush creativity;
4 they can crowd out good behaviour;
5 they can encourage cheating, shortcuts and unethical behaviour;
6 they can become addictive;
7 they can foster short-term thinking.

The first deadly sin is the one most commonly referred to by critics of financial rewards. Pink's argument is based on the research of Deci, who is credited with recognizing the importance of intrinsic satisfaction as a powerful source of motivation. His conclusions were based largely on student experiments. The caveat is that the research where rewards are at issue has focused on simple tasks in artificial situations. That is best illustrated in the introduction to Pink's book, which is largely devoted to a Deci experiment where students rearranged blocks – with their performance rewarded with what today is equivalent to US $6. He also discusses an experiment with monkeys. Both the students and the monkeys apparently experienced intrinsic satisfaction. Pink supplied no convincing evidence from work-based research for the other deadly sins. Of course, any of them might arise in a badly designed or managed financial incentive scheme; for example, excessive bonuses for City traders have produced short-term thinking and unethical behaviour. But a typical merit pay scheme as described in Chapter 17 seldom offers payouts of more than 10 per cent for top performers at the end of the year and the average is likely to be about 3 per cent. The extent to which this level of payment can detrimentally affect behaviour must be severely limited. The corollary to this is that neither will such payments have much effect on performance. In other words, they act as rewards rather than incentives and are justifiable on that basis.

The *reductio ad absurdum* of the stance taken by the opponents of financial rewards is that everyone should be paid the same!

Arguments for and against financial rewards

As we have seen, the use of financial rewards has aroused strong feelings amongst those who support and those who oppose them. The arguments for and against are set out below.

Arguments for

The most powerful argument advanced for financial rewards is that those who contribute more should be paid more. It is right and proper to recognize achievement with a financial and therefore tangible reward. This is in accordance with the principle of distributive justice, which, while it states that rewards should be provided equitably, does not require them to be equal except when the value of contribution is equal.

Arguments against

The main arguments against financial rewards, especially merit pay, are that:

- Money by itself will not result in sustained motivation; intrinsic motivation provided by the work itself goes deeper and lasts longer.
- The extent to which merit pay schemes motivate is questionable – the amounts available for distribution are usually so small that they cannot act as an incentive.

- The requirements for success are exacting and difficult to achieve.
- People react in widely different ways to any form of motivation – it cannot be assumed that money will motivate all people equally, yet that is the premise on which merit pay schemes are based.
- Financial rewards may possibly motivate those who receive them but they can demotivate those that don't, and the numbers who are demotivated could be much higher than those who are motivated.
- Merit pay and bonus schemes can create more dissatisfaction than satisfaction if they are perceived to be unfair, inadequate or badly managed.
- Employees can be suspicious of schemes because they fear that performance bars will be continuously raised; a scheme may therefore only operate successfully for a limited period.
- Merit pay schemes depend on the existence of accurate and reliable methods of measuring performance competence, contribution, or skill, which can be very difficult and frequently do not exist.
- Merit pay and bonus pay decisions depend on the judgement of managers, which in the absence of reliable criteria can be partial, prejudiced, inconsistent or ill-informed.
- The concept of merit pay is based on the assumption that performance is completely under the control of individuals when in fact it is affected by the system in which they work.
- Merit pay, especially performance-related pay, can militate against quality and teamwork.
- Merit pay, according to Heery (1996), poses a threat to employee well-being because it contradicts employees' needs for a stable and secure income.
- Individuals are encouraged to emphasize only those aspects of performance that are rewarded.
- Performance pay for sales staff may lead to the unintended consequence of overselling in order to maximize financial rewards.

Another powerful argument against merit pay is that it has proved difficult to manage. Organizations, including the British Civil Service, rushed into performance-related pay in the 1980s without really understanding how to make it work. Inevitably problems of implementation arose. Studies such as those mentioned earlier have all revealed these difficulties. Failures may arise because insufficient attention has been given to fitting schemes to the context and culture of the organization. But they may also be rooted in implementation and operating processes, especially those concerned with performance management, the need for effective communication and involvement, and line management capability.

The last factor is crucial. As Thompson (1992) explained, the success of merit pay rests largely in the hands of front-line managers. They have to believe in it as something that will help them as well as the organization. They must also be good at practising the crucial skills of agreeing targets, measuring performance fairly and consistently, and providing feedback to their staff on the outcome of performance management and its impact on pay. Line managers can make or break merit pay schemes. Vicky Wright (1991) summed it up: 'Even the most ardent supporters of performance-related pay recognize that it is difficult to manage well', and Oliver (1996) made the point that 'performance pay is beautiful in theory but difficult in practice'.

There is also the problem of moral hazard inherent in financial incentives. This concept originated in insurance, where it describes the phenomenon of people who, because they are insulated from risk by being insured, proceed to take unnecessary risks. The term was extended to incentives by Prendergast (1999), who pointed out that 'Contracts offering incentives can give rise to dysfunctional behaviour whereby agents emphasize only those objects of performance that are rewarded... Compensation on any sub-set of tasks will result in reallocation of activities towards those that are directly compensated and away from the uncompensated activities.' A moral hazard exists when incentive schemes, for example huge bonuses, encourage undesirable behaviour in which people strive to obtain higher rewards by manipulating results, hiding or even falsifying poor figures, focusing on easy short-term gains rather than the tougher long-term demands or going for one result and neglecting another important outcome, as when they pursue output increases at the expense of quality. These problems can be difficult to spot, especially if everyone's attention is focused on headline figures and not what lies beneath them. As Lawler (1971) warned: 'It is quite difficult to establish criteria that are both measurable quantitatively and inclusive of all the important job behaviours.'

Criteria for effectiveness

The effectiveness of financial rewards depends on the following 12 factors:

1 There is a clear line of sight between effort and reward.
2 Rewards are attainable and worth attaining.
3 It must be possible to measure performance accurately, fairly and consistently.
4 Rewards follow performance quickly.
5 Pay differences can be related to performance or contribution differences and can be seen to be related.
6 There is a climate of trust in the organization – as Thompson (1992b) commented: 'Where there is trust, involvement and a commitment to fairness, the (PRP) schemes work.'
7 Performance management systems function well.
8 Line managers have the necessary skills and commitment.
9 The scheme is appropriate to the context and culture of the organization.

10 The scheme is not unduly complex.

11 Stakeholders, including line managers, employees and employee representatives, have been involved in the design of the scheme.

12 The purpose, methodology and effect of the scheme have been communicated and understood.

These are tough criteria. Merit pay schemes as described in Chapter 17 seldom if ever meet them, especially the first five. They are therefore less likely to effectively provide financial incentives and act as motivators. Schemes where measurement can be based on reliable data such as some bonus schemes (see Chapter 18), commission schemes for sales representatives (see Chapter 23) and piecework and payment-by-result schemes for manual workers (see Chapter 25) are more likely to be effective. Summaries of the factors that have been found in various research projects to relate to the success of financial rewards are shown in Table 9.1.

Gupta and Shaw (1998) summed up the dos and don'ts of financial incentives admirably, as set out in Table 9.2.

It is interesting to note the emphasis on involvement or communication in all these studies. A top-down approach can easily fail.

TABLE 9.1 Factors relating to the success of financial rewards

Study	Factors affecting the success of financial rewards
Bowey and Thorpe (1982)	Staff involvement in design Amount of consultation Supervisory skills Fit to context and culture
Bullock and Tubbs (1990)	Staff involvement in design Favourable attitude of employees Participative management style Productivity rather than profit orientation
De Matteo *et al* (1997)	Communication and understanding of schemes Clarification of team goals Team independence
Towers Perrin (1997)	Senior management commitment Employee involvement Employee support Emphasis on communications Related HR activities, eg training

TABLE 9.2   The dos and don'ts of financial incentives

Do:	Don't:
• involve managers and staff in the design of the scheme	• give in to hope and fad
• have good communications	• equate rewards and punishments
• tie financial incentives to valued behaviours	• rely on invalid behaviour measurement tools
• have good measurement systems	• keep things secret
• make the system complete, ie cover all relevant and valued aspects of performance	• violate employee expectations
• use other rewards to supplement financial incentives	
• make meaningful differentiations	
• set realistic goals	
• provide relevant skills and resources – managers need to be trained in their role in operating the scheme and need to be supported in implementing it	
• emphasize long-term as well as short-term success	
• accept reality – use incentives that *do* work rather than those that *should* work	

SOURCE: Adapted from Gupta and Shaw, 1998

Using financial rewards: six tips

1   Ensure in accordance with expectancy theory that there is a clear line of sight between effort and reward and that the rewards provided by the scheme are attainable and worth attaining.

2   Provide for the accurate, consistent and fair assessment of performance or contribution.

3   Fit the scheme to the context and culture of the organization.

4   Keep it simple.

5   Involve stakeholders, including line managers, employees and employee representatives, in the design of the scheme.

6   Communicate the purpose, methodology and effect of the scheme.

References

Abowd, J M (1990) Does Performance-Based Managerial Compensation Affect Corporate Performance? *Industrial and Labor Relations Review*, **43** (3), pp 52–73

Blackburn, R M and Mann, R (1979) *The Working Class in the Labour Market*, Macmillan, London

Booth, A L and Frank, J (1999) Earnings, Productivity and Performance-Related Pay, *Journal of Labor Economics*, **17** (3), pp 447–63

Bowey, A and Thorpe, R (1982) *The Effects of Incentive Pay Systems*, Department of Employment, London

Brayfield, A H and Crockett, W H (1955) Employee Attitudes and Employee Performance, *Psychological Bulletin*, **52**, pp 346–424

Bullock, R J and Tubbs, M E (1990) A Case Meta-Analysis of Gainsharing Plans as Organizational Development Interventions, *Journal of Applied Behavioural Science*, **26** (3), pp 383–406

Deci, E L and Ryan, R M (1985) *Intrinsic Motivation and Self-determination in Human Behavior*, Plenum Press, New York, NY

Deci, E L, Koestner, R and Ryan, R M (1999) A Meta-Analytical Review of Experiments Examining the Effects of Extrinsic Rewards on Intrinsic Motivation, *Psychological Bulletin*, **25**, pp 627–68

De Matteo, J S, Rush, M C, Sundstorm, E and Eby, L T (1997) Factors Relating to the Successful Implementation of Team-Based Reward, *ACA Journal*, Winter, pp 16–28

Fang, M and Gerhart, B (2012) Does Pay for Performance Erode Intrinsic Interest? *The International Journal of Human Resource Management*, **23** (6), pp 1176–96

Furnham, A (2006) Pouring Money Down the Drain? *British Journal of Administrative Management*, June/July, pp 26–27

Gerhart, B and Rynes, S L (2003) *Compensation: Theory, evidence and strategic implications*, Sage, Thousand Oaks, CA

Gupta, N and Shaw, J D (1998) Financial Incentives, *Compensation & Benefits Review*, March/April, pp 26, 28–32

Guzzo, R A, Jette, R D and Katzell, R A (1985) The Effects of Psychologically Based Intervention Programs on Worker Productivity: A meta-analysis, *Personnel Psychology*, **38** (2), pp 275–91

Hackman, J R and Oldham, G R (1974) Motivation Through the Design of Work: Test of a theory, *Organizational Behaviour and Human Performance*, **16** (2), pp 250–79

Heery, E (1996) Risk, Representation and the "New Pay", *Personnel Review*, **25** (6), pp 54–65

Heneman, R L (1992) *Merit Pay: Linking pay increases to performance ratings*, Addison-Wesley, Reading, MA

Herzberg, F (1966) *Work and the Nature of Man*, Staple Press, New York

Herzberg, F (1987) One More Time: How do you motivate employees? *Harvard Business Review*, January–February, pp 109–20 (first published 1967)

Jaques, E (1961) *Equitable Payment*, Heinemann, London

Jenkins, D G, Mitra, A, Gupta, N and Shaw, J D (1998) Are Financial Incentives Related to Performance? A meta-analytic review of empirical research, *Journal of Applied Psychology*, **3**, pp 777–87

Jurgensen, C E (1978) Job Preferences (What Makes a Job Good or Bad?), *Journal of Applied Psychology*, **63**, pp 267–76

Kessler, I and Purcell, J (1992) Performance-Related Pay: Objectives and application, *Human Resource Management Journal*, **2** (3), pp 16–33

Kohn, A (1993) Why Incentive Plans Cannot Work, *Harvard Business Review*, September–October, pp 54–63

Kohn, A (1998) Challenging Behaviourist Myths about Money and Motivation, *Compensation & Benefits Review*, March/April, pp 27, 33–37

Lawler, E E (1971) *Pay and Organizational Effectiveness*, McGraw-Hill, New York, NY

Lawler, E E (1990) *Strategic Pay*, Jossey-Bass, San Francisco, CA

Lazear, E P (1999) Performance Pay and Productivity, *American Economic Review*, 90, pp 1346–61

Locke, E A, Feren, D B, McCaleb, V M, Shaw, K N and Denny, A T (1980) The Relative Effectiveness of Four Methods of Motivating Employee Performance, in *Changes in Work, Changes in Working Life,* eds K D Duncan, M M Gruneberg and D Wallis, Wiley, New York, NY

Marsden, D (2004) The Role of Performance-Related Pay in Renegotiating the 'Effort Bargain': The case of the British public service, *Industrial and Labor Relations Review*, 57 (3), pp 350–70

Marsden, D and Richardson, R (1994) Performing For Pay? The effects of 'merit pay' on motivation in a public service, *British Journal of Industrial Relations*, 32 (2), pp 243–61

Maslow, A (1954) *Motivation and Personality*, Harper & Row, New York, NY

McDougall, C (1973) How Well do You Reward Your Managers? *Personnel Management*, March, pp 12–14

Oliver, J (1996) Cash on Delivery, *Management Today*, August, pp 52–55

Pfeffer, J (1998) Six Dangerous Myths About Pay, *Harvard Business Review*, May–June, pp 109–19

Pink, D H (2009) *Drive: The surprising truth about what motivates us*, Riverhead Books, New York, NY

Porter, L W and Lawler, E E (1968) *Managerial Attitudes and Performance*, Irwin-Dorsey, Homewood, IL

Prendergast, C (1999) The Provision of Financial Incentives in Firms, *Journal of Economic Literature*, 37, pp 7–63

Prentice, G, Burgess, S and Propper, C (2007) *Performance Pay in the Public Sector: A review of the issues and evidence*, Office of Manpower Economics, London

Ritchie, S and Martin, P (1999) *Motivation Management*, Gower, Aldershot

Ryan, R M and Deci, E L (2000) Self-Determination Theory and the Facilitation of Intrinsic Motivation, Social Development and Well-Being, *American Psychologist*, 55 (1), pp 67–78

Rynes, S L, Gerhart, B and Parks, L (2005) Personnel Psychology, Performance Evaluation and Pay for Performance, *Annual Review of Psychology*, 56, pp 571–600

Slovic, P and Lichtenstein, S (1971) Comparison of Bayesian and Regression Approaches to the Study of Information Processing in Judgment, *Organizational Behavior and Human Performance*, 6, pp 649–744

Stajkovic, A D and Luthans, F (2001) Differential Effects of Incentive Motivators on Work Performance, *Academy of Management Journal*, 4 (3), pp 580–90

Sturman, M C, Trevor, C O, Boudreau, J W and Gerhart, B (2003) Is it Worth it to Win the Talent War? Evaluating the utility of performance-based pay, *Personnel Psychology*, 56 (4), pp 997–1035

Thompson, M (1992) *Pay and Performance: The employer experience*, IMS, Brighton

Thompson, M (1998) HR and the Bottom Line, *People Management*, 16 April, pp 38–41

Towers Perrin (1997) *Learning From the Past: Changing for the future*, Towers Perrin, London

Vroom, V (1964) *Work and Motivation*, Wiley, New York, NY

Wallace, M J and Szilagyi, A D (1982) *Managing Behaviour in Organizations*, Scott, Glenview, IL

West, M, Fisher, G, Carter, M, Gould, V and Scully, J (2005) *Rewarding Customer Service? Using reward and recognition to deliver your customer service strategy*, CIPD, London

Wright, V (1991) Performance-Related Pay, in *The Performance Management Handbook*, ed E Neale, IPM, London

10
Non-financial rewards

LEARNING OUTCOMES

On completing this chapter you should be able to define these key concepts. You should also know about:

- The significance of non-financial rewards
- Extrinsic non-financial rewards
- Intrinsic non-financial rewards
- Using non-financial rewards

Introduction

Non-financial rewards are those that focus on the needs people have to varying degrees for recognition, achievement, responsibility, autonomy, influence and personal growth. They incorporate the notion of relational rewards, which are the intangible rewards concerned with the work environment (quality of working life, work–life balance), recognition, performance management, and learning and development.

Non-financial rewards can be extrinsic, such as praise or recognition, or intrinsic, arising from the work itself associated with job challenge and interest and feelings that the work is worthwhile.

This chapter starts with an exploration of the significance of non-financial rewards. It then deals with each of the major aspects of non-financial rewards and ends with a discussion on how they can be developed.

The significance of non-financial rewards

Latham and Locke (1979) noted that 'Money is obviously the primary incentive' but they went on to say that 'money alone is not enough to motivate high performance'. Money may be an important factor in attracting and retaining people (the sorting effect). It can produce satisfaction, but this may be short-lived. And if the principles of distributive and procedural justice are not followed, it can cause lasting dissatisfaction.

It can be said that money will motivate some of the people all of the time and, perhaps, all of the people some of the time. But it cannot be relied on to motivate all of the people all of the time. To rely on it as the sole motivator is misguided. Money has to be reinforced by non-financial rewards, especially those that provide intrinsic motivation.

When motivation is achieved by intrinsic rewards it can have a more powerful and longer-lasting effect on people, and financial and non-financial rewards can be mutually reinforcing.

Reward systems should therefore be designed and managed in such a way as to provide the best mix of all kinds of motivators according to the needs of the organization and its members.

Types of non-financial rewards

Non-financial rewards can be classified as follows:

- individual extrinsic rewards: non-financial recognition, praise, feedback;
- individual intrinsic rewards: fulfilling work, opportunity to grow;
- collective extrinsic rewards: work–life balance policies, employee well-being services, concierge services, voluntary benefits, learning and development and talent management programmes;
- collective intrinsic rewards: work environment enhancement, work system design.

Individual extrinsic rewards

Non-financial recognition

Recognition is one of the most powerful methods of rewarding people. People need to know not only how well they have achieved their objectives or carried out their work but also that their achievements are appreciated. Recognition needs are linked to the esteem needs in Maslow's (1954) hierarchy of needs. They are defined by Maslow as the need to have a stable, firmly based, high evaluation of oneself (self-esteem) and to have the respect of others (prestige). These needs are classified into two subsidiary sets: first, 'the desire for achievement, for adequacy, for confidence in the face of the world, and for independence and freedom', and second, 'the desire for reputation or status defined as respect or esteem from other people, and manifested by recognition, attention, importance or appreciation'.

Belief in the motivational value of recognition is supported by Herzberg's (1966, 1987) research, which identified recognition as an important 'satisfier'. Although the methodology he used has been criticized, the proposition rings true that recognizing people for what they achieve makes them feel good and therefore helps to enlist their engagement.

Recognition is a form of feedback that lets people know that they have done well and therefore provides positive reinforcement. Research by Brand *et al* (1982) found that a feedback programme in a US government agency that involved public recognition brought about an increase in productivity of 26 to 149 per cent in different sections. A meta-analysis by DeNisi and Kluger (2000) of 131 empirical studies that had tested how well feedback interventions worked indicated a modest but positive effect of feedback on performance overall.

Recognition can be provided by positive and immediate feedback from managers and colleagues that acknowledges individual contributions, and by managers who listen to and act upon the suggestions of their team members. Other actions that provide recognition include allocation to a high-profile project and enrichment of the job to provide scope for more interesting and rewarding work.

There are other forms of recognition such as public 'applause', status symbols of one kind or another, sabbaticals, treats, trips abroad and long-service awards, all of which can function as rewards. But they must be used with care. One person's recognition implies an element of non-recognition to others and the consequences of having winners and losers need to be carefully managed. Recognition schemes are examined more thoroughly in Chapter 21.

Praise

Praise is, of course, a form of recognition. It can be given privately during the course of work or in a performance review meeting. Public praise can be even more rewarding. But the praise must be genuine and saved for real achievements. It should not be fulsome.

Feedback

Feedback is another type of recognition. If done properly it can increase self-belief and provide the basis for self-directed learning.

Individual intrinsic rewards

Fulfilling work

Work can be fulfilling and therefore motivating when individuals feel that what they do is worthwhile and adds value. This implies that they should ideally work on a complete process or product, or a significant part of it that can be seen as a whole. Work is also fulfilling when it requires people to use abilities they value to perform it effectively and scope is provided for achievement, responsibility, autonomy and influence.

Use of abilities

Fulfilling work enables people to use and develop their abilities. This is particularly the case when people are stretched, but not too hard, to achieve more than they expected they could achieve.

Achievement

The need to achieve applies in varying degrees to all people in all jobs, although the level at which it operates will depend on the orientation of the individual and the scope provided by the work to fulfil a need for achievement. People feel rewarded and motivated if they have the scope to achieve as well as being recognized for the achievement.

Responsibility

Individuals can be motivated by being given more responsibility for their work. People are in positions of responsibility when they are held to account for what they do. They are in charge of their work and the resources required to do it. Being given more responsibility can satisfy needs for achievement and increase self-esteem. It is also a form of recognition.

Autonomy

Autonomy exists when an individual has freedom to make decisions and act independently without reference to higher authority. It enhances self-belief, gives people more opportunity to achieve and provides an opportunity to develop skills.

Influence

Jobs are more fulfilling if people can influence what they do or exert wider influence on policy and operational decisions.

Opportunity to grow

Alderfer (1972) emphasized the importance of providing people with opportunities for personal growth as a means of rewarding and therefore motivating them. He believed that satisfaction of growth needs takes place when individuals have the opportunity to be what they are most fully and to become what they can. Most learning and development opportunities take place in the course of everyday work, and the organization can encourage this through coaching, mentoring and support in the implementation of personal development plans created as part of the performance management process.

Collective extrinsic rewards

Collective extrinsic rewards are provided by the organization in the shape of policies, procedures, services and programmes such as the following:

- Work–life balance policies reward people by recognizing their needs outside work by, for example, adopting family-friendly policies, including the provision of more flexible working arrangements.
- Employee well-being services can be provided for individuals to help them deal with their problems. This may involve counselling or personal casework where the aim is as far as possible to get individuals to help themselves.
- Concierge services provide employees with help by undertaking mundane personal tasks such as getting their car serviced, home repairs or waiting at home for deliveries.
- Voluntary benefit schemes provide opportunities for employees to buy goods or services at discounted prices. The employer negotiates deals with the suppliers.
- Learning and development programmes give employees the chance to develop their skills and careers.

Collective intrinsic rewards

Collective intrinsic rewards are provided mainly through the work environment. They relate to the quality of working life provided and the organization's core values.

Quality of working life

The quality of working life refers to the feelings of satisfaction and well-being arising from the work itself and the way people are treated. On the basis of their longitudinal research in 12 companies Purcell *et al* (2003) concluded that:

> What seems to be happening is that successful firms are able to meet people's needs both for a good job and to work 'in a great place'. They create good work and a conducive working environment. In this way they become an 'employer of choice'. People will want to work there because their individual needs are met – for a good job with prospects linked to training, appraisal and working with a good boss who listens and gives some autonomy but helps with coaching and guidance.

Specifically, the quality of working life depends on having a system of work that enables jobs to be designed that provide for intrinsic motivation, on good working conditions and on the leadership qualities of line managers and team leaders.

Core values

The significance of the core values of an organization as a basis for creating a rewarding work environment was identified by the research conducted by John Purcell and his colleagues referred to above. The most successful companies had what the researchers called 'the big idea'. They had a clear vision and a set of integrated values that were embedded, enduring, collective, measured and managed. They were concerned with sustaining performance and flexibility. Clear connections existed between positive attitudes towards HR policies and practices, levels of satisfaction, motivation and commitment, and operational performance.

Using non-financial rewards: six tips

1   Develop the use of non-financial rewards as part of a total rewards policy (see Chapter 11).

2   Introduce employment practices designed to ensure the fair and ethical treatment of employees.

3   Involve employees as stakeholders in drawing up a set of core values associated with the employment relationship and in planning and implementing the steps required to ensure that everyone concerned 'lives the values'.

4   Review the features of the work environment and introduce changes that will improve the quality of working life and deal with any issues that may affect it.

5   Examine ways in which the design of the work system and jobs can be improved to make them more rewarding. Ensure that all those involved in work or job design (which means line managers) know what they can do and why and how they should do it.

6   Develop and implement specific policies and practices in such areas as recognition, work–life balance, well-being programmes, concierge services, voluntary benefits, performance management, learning and development and talent management.

References

Alderfer, C (1972) *Existence, Relatedness and Growth*, The Free Press, New York, NY

Brand, D D, Staelin, J R, O'Brien, R M and Dickinson, A M (1982) Improving White Collar Productivity at HUD, in *Industrial Behavior Modification*, ed R M O'Brien, A M Dickinson and M P Rosow, Pergamon, New York, NY

DeNisi, A S and Kluger, A N (2000) Feedback effectiveness: Can 360-degree appraisals be improved? *Academy of Management Executive*, **14** (1) pp 129–39

Herzberg, F (1966) *Work and the Nature of Man*, Staple Press, New York, NY

Herzberg, F (1987) One More Time: How do you motivate employees? *Harvard Business Review*, January–February, pp 109–20 (first published 1967)

Latham, G and Locke, R (1979) Goal Setting: A motivational technique that works, *Organizational Dynamics*, Autumn, pp 68–80

Maslow, A (1954) *Motivation and Personality*, Harper & Row, New York, NY

Purcell, J, Kinnie, K, Hutchinson, S, Rayton, B and Swart, J (2003) *People and Performance: How people management impacts on organizational performance*, CIPD, London

References

11
Total rewards

LEARNING OUTCOMES

On completing this chapter you should be able to define these key concepts. You should also know about:

- The overall concept of total rewards
- The underpinning concepts of total rewards
- How to introduce total rewards

Introduction

The concept of total rewards describes an approach to reward management that aims to blend the financial and non-financial elements of reward. The first person to refer in effect to total rewards was Adam Smith in 1776. He identified several components of what he called total net advantage besides pay, namely: agreeableness or disagreeableness of work, difficulty and expense of learning it, job security, responsibility and the possibility of success or failure.

The concept of total rewards

The basic premise of total rewards is that there is more to rewarding people than throwing money at them. The total rewards concept is that all aspects of reward should be linked together and treated as an integrated and coherent whole. It means that when developing the reward system employers must consider all aspects of the work experience that employees value. Sandra O'Neal (1998), one of the first people to write about total rewards after Adam Smith, commented that 'Total reward embraces everything that employees value in the employment relationship.'

The concept of total rewards recognizes that it is necessary to get financial rewards (pay and benefits) right. But it also appreciates the importance of providing people with rewarding experiences that arise from the work they do, their work environment, how they are managed and the opportunity to develop their skills and careers. It contributes to the production of an employee value proposition that provides a clear, compelling reason why talented people should work for a company.

However, Industrial Data Services (2008) commented that 'While as a philosophy, total reward emphasizes the value of the non-financial aspects of the employee value proposition, pay remains the foundation upon which everything else is built.'

The notion of total rewards influences those aspects of reward management concerned with the nature and choice of rewards but does not specifically deal with the reward management functions of market pricing, job evaluation, grade and pay structure design and the administration of reward systems. Its premise is persuasive but as discussed later in this chapter there are problems in applying it.

The approach to total rewards

A total rewards model produced by Towers Perrin (2007) is shown in Figure 11.1.

This consists of a matrix with four quadrants. The upper two quadrants – pay and benefits – represent transactional or tangible rewards. These are financial in nature and are essential to recruit and retain staff but can be easily copied by competitors. By contrast, the relational or intangible non-financial rewards represented in the lower two quadrants cannot be imitated so readily and can therefore create the human capital advantage which arises from employing people with competitively valuable knowledge and skills. They are essential to enhancing the value of the upper two quadrants. It is suggested that the real power comes when organizations combine relational and transactional rewards.

An argument for a total rewards approach was produced by Pfeffer (1998):

> Creating a fun, challenging, and empowered work environment in which individuals are able to use their abilities to do meaningful jobs for which they are shown appreciation is likely to be a more certain way to enhance motivation and performance – even though

FIGURE 11.1 Model of total rewards at Towers Perrin

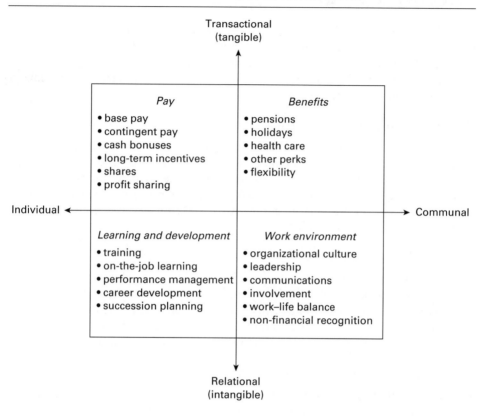

creating such an environment may be more difficult and take more time than simply turning the reward lever.

Advocates of total rewards claim that the combined effect of the different types of rewards will enhance the employment relationship and make a deeper and longer-lasting impact on engagement and performance. This may be so but there is no research evidence to prove it.

And total rewards is not an easy option. WorldatWork (2000) commented that total rewards are 'simple in concept and, at best, complex in execution'. Duncan Brown (2014) pointed out that there is a lot of rhetoric about total rewards but it often fails to work in practice. He commented on this as follows:

Professor Stephen Bevan at Lancaster University believes this HR 'rhetoric–reality' gap is widest in the rewards field. Fewer than half of UK employers actually have a defined total rewards strategy, according to the annual rewards survey from the CIPD (Chartered Institute of Personnel and Development), and in my experience policies are often based on copying rather than differentiating yourself from competitors. Even if you have a total rewards strategy in theory, 9 out of 10 firms feel their rewards are not well implemented and operated in practice. (Armstrong et al, 2010)

Bridging the gap

There is much to be said for the idea of developing and implementing reward policies that are concerned with maximizing the combined impact of both non-financial and financial reward practices. But it is necessary to consider how to bridge the reward rhetoric–reality gap when introducing a total rewards strategy. This is not easy but carrying out the following steps should help.

1 Clarify the concept of total rewards

A programme for developing total rewards should start with a clarification of the meaning of the concept to the organization and a definition of its objectives, taking into account the circumstances and requirements of the business and the views and needs of its employees and other stakeholders. Statements of meaning and purpose provide the basis for further discussions with stakeholders and decisions on the elements of a total rewards policy.

2 Involve stakeholders

Stakeholders should be involved as much as possible in developing total rewards. These include line managers, employees and employee representatives. Their commitment to the programme will be enhanced if they can contribute their ideas at the stages when the broad aims and features of the concept are defined and when the elements of total rewards are selected and their introduction prioritized.

3 Identify total rewards elements

In its basic form, a total rewards approach means simply getting the financial reward elements right and consciously doing whatever is possible progressively to enhance the elements that contribute to non-financial rewards. These include HR practices and policies such as learning and development, career management, leadership development programmes, job and work design, work–life balance initiatives and anything else that will improve the working environment. It could also include recognition schemes and flexible benefits.

4 Prioritize

The best way to bridge the gap is to avoid being over-ambitious. Start with initiatives that can be introduced easily but are still likely to make a positive impact on employee engagement. Priorities can then be established and the introduction of the less immediate elements phased.

Examples of possible developments are:

- Revise grade and pay structure, possibly instituting a career-family structure that defines career paths.
- Revise contingent pay scheme or develop new one. Include leadership and upholding core values as important factors in a contribution-related pay scheme.

- Introduce a flexible benefits scheme.
- Issue total rewards statements that spell out to employees the value of all the benefits they receive in addition to pay.
- Introduce a non-financial recognition scheme.
- Improve the performance management system, including leadership and upholding core values as important factors.
- Enhance learning and development, talent management and career development programmes.
- Focus management development programmes on improving the ability of line managers to play a major part in providing relational rewards.
- Take steps to improve work–life balance.
- Educate line managers in the principles of job design and provide guidance to them on developing roles that provide for intrinsic motivation.

5 Communicate

The nature of the total rewards concept – how it will be introduced and managed and how people will benefit – needs to be communicated.

Total rewards statements tell employees about the value of the employee benefits they receive in addition to their pay such as pensions, holidays, company cars, free car parking and subsidized meals. They also describe any other rewards they get such as learning and development opportunities. The aim is to ensure that they appreciate the total value of their reward package.

6 Implement

While planning a total rewards programme may be hard, implementing it can be even more difficult. It is an exercise in change management, for employees generally when new reward practices are being introduced and for line managers in particular if they are expected to change their behaviour. Continuing communications and involvement of stakeholders are essential.

7 Monitor and evaluate

It is essential to monitor the implantation of total rewards carefully and then to evaluate how well each element has worked against the objectives set for it. This can lead to a re-clarification of the concept and amendments to reward practices as required.

Total rewards in practice

Aegon

A model of the total rewards policy developed by Aegon is shown in Figure 11.2.

FIGURE 11.2   Model of total rewards at Aegon

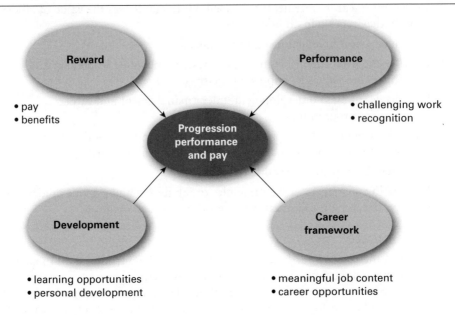

The commitment to total rewards made by senior management was to:

- recognize their best people through career opportunities and reward packages;
- develop all staff to their full potential;
- widen career opportunities for all;
- provide managers with the means to recognize and reward performance locally.

There is a notable emphasis on learning and development.

Cabinet Office

The total rewards approach adopted by the Cabinet Office in the form of a toolkit for government departments is derived from the Hay Engaged Performance model. As explained by the Cabinet Office, it draws together all the financial and non-financial investments an employer makes in its workforce. It emphasizes all aspects of reward as an integrated and coherent whole, from pay and benefits through flexible working to learning and development and the quality and challenge of the work itself.

The Cabinet Office suggests that the benefit of the total rewards approach to public sector organizations is that it will help them to recruit, retain and win the engagement of high-quality staff, align their investment with employee expectations and needs and secure better value for money. For employees a properly developed total rewards strategy will respond to employee preferences and values to create an environment that brings out the best in them.

Centrica

The total rewards approach at Centrica concentrates overall on developing reward management as a strategic, innovative and integrative process that is designed to meet the evolving needs of the organization and the people it employs. It involves the use of both:

- financial rewards: base pay, contingent or variable pay, share ownership and employee benefits;
- non-financial rewards: the work environment, recognition, quality of working life, opportunity to develop and learn skills, and work–life policies.

Nationwide

Total rewards are defined at Nationwide as 'a mixture of pay elements, with a defined cash value, benefits which have an intrinsic value, a positive and enjoyable work environment and opportunities for learning and development, all designed to make Nationwide an employer of choice.'

The Nationwide model of total rewards is shown in Figure 11.3.

FIGURE 11.3   Model of total rewards at Nationwide

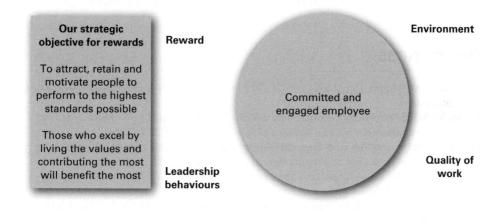

Unilever

Unilever believes that total rewards encompass all the elements in 'what it means to come to work'. It supports the Towers Perrin model of total rewards covering pay, benefits, learning and development and the work environment, which for Unilever means that it is essential to create an environment worth working in. For managers, development has been at the heart of the company's employment offering.

Conclusions

The rhetoric of the total rewards concept is compelling. Even if the prescriptions in the models for non-financial rewards are simply good HR practices or typical components in a high-performance work system, they do clarify that these should be associated with the reward system. As Giancola (2009) suggested, the main purpose of total rewards is 'to consider the standard list of human resource programmes from a reward perspective when developing strategy'. When dealing with performance and rewards it is necessary to consider these elements as well as the more obvious financial rewards.

But the reality of total rewards – making them work – is difficult. It requires a lot of effort on the part of top management and line managers, with the determined encouragement and guidance of HR.

Duncan Brown (2014) argues that the terminology and concept of total rewards is become increasingly meaningless and outdated in our post-recessionary economy of austerity and inequality. Its generic and unthinking application in uniform packages risks isolating the rewards profession into an administrative backwater.

Instead he argues for a new approach that he calls 'smart rewards'. He discerns four components of this emerging reward management approach: a simpler and clearer focus on a few core values and principles, a stronger basis in evidence and measurement, more emphasis on employee engagement through rewards, and improved and more open communications and line management of reward. He concludes that adapting and tailoring this type of approach is much more likely to create the genuinely business-enhancing and employee-engaging reward practices in our contemporary context that reward professionals and their policies aspire to.

References

Armstrong, M, Brown, D and Reilly, P (2010) *Evidence-Based Reward Management*, Kogan Page, London

Bevan, S (2013) Performance-Related Pay and the Rhetoric Gap, *The Work Foundation* [online] www.theworkfoundation.com/blog/1479/ [accessed 22 July 2015]

Brown, D (2014) The Future of Reward Management: From total reward strategies to smart rewards, *Compensation & Benefits Review*, **46** (3), pp 147–51

Chartered Institute of Personnel and Development (2013) *Reward Management Annual Survey Report*, CIPD, London

Giancola, F L (2009) Is Total Rewards a Passing Fad? *Compensation & Benefits Review*, **41** (4), pp 29-35

Industrial Data Services (2008) *Total Reward*, IDS Study 871, IDS, London

O'Neal, S (1998) The Phenomenon of Total Rewards, *ACA Journal*, 7 (3), pp 8–14

Pfeffer, J (1998) *The Human Equation: Building profits by putting people first*, Harvard Business School Press, Boston, MA

Smith, Adam (1776) *The Wealth of Nations*, published by Penguin Books, Harmondsworth, 1986

Towers Perrin (2007) *Adapting Total Rewards to Support a Changing Business Strategy*, Towers Perrin, New York, NY

WorldatWork (2000) *Total Rewards: From strategy to implementation*, WorldatWork, Scottsdale, AZ

12
The ethical approach to reward and performance management

LEARNING OUTCOMES

On completing this chapter you should be able to define these key concepts. You should also know about:

- The rationale for ethical reward and performance management
- The requirements of an ethical approach
- Resolving ethical dilemmas
- Key ethical issues
- An ethical code of practice for reward
- The ethical role of reward professionals

Introduction

An ethical approach to reward and performance management involves taking into account ethical considerations in the design, management and operation of reward and performance management systems. Reward and performance management necessarily means making ethical decisions. As defined by Jones (1991) an ethical decision is one that is morally acceptable to the larger community. He also noted that 'A moral issue is present where a person's actions, when freely performed, may harm or benefit others. In other words, the action or decision must have consequences for others and must involve choice, or volition, on the part of the actor or decision maker.'

Winstanley and Woodall (2000a) observed that:

> Ethics is not about taking statements of morality at face value; it is a critical and challenging tool. There are no universally agreed ethical frameworks... Different situations require ethical insight and flexibility to enable us to encapsulate the grounds upon which competing claims can be made. Decisions are judgements usually involving choices between alternatives, but rarely is the choice between right and wrong... Moral disagreement and judgements are concerned with attitudes and feelings, not facts.

Clegg *et al* (2007) emphasized that: 'Ethical decisions emerge out of dilemmas that cannot be managed in advance through rules.' People have to make choices. Foucault (1997) asked: 'What is ethics, if not the practice of freedom?'

Ethical decisions in reward and performance management

Ethical decisions in reward and performance management are concerned generally with ensuring fair pay and fair dealing and specifically with:

- the achievement of equity in the design and operation of pay systems;
- the fair operation of performance management and performance pay systems;
- the achievement of equal pay for work of equal value;
- the extent of dispersion, namely, the gap between the pay of the chief executive and that of the lowest-paid member of the organization or the median earnings of employees – this is often expressed as a multiple, eg a ratio of 50:1.

These issues are discussed in detail later in this chapter. However, it is necessary first to answer the question 'Why is an ethical approach desirable?' and second, to analyse the requirements of such an approach.

Why is an ethical approach desirable?

The fundamental argument for adopting an ethical approach is that there is a moral imperative for businesses to 'do the right thing'. This means creating a working environment in which personal and employment rights are upheld and HR policies and practices, including those concerned with reward and performance, provide for the fair treatment of employees. A survey conducted by Industrial Relations Services (Egan, 2006) established that the issue of ethics in employment was often viewed by employers as part of a broader social responsibility package.

There is also an element of 'doing well by doing good'. An ethical approach can boost the reputation of an organization and enhance its employee value proposition. The IRS survey (Egan, 2006) found that most employers believe that employment practices designed to ensure the fair and ethical treatment of staff could boost recruitment and retention.

Importantly, an ethical approach can help to generate trust and, therefore, a positive and cooperative climate of employee relations as considered below.

Generating trust

A climate of trust is an essential ingredient in a positive employment relationship. Trust, as defined by the *Oxford English Dictionary*, is a firm belief that a person may be relied on. It was suggested by Herriot *et al* (1988) that trust should be regarded as social capital – the fund of goodwill in any social group that enables people within it to collaborate with one another.

As Thompson (1998) noted, trust is an outcome of good management. Trust is created and maintained by managerial behaviour and by the development of better mutual understanding of expectations – employers of employees, and employees of employers. The sort of behaviour that is most likely to engender trust is when management is honest with people, keeps its word (delivers the deal) and practises what it preaches. Organizations which espouse core values ('people are our greatest asset') and then proceed to ignore them will be low-trust organizations.

In managing reward, trust will be developed if management acts fairly, equitably and consistently, if a policy of transparency is implemented, if intentions and the reasons for proposals or decisions are communicated both to employees generally and to individuals, if there is full involvement in developing reward processes, and if mutual expectations are agreed through performance management. An unethical approach to reward or performance management can do long-lasting damage to the climate of trust in an organization and therefore to levels of commitment and engagement.

Fairness

Fairness means giving people what they deserve. This is the concept of 'due desert' – that individuals should be rewarded for their performance, diligence, effort and application but should not benefit from circumstances beyond their control. To be fair, pay should be proportional to each individual's contribution. It should reflect both the nature of the post and the performance of the post holder.

Treating people justly

Treating people justly means that they are dealt with in ways which are inherently fair, right and proper. An egalitarian theory of justice was proposed by Rawls (2005). His preferred system involved guiding the distribution of economic and social benefit by the 'difference principle', the notion that inequality is permissible only to the extent that those at the bottom can be said to benefit from arrangements which allow others to be much richer.

The two types of justice most relevant to reward and performance management are distributive justice and procedural justice.

Distributive justice

As defined by Homans (1961) and Leventhal (1980), distributive justice refers to how rewards are provided to people. Employees will feel that they have been treated justly if they believe that the rewards have been distributed in accordance with the value of their contribution (they get what they deserve), that they receive what was promised to them (management delivers the deal) and that they get what they need.

Procedural justice

Procedural justice (Adams, 1965; Leventhal, 1980) is concerned with the perceptions employees have about the fairness with which company procedures in reward and performance management are operated. It refers to the ways in which managerial decisions are made and reward policies are put into practice. The five factors that affect perceptions of procedural justice identified by Tyler and Bies (1990) are:

1 The viewpoint of employees is given proper consideration.
2 Personal bias towards employees is suppressed.
3 The criteria for decisions are applied consistently to all employees.
4 Employees are provided with early feedback about the outcome of decisions.
5 Employees are provided with adequate explanations of why decisions have been made.

It was established by Folger and Konovsky (1989) that while distributive justice had most effect on pay satisfaction, procedural justice was far more influential in terms of organizational trust and commitment.

Fair process

Procedural justice is sometimes referred to as 'fair process' which, as described by Shields (2007), means fair hearing, judgement based on evidence, and meaningful employee input at all stages of system design and implementation.

The features of a fair process were defined in the Hutton Interim Report (2010) as:

Dignity – A fair process must treat all parties involved with respect, including giving all concerned a voice, and the opportunity to make their case.

Equality – A fair process must treat (and be seen to treat) all individuals the same, applying consistent, transparent rules in all cases with no scope for favouritism.

Accuracy – A fair process must take full account of all available information, exhaustively establishing the facts of each particular case.

Legitimacy – Flowing from the above criteria, a fair process must be trusted by all parties to be seeking a fair outcome for all.

Fair process includes the requirements for consistency and transparency. A consistent approach to reward management means that decisions on pay do not vary arbitrarily – without due cause – between different people or at different times. They do not deviate irrationally from what would generally be regarded as fair and equitable practice. Transparency exists when people understand how reward processes function and how they are affected by them. The reasons for pay decisions are explained at the time they are made. Employees have a voice in the development of reward policies and practices.

The felt-fair principle

An earlier and influential approach to fairness was produced by Eliot Jaques (1961). He formulated the 'felt-fair' principle, which states that pay systems will be fair if they are felt to be fair. The assumptions underpinning the theory are that:

- there is an unrecognized standard of fair payment for any level of work;
- unconscious knowledge of the standard is shared among the population at work;
- pay must match the level of work and the capacity of the individual to do it;
- people should not receive less pay than they deserve by comparison with their fellow workers.

This felt-fair principle has passed into the common language of those involved in reward management. It is sometimes used as the final arbiter of how a job should be graded, possibly overriding the conclusions reached by an analytical job evaluation exercise (the so-called 'felt-fair' test). But such tests are in danger of simply reproducing existing prejudices about relative job values.

Equity

To be dealt with equitably is to be treated fairly in comparison with another group of people (a reference group) or a relevant other person. Equity involves feelings and perceptions and it is always a comparative process. It is not synonymous with equality, which means treating everyone the same and would be inequitable if they deserve to be treated differently.

Duncan Brown (2010) produced the following thoughts on equity:

> Ever since Adams outlined his equity theory in the 1960s, a wide variety of research studies have reinforced his ideas on the importance of relative assessments in determining our satisfaction with rewards. The bulk of those studies appear to suggest that we place most weight on comparisons with those closest to us in our organizations, rather than the abstract concept of the external market which reward managers now spend so much time obsessing about.

It was suggested by Shields (2007) that in an effort to restore equity an employee might take one or more of six possible courses of action:

1 Leave the organization for a more rewarding position elsewhere.
2 Change outcomes within the organization.
3 Change inputs.
4 Rationalize away the inequity by altering their perception of their inputs and outcomes.
5 Psychologically distort the inputs and outputs of others to eliminate felt inequity.
6 Change the comparison order (referent).

Equitable reward processes ensure that relativities between jobs are measured as objectively as possible and that equal pay is provided for work of equal value.

Resolving ethical dilemmas

Adam Smith (1759) wrote in *The Theory of Modern Sentiments* that:

> When ethically perplexed, the question we should always ask is: would a disinterested observer, in full possession of the relevant facts, approve or disapprove of our actions?

This guidance is just as compelling and relevant today.

Woodall and Winstanley (2000) proposed that 'being ethical is not so much about finding one universal principle to govern all action, but more about knowing how to recognize and mediate between often unacknowledged differences of view'. By definition, an ethical dilemma is one that will be difficult to resolve. There may be all sorts of issues surrounding the situation, some of which will be unclear or contentious. The extent to which people react or behave rationally may be limited by their capacity to understand the complexities of the situation they are in and affected by their emotional reactions to it (the concept of bounded rationality). As Harrison (2009) explained: 'Some of the factors that militate against a purely "rational" approach include confused, excessive, incomplete or unreliable data, incompetent processing or communicating of information, pressures of time, human emotions, and differences in individuals' cognitive processes, mental maps and reasoning capacity.' Faced with factors such as these the process of ethical dilemma resolution can be hard going.

There is no one right way to deal with an ethical dilemma, but an approach based on systematic questioning, analysis, and diagnosis to get at the facts and establish the issues involved is more likely to produce a reasonably satisfactory outcome than one relying purely on 'gut feeling'. The following checklist – used judiciously and selectively according to the circumstances – can provide a basis for such questioning and analysis:

1 Will the proposed action benefit the organization and if so, how?

2 Will the proposed action be harmful to the individual affected or to employees generally in any way and if so, how?

3 Does the proposed action benefit one stakeholder (eg shareholders) to the detriment of others (eg employees)?

4 Are the proposed action and any investigations leading to it consistent with the principles of procedural and distributive justice?

5 Is the reason for taking the proposed action clear to all concerned?

6 Is there any risk of the proposed action doing harm to the organization's reputation for fair dealing?

7 Do the facts as identified and confirmed justify the proposed action?

8 Is the action consistent with established guiding principles or value statements?

9 Have different versions or interpretations of the facts and circumstances been offered and if so, what steps can be taken to obtain the true and full picture?

10 Is the proposed action in line with both the letter and the spirit of the law?

The application of these will, of course, depend on the context and the issues to be dealt with. Typical issues as discussed below are concerned with pay dispersion, equity, equal pay, performance management and performance-related pay.

Pay dispersion

Pay dispersion refers to the differentials or gaps in pay between jobs in an organization. The major ethical issue raised by dispersion is the ratio of the pay of a chief executive to that of the lowest-paid employee or to the median pay of all employees. What amount of dispersal is justified?

The pay of chief executives had grown from 60 times that of the average worker in 1998 to 160 times in 2012. How can that be explained or justified?

Equity

The ethical issue with equity is that while most managers would accept that it is right in principle, in practice they may be faced with ethical dilemmas. Here are some examples:

● What should be done when someone urgently required by the organization can only be recruited at a salary significantly higher than a number of existing members of staff carrying out essentially the same job?

● How is it possible to reconcile the often conflicting view that pay levels should be both internally equitable and externally competitive?

- How can the pressure to devolve more pay decisions to line managers be achieved without prejudicing equitable pay because of inconsistent decisions?
- What can be done about a job-family structure (see Chapter 15) consisting of separate market groups for each family, which results in pay inequities between comparable jobs in different families?
- Should pay be protected so that employees do not suffer a reduction of salary after a pay structure redesign (see Chapter 16) and if so for how long?

Equal pay

The equal pay ethical dilemma facing organizations is the extent to which they go beyond compliance with the law in order to meet the moral obligation to reward men and women equally for work of equal value. The issues that may need to be addressed include:

- whether or not to conduct an equal pay review and, if one is carried out, what action to take if it reveals unjustifiable variations between the pay of men and women in comparable jobs which can only be corrected at considerable expense;
- what to do about women who have been on maternity leave and whose pay then falls behind those of men in comparable jobs who have continued to receive pay increments;
- decisions on recruiting men at an attractive salary which would place them at a higher point in the pay range than women in similar jobs;
- whether the factor plan for a job evaluation scheme (see Chapter 14) should include factors which may be particularly relevant for women workers such as emotional demands and manual dexterity.

Performance management

Performance management schemes can be ethical minefields. The overriding ethical issue is how they can be operated fairly. The specific ethical issues are:

- the extent to which the standards used to judge performance are fair in the sense that they are both valid and reliable, ie are based on correct and consistently applied criteria, adequate performance information and unbiased judgements;
- how well equipped managers are to make judgements about the performance of their staff;
- the degree to which judgements about performance are imposed from above;
- the use of ranking or the forced distribution of assessments (see Chapter 2) to inform decisions on who should be dismissed for underperformance ('rank and yank' systems);
- how performance ratings, which may be largely subjective or biased, will govern pay increases;

- what scope employees have, in the words of Shields (2007), 'to challenge, test, refute and have corrected any assessment evidence or judgement that the assessee believes to be inaccurate, unrepresentative, biased, unethical or which is perceived as being unfair in any other way'.

The following four performance management ethical principles were defined by Winstanley and Stuart-Smith (1996):

1 *Respect for the individual* – people should be treated as 'ends in themselves' and not merely as 'means to other ends'.

2 *Mutual respect* – the parties involved in performance management should respect each other's needs and preoccupations.

3 *Procedural fairness* – the procedures incorporated in performance management should be operated fairly in accordance with the principles of procedural justice.

4 *Transparency* – people affected by decisions emerging from performance management processes should have the opportunity to scrutinize the basis upon which decisions were made.

These principles are equally valid for any other aspect of reward management.

Performance-related pay

The fundamental ethical issue concerning performance-related pay is the extent to which fair, equitable and consistent judgements can be made about performance to inform decisions on the amount of pay increases. The degree to which performance-related pay is ethical depends on fair performance management processes (ie procedural justice). And for the reasons given above this is difficult to achieve.

As cited by Shields (2007), Heery (1996) argued that performance-related pay poses a threat to employee well-being because it can contradict employees' need for a stable and secure income and expose their pay to disproportionate risk. Rubery (1995) contended that women may be worse off under performance-related pay in situations where supervisory positions tend to be male dominated, as in service work.

The ethical role of reward professionals

Winstanley and Woodall (2000b) remarked that: 'HR professionals [including reward specialists] have to raise awareness of ethical issues, promote ethical behaviour, disseminate ethical practices widely among line managers, communicate codes of ethical conduct, ensure people learn about what constitutes ethical behaviours, manage compliance and monitor arrangements.'

Reward professionals need to do whatever they can to embed the consistent application of ethical values in the organization so that they can become values in use rather than simply professed values in a code of practice or a set of guiding principles. As recommended by the Institute of Business Ethics (2003), they need to find a champion, gain the endorsement of the chief executive officer and the board, communicate the guiding principles or code widely and ensure through constant monitoring and contacts with line managers that the code is put into practice.

Ann Cummins (Humanus Consultants) produced the following checklist for reward practitioners in 2009:

- Don't create pay plans that you wouldn't be proud of.
- When you're designing pay structures, ask yourself, 'Is this just?' as often as you ask, 'Will this make money?'
- Coach your business leaders to do the right thing. It's not enough and not professional to 'take orders'.
- If you know it's wrong, it is wrong. Stand up, speak out. Get a backbone. That's your job.

An ethical code of practice for reward and performance management

1 Apply the principles of distributive and procedural justice, ie ensure that people get the pay they deserve and that the processes used in managing pay are fair.

2 Ensure that reward and performance management policies and practices are fair, equitable and transparent and that they are applied consistently.

3 Reward people fairly according to their contribution.

4 Ensure that people know in general the basis upon which rewards are provided and how their own reward package is determined.

5 Maintain reasonable and defensible pay differentials.

6 Ensure that equal pay is provided for work of equal value.

7 Ensure that the standards used to judge performance are fair in the sense that they are both valid and reliable, ie are based on correct and consistently applied criteria, adequate performance information and unbiased judgements.

8 Base decisions on performance pay or bonuses on fair and equitable criteria.

9 Avoid bonus schemes which encourage undesirable behaviour or reward for failure.

10 Involve employees in the development of reward and performance management systems.

References

Adams, J S (1965) Injustice in Social Exchange, in *Advances in Experimental Psychology*, ed L Berkowitz, Academic Press, New York, NY

Brown, D (2010) Fairness: The ultimate reward goal, *Institute for Employment Studies* [online] www.employment-studies.co.uk/resource/fairness-ultimate-reward-goal [accessed 11 November 2011]

Clegg, S, Kornberger, M and Rhodes, C (2007) Business Ethics as Practice, *British Journal of Management*, **18** (2), pp 107–22

Cummins, A (2009) *A Fair Day's Wage for a Fair Day's Work?* Unpublished presentation at e-reward annual update, November

Egan, J (2006) Doing the Decent Thing: CSR and ethics in employment, *IRS Employment Review*, 858, 3 November, pp 9–16

Folger, R and Konovsky, M A (1989) Effects of Procedural and Distributive Justice in Reaction to Pay Rise Decisions, *Academy of Management Journal*, **32** (1), pp 115–39

Foucault, M (1997) *Ethics, Subjectivity and Truth: Essential Works of Foucault, 1954–1984*, ed P Rabinow, The New Press, New York, NY

Harrison, R (2009) *Learning and Development*, 5th edn, CIPD, London

Heery, E (1996) Risk, Representation and the New Pay, *Personnel Review*, **25** (6), pp 54–65

Herriot, P, Hirsh, W and Riley, P (1988) *Trust and Transition: Managing the employment relationship*, Wiley, Chichester

Homans, G C (1961) *Social Behaviour: Its elementary forms*, Brace & World, New York, NY

Hutton Review of Fair Pay in the Public Sector: Interim report (2010) HM Treasury, London

Institute of Business Ethics (2003) Developing a Code of Business Ethics, *Institute of Business Ethics* [online] www.ibe.org.uk/userfiles/developingsumm.pdf [accessed 16 November 2011]

Jaques, E (1961) *Equitable Payment*, Heinemann, London

Jones, T M (1991) Ethical Decision Making by Individuals in Organizations: An issue-contingent model, *Academy of Management Review*, **16** (2), pp 366–95

Leventhal, G S (1980) What Should be Done with Equity Theory? in *Social Exchange: Advances in theory and research*, eds G K Gergen, M S Greenberg and R H Willis, Plenum, New York, NY

Rawls, J (2005) *A Theory of Justice*, Harvard University Press, Cambridge, MA

Rubery, J (1995) Performance-Related Pay and the Prospects for Gender Pay Equality, *Journal of Management Studies*, **32** (5), pp 637–53

Shields, J (2007) *Managing Employee Performance and Reward*, Cambridge University Press, Port Melbourne

Smith, A (1759) *The Theory of Modern Sentiments*, available from A Millar, London

Thompson, M (1998) Trust and Reward, in *Trust, Motivation and Commitment: A reader*, eds S Perkins and St John Sandringham, Strategic Remuneration Research Centre, Farringdon

Tyler, T R and Bies, R J (1990) Beyond Formal Procedures: The interpersonal context of procedural justice, in *Applied Social Psychology and Organizational Settings*, ed J S Carrol, Lawrence Erlbaum, Hillsdale, NJ

Winstanley, D and Stuart-Smith, K (1996) Policing Performance: The ethics of performance management, *Personnel Review*, **25** (6), pp 66–84

Winstanley, D and Woodall, J (2000a) Introduction to *Ethical Issues in Contemporary Human Resource Management*, eds D Winstanley and J Woodall, Macmillan, Basingstoke

Winstanley, D and Woodall, J (2000b) The Ethical Dimension of Human Resource Management, *Human Resource Management Journal*, **10** (2), pp 5–20

Woodall, J and Winstanley, D (2000) Concluding Comments: Ethical frameworks for action, in (eds) D Winstanley and J Woodall, *Ethical Issues in Contemporary Human Resource Management*, Macmillan, Basingstoke, pp 3–22

PART TWO
Base pay management

13
Market pricing

LEARNING OUTCOMES

On completing this chapter you should be able to define these key concepts. You should also know about:

- The aims of market rate analysis
- The concept of a market rate
- Factors affecting the validity and reliability of market rate data
- Job matching
- Uses of benchmark jobs
- Sources of data
- Interpreting and presenting market rate data
- Using survey data

Introduction

Market pricing is the process of analysing market rates to establish external relativities and provide a guide to the development of a competitive pay structure, ie one in which levels of pay enable the organization to attract and retain the talented people it needs.

Market pricing is based on the collection and analysis of market rate data through surveys that produce information data on the levels of pay and benefits for similar jobs in comparable organizations. It is the basis either for the method of valuing jobs known as extreme market pricing (see Chapter 14) or for deciding on rates of pay for specific jobs or pay ranges in a grade and pay structure.

Decisions on levels of pay following market rate analysis will be guided by the pay policy of the organization or its 'market stance' – that is, how it wants its pay levels to relate to market levels.

Aims of market pricing

Market rate pricing aims to:

- obtain relevant, accurate and representative data on market rates;
- compare like with like, in terms of data, regional and organizational variations and, importantly, type and size of job or role;
- obtain information that is as up to date as possible;
- interpret data in a way that clearly indicates the action required in the shape of decisions on pay structures or the rate of pay for individual jobs.

Achieving these aims depends on understanding the concept of a market rate and the factors affecting the validity and reliability of market rate data, as considered in the next two parts of this chapter. The rest of the chapter deals with selecting the benchmark jobs used for comparison, the sources of market rate data and how it should be used.

The concept of a market rate

People often refer to the market rate, but this is a much more elusive concept than it seems. There is no such thing as a definitive market rate for any job, even when comparing identically sized organizations in the same industry and location. There are local markets and there are national markets, and none of them is perfect in the economists' sense. Different market information sources for the same types of jobs produce different results because of variations in the sample, the difficulty of obtaining precise comparisons between jobs in the organization and jobs elsewhere (job matching), and timing (the dates on which the data is collected may differ).

This means that market rate analysis is most unlikely to produce totally reliable information on the rate for the job. The possibly incomplete data from a number of sources, some more accurate than others, has to be interpreted to indicate what the organization should do about it. The result of a market rate survey is often what is called a derived market rate, which is a judgement on what appears to be a reasonable rate made on the basis of an analysis of the data obtained from a number of sources.

The factors determining the accuracy of market rate comparisons are as follows:

- *Job matching*: the extent to which the external jobs with which the internal jobs are being compared are similar; in other words, like is being compared with like.
- *Sample frame*: the degree to which the sample of organizations from which the data has been collected is fully representative of the organizations with which comparisons need to be made in such terms as sector, technology or type of business, size and location.
- *Timing*: the extent to which the information is up to date or can be updated reliably. By their very nature, published surveys, upon which many people rely, can soon become out of date. This can happen even at the moment they are published – pay levels may have changed and people may have moved in or out since the date of the original survey. Whilst it is not possible to overcome this completely, as data must be gathered and analysed, surveys that aim to have as short a time as possible between data collection and the publication of results are likely to be of more use than those with longer lead times. Estimates can be made of likely movements since the survey took place, but they are mainly guesswork.

Job matching

Inadequate job matching is a major cause of inaccuracies in the data collected by market analysis. So far as possible, the aim is to match the jobs within the organization and those outside (the comparators) so that like is being compared with like. It is essential to avoid crude and misleading comparisons based on job titles alone or vague descriptions of job content. It is first necessary to ensure that a broad match is achieved between the organization concerned and the types of organizations used as comparators in terms of sector, industry classification, size and location.

The next step is to match jobs within the organizations concerned. The various methods in ascending order of accuracy are:

- Job title: this can be misleading. Job titles by themselves give no indication of the range of duties or the level of responsibility, and are sometimes used to convey additional status to employees or their customers regardless of the real level of work done.
- Brief description of duties and level or zone of responsibility: national surveys frequently restrict their job-matching definitions to a two- or three-line description of duties and an indication of levels of responsibility in rank order. The latter is often limited to a one-line definition for each level or zone

in a hierarchy. This approach provides some guidance on job matching, which reduces major discrepancies, but it still leaves considerable scope for discretion and can therefore provide only generalized comparisons.

- Capsule job descriptions: club or specialist bespoke surveys frequently use capsule job descriptions that define main responsibilities and duties in about 100 to 200 words. To increase the refinement of comparisons, modifying statements may be made indicating where responsibilities are higher or lower than the norm. Capsule job descriptions considerably increase the accuracy of comparisons as long as they are based on a careful analysis of actual jobs and include modifying statements. But they are not always capable of dealing with specialist jobs and the accuracy of comparisons in relation to levels of responsibility may be limited, even when modifiers are used.

- Full role profiles, including a factor analysis of the levels of responsibility involved, may be used in special surveys when direct comparisons are made between jobs in different organizations. They can be more accurate on a one-for-one basis but their use is limited because of the time and labour involved in preparing them. A further limitation is that comparator organizations may not have available, or not be prepared to make available, their own full role profiles for comparison.

- Job evaluation: can be used in support of a capsule job description or a role profile to provide a more accurate measure of relative job size. A common method of evaluation is necessary. An increasing number of international and UK consultancies now claim to be able to make this link, either through a point-factor scheme or a matching approach. This approach will further increase the accuracy of comparisons but the degree of accuracy will depend on the quality of the job evaluation process.

Use of benchmark jobs

A market rate survey should aim to collect data on a representative sample of benchmark jobs, which are defined as typical jobs with which comparisons of other jobs can be made. They will be used to provide guidance on the design of a pay structure or as a basis for market pricing. The jobs selected should be ones for which it is likely that market data will be available. There are usually some jobs that are unique to the organization and for which comparisons cannot be made. When conducting a market pricing exercise, it is necessary to make a judgement on the positioning of these jobs in the structure on the basis of comparisons with the benchmark jobs. A point-factor evaluation scheme, if available, helps to make these comparisons more accurate.

Sources of market data

There is a wide variety of sources of varying quality, as summarized in Table 13.1. They include published surveys, special surveys conducted by organizations, pay clubs (groups of organizations that exchange information on pay and benefits) and advertisements. It is not advisable to rely on only one possibly unreliable source.

Should improvements in the quality of job matching be desirable, an individual survey can be conducted or a salary club can be joined, if there is one available. If several sources are used, it may be possible to produce an objective justification for any market supplement or premium (an addition to the normal rate for the job to reflect the market value of a job) that might create unequal pay.

In choosing data sources it is important to take account of how easily replicable the analysis will be in future years. Trends can only be identified if a consistent set of sources is used, and if those sources are reasonably stable.

Published surveys

Published surveys are readily accessible and are commonly based on a large sample. If the information can be obtained online, so much the better. For example, IDS in the UK offers an extensive pay database to subscribers.

But the sources have to be relevant to the needs of the organization and particular attention should always be paid to the range of data and the quality of job matching. Published surveys are of widely varying content, presentation and quality, and are sometimes expensive. They can be national, local, sector, industrial or occupational.

When selecting a published survey the following questions should be considered:

1 Does it cover relevant jobs in similar organizations?
2 Are there effective arrangements for job matching?
3 Does it provide the required information on the relevant pay and benefits?
4 Are there enough participants to provide acceptable comparisons?
5 So far as can be judged, is the survey conducted properly in terms of its sampling techniques?
6 Is it reasonably up to date?
7 Are the results well presented?
8 Does it provide value for money?

Consultants' databases

Many consultancies concerned with reward management have databases of market rates produced by their own surveys and contacts and often linked to their proprietary job evaluation scheme.

Special surveys

Special surveys can be 'do it yourself' affairs or they can be conducted for companies by management consultants or IDS. The latter method costs more but it saves a lot of time and trouble, and some organizations may be more willing to respond to an enquiry from a reputable consultant.

Conducting your own special survey

1   Decide what information is wanted.

2   Identify the 'benchmark' jobs for which comparative pay data is required. This could have been done as part of a job evaluation exercise as described in Chapter 14.

3   Produce capsule job descriptions for those jobs.

4   Identify the organizations that are likely to have similar jobs.

5   Contact those organizations and invite them to participate. It is usual to say that the survey findings will be distributed to participants (this is the quid pro quo) and that individual organizations will not be identified.

6   Provide participants with a form to complete, together with notes for guidance and capsule job descriptions. This includes provision for participants to indicate by a + or − whether the size or scope of the job is larger or smaller than the capsule job description indicates. Give them a reasonable amount of time to complete and return the form, say two to three weeks.

7   Analyse the returned forms and distribute a summary of the results to participants.

Special surveys can justify the time and trouble, or expense, by producing usefully comparable data. It may, however, be difficult to get a suitable number of participants to take part, either because organizations cannot be bothered or because they are already members of a survey club or take part in a published survey.

Club surveys

Club surveys (pay clubs) are conducted by a number of organizations that agree to exchange information on pay in accordance with a standard format and on a regular basis. They have all the advantages of special surveys plus the additional benefits of saving a considerable amount of time and providing regular information. It is well worth joining one if you can. If a suitable club does not exist you could always try to start one, but this takes considerable effort.

Advertisements

Many organizations rely on the salary levels published in recruitment advertisements. But these can be very misleading as you will not necessarily achieve a good match and the quoted salary may not be the same as what is finally paid. However, although it is highly suspect, data from advertisements can be used to supplement other more reliable sources.

Other market intelligence

Other market intelligence can be obtained from the publications of IDS and the IRS. This may include useful information on trends in the 'going rate' for general, across-the-board pay increases that can be used when deciding on what sort of uplift, if any, is required to pay scales.

The features of the main sources and their advantages and disadvantages are listed in Table 13.1.

Interpreting and presenting market rate data

Market rate data needs to be interpreted by reference to the details provided from each source and by assessments of their reliability, accuracy and relevance.

Data can be presented as measures of central tendency or measures of dispersion. Measures of central tendency consist of the arithmetic mean (average) and the median – the middle item in a distribution of individual items. The latter is the most commonly used measure because it avoids the distortions to which arithmetic averages are prone. Measures of dispersion consist of:

- The upper quartile: the value above which 25 per cent of the individual values fall (this term is often used more loosely to indicate any value within the top 25 per cent).
- The lower quartile: the value below which 25 per cent of the individual values fall.
- The inter-quartile range: the difference between the upper and lower quartiles.

Using survey data

The use of market survey data as a guide on pay levels is a process based on judgement and compromise. Different sources may produce different indications of market rate levels. As a result it is often necessary to produce a derived market rate based on an assessment of the relative reliability of the data. This would strike a reasonable balance between the competing merits of the different sources used. It is an intuitive process.

Once all the data available has been collected and presented in the most accessible manner possible (ie job by job for all the areas the structure is to cover), reference points can be determined for each pay range in a graded pay structure, as described in Chapter 15. This process will take account of how the business wants to relate its internal rates to the market rates, that is, its market stance or posture. A market stance policy can be expressed in such terms as 'pay upper quartile rates' to keep ahead of the market and attract high-quality people. But this policy may be difficult to apply if accurate market rate information is not available. And if everyone in a confined labour market adopted it, the outcome would be an increase in average pay levels through a ratchet effect.

TABLE 13.1 Analysis of market rate data sources

Source	Brief description	Advantages	Disadvantages
Online data	Access data from general surveys.	Quick, easy, can be tailored.	May not provide all the information required.
General national published surveys	Available for purchase – provide an overall picture of pay levels for different occupations in national and regional labour markets.	Wide coverage, readily available, continuity allows trend analyses over time, expert providers.	Risk of imprecise job matching, insufficiently specific, quickly out of date.
Local published surveys	Available for purchase – provide an overall picture of pay levels for different occupations in the local labour market.	Focus on local labour market, especially for administrative staff and manual workers.	Risk of imprecise job matching, insufficiently specific, quickly out of date; providers may not have expertise in pay surveys.
Sector surveys	Available for purchase – provide data on a sector such as charities.	Focus on a sector where pay levels may differ from national rates; deal with particular categories in depth.	Risk of imprecise job matching, insufficiently specific, quickly out of date.
Industrial/ occupational surveys	Surveys, often conducted by employer and trade associations on jobs in an industry or specific jobs.	Focus on an industry; deal with particular categories in depth; quality of job matching may be better than general or sector surveys.	Job matching may still not be entirely precise; quickly out of date.
Management consultants' databases	Pay data obtained from the databases maintained by management consultants.	Based on well-researched and matched data. Often highly tailored to specific market segments.	May be restricted to clients

TABLE 13.1 *continued*

Source	Brief description	Advantages	Disadvantages
Special surveys	Surveys specially conducted by an organization.	Focused, reasonably good job matching, control of participants, control of analysis methodology.	May not provide all the information required.
Pay clubs	Groups of employers who regularly exchange data on pay levels.	Focused, precise job matching, control of participants, control of analysis methodology, regular data, trends data, more information may be available on benefits and pay policies.	Risk of imprecise job matching, insufficiently specific, quickly out of date.
Published data in journals	Data on settlements and pay levels available from IDS or IRS, and on national trends in earnings from the New Earnings Survey.	Readily accessible.	Risk of imprecise job matching, insufficiently specific, quickly out of date; providers may not have expertise in pay surveys.
Analysis of recruitment data	Pay data derived from analysis of pay levels required to recruit staff.	Immediate data.	Risk of imprecise job matching, insufficiently specific, quickly out of date.
Job advertisements	Pay data obtained from job advertisements.	Readily accessible, highly visible (to employees as well as employers), up to date. Data can be quite specific for public and voluntary sector roles.	Job matching may still not be entirely precise; quickly out of date.
Other market intelligence	Pay data obtained from informal contacts or networks.	Provide good background.	Imprecise, not regularly available

Market pricing: six tips

1 Select benchmark jobs for which external market data is available.

2 Identify all the sources of market rate information available, including pay clubs, published data, consultancies and agencies and other sources of market rate intelligence.

3 Evaluate the sources to assess the likelihood of their producing valid and reliable information.

4 Use more than one source to collect as much comparative data as possible.

5 Make every attempt to match internal benchmark jobs with jobs covered in the data sources in order to compare like with like.

6 Analyse the data from each source and if variable results are obtained (which is likely), use judgement to produce a 'derived market rate' using the most reliable results.

14
Job evaluation

KEY CONCEPTS AND TERMS

- Analytical job evaluation
- Analytical job matching
- Benchmark job
- Computer-aided job evaluation
- Explicit weighting
- Extreme market pricing
- Factor (job evaluation)
- Factor comparison
- Factor level
- Factor plan
- Going rates
- Implicit weighting
- Internal benchmarking
- Internal relativities
- Job classification
- Job evaluation
- Job ranking
- Job size
- Job slotting
- Job worth
- Levelling
- Market driven
- Market pricing
- Market rates
- Non-analytical job evaluation
- Paired comparison ranking
- Point-factor job evaluation
- Proprietary brand
- Tailor-made job evaluation scheme
- Time span of discretion
- Weighting

LEARNING OUTCOMES

On completing this chapter you should be able to define these key concepts. You should also know about:

- The purposes of job evaluation
- Approaches to achieving the purposes
- Analytical job evaluation schemes
- Non-analytical job evaluation schemes

- Market pricing
- Levelling
- Job and role analysis
- Computer-aided job evaluation
- Choice of approach
- Designing a point-factor scheme

Introduction

Decisions about what jobs are worth take place all the time. The decisions may be made informally, based on assumptions about the value of a job in the marketplace or by comparison with other jobs in the organization. Or there may be a formal approach, either some type of job evaluation or 'levelling', as described in this chapter, or a systematic comparison with market rates. It has been stated by Gupta and Jenkins (1991) that the basic premise of job evaluation is that certain jobs 'contribute more to organizational effectiveness and success than others, are worth more than others and should be paid more than others'.

A formal approach to evaluating 'worth' leads to where a job is placed in a level or grade within a hierarchy and can therefore determine how much someone is paid. The performance of individuals also affects their pay, but this is not a matter for job evaluation, which is concerned with valuing the jobs people carry out, not how well they perform their jobs.

This chapter contains a definition of job evaluation and a description of the different types of analytical and non-analytical formal schemes and the processes of market pricing and levelling. This is followed by an examination of job and role analysis techniques as these provide the factual basis for all formal evaluations. Consideration is then given to the use of computers as an aid to evaluation. Finally the factors affecting the choice of a scheme are discussed and methods of developing the most typical form of job evaluation – the point-factor scheme – are described.

Job evaluation defined

Job evaluation is a systematic process for deciding on the relative worth or size of jobs within an organization. It was defined by the Equality and Human Rights Commission (2011) as a mechanism for establishing agreed differentials within organizations. However, the Commission noted that: 'It is important to recognize that to some extent any assessment of a job's total demands relative to another will always contain elements of subjectivity.'

Aims of job evaluation

The Equality and Human Rights Commission (2011) stated that the aim of job evaluation is 'to minimize subjectivity and make decisions about jobs as rational, consistent and transparent as possible'. As described by Armstrong and Cummins (2008), job evaluation has three specific purposes:

1 To generate the information required to develop and maintain an internally equitable grade and pay structure by establishing the relative value of roles or jobs within the organization (internal relativities) based on fair, sound and consistent judgements.

2 To provide the data required to ensure that pay levels in the organization are externally competitive, by making valid market comparisons with jobs or roles of equivalent complexity and size.

3 To ensure transparency so that the basis upon which grades are defined, jobs graded and rates of pay determined is clear to all concerned.

Achieving the aims

Approaches to achieving these purposes can either use a formal analytical or non-analytical job evaluation scheme or value jobs informally. Some organizations rely entirely on comparisons with external market rates to determine internal levels of pay, a process called 'extreme market pricing'. The argument for this approach is that businesses must take account of market rates as a fundamental part of the process of valuing jobs in order to be competitive in the external labour market. Market pricing as described later in this chapter is by far the most common method of valuing jobs in the United States.

In formal schemes the basis of the job evaluation is a detailed analysis of the job or role, which leads to the production of a job description or role profile. Although formal job evaluation schemes are still common there is much less reliance on the elaborate and time-consuming traditional point-factor versions which, when adopted, do no more than support the simpler processes of levelling and analytical matching. Informal evaluation is based on assumptions about what the job contains but may possibly refer to an existing job description that could be inaccurate and out of date.

Arguments for and against job evaluation

Among the arguments for a systematic approach to job evaluation is that it enables organizations to make decisions on the worth of their employees. It also brings order and discipline to situations, which can too easily become chaotic without the structure developed by job evaluation. It is also a means of establishing situations where work of equal value should be paid equally.

The most common argument against traditional approaches to job evaluation is that they focus on internal relativities and ignore the importance of the external market. Nielsen (2002) took exception to the fact that such approaches are not concerned with external relativities, which, he claims, are what really matter.

But formal job evaluation techniques like point-factor rating are also criticized for being cumbersome, bureaucratic, inflexible, time-consuming and inappropriate for the types of roles found in today's organizations.

Formal job evaluation

Formal approaches use standardized methods to evaluate jobs, which can be analytical or non-analytical. Such schemes deal with internal relativities and the associated process of establishing and defining job grades or levels in an organization. Schemes may be used to evaluate all jobs or they may focus on a sample of typical benchmark jobs.

An alternative approach is extreme market pricing, in which formal pay structures and individual rates of pay are entirely based on systematically collected and analysed information on market rates and no use is made of job evaluation to establish internal relativities. Extreme market pricing should be distinguished from the process of collecting and analysing market rate data used to establish external relativities after internal relativities have been determined through formal job evaluation.

In the 1980s and 1990s formal job evaluation fell into disrepute for the reasons given above. However, job evaluation is still practised widely (60 per cent of the respondents to the 2007 e-reward job evaluation survey had a formal scheme) and, indeed, its use is increasing in the UK, not least because of the pressures to achieve equal pay. Although formal job evaluation may work systematically it should not be treated as a rigid, monolithic and bureaucratic system. It should instead be regarded as an approach that may be applied flexibly. Process – the way job evaluation is used – can be more important than the system itself when it comes to producing reliable and valid results.

Informal job evaluation

Informal approaches price jobs either on the basis of assumptions about internal and external relativities or simply by reference to going or market rates when recruiting people unsupported by any systematic analysis. There are, however, degrees of informality. A semi-formal approach might require some firm evidence to support a market pricing decision, and the use of role profiles to provide greater accuracy to the matching process.

Analytical job evaluation schemes

Analytical job evaluation is based on a methodology of breaking whole jobs down into a number of defined elements or factors such as responsibility, decisions and the knowledge and skill required. In point-factor and fully analytical matching schemes, jobs are then compared factor by factor, either with a graduated scale of points attached to a set of factors or with grade or role profiles analysed under the same factor headings.

The advantages of an analytical approach are that, first, evaluators have to consider each of the characteristics of the job separately before forming a conclusion about its relative value, and second, they are provided with defined yardsticks or guidelines that help to increase the objectivity and consistency of judgements. It can also provide a defence in the UK against an equal pay claim. The main analytical schemes as described below are point-factor rating, analytical matching and factor comparison.

Point-factor rating

Point-factor schemes are the most common forms of analytical job evaluation. They were used by 70 per cent of those with job evaluation schemes who responded to the e-reward 2007 job evaluation survey. The basic methodology is to break down jobs into factors such as those mentioned above that represent the demands made by the job on job holders and are used as criteria for judging the value of a job in an aspect of the work involved. For job evaluation purposes it is assumed that each of the factors will contribute to the value of the job and is present in all the jobs to be evaluated, but to different degrees. The 2007 e-reward job evaluation survey established that the respondents' schemes had between three and 14 factors, the average number being five.

Each factor is divided into a hierarchy of levels, typically five or six. Definitions of these levels are produced to provide guidance on deciding the degree to which the factor applies in the job to be evaluated. A maximum points score is allocated to each factor. The scores available may vary between different factors in accordance with beliefs about their relative significance. This is termed explicit weighting. If the number of levels varies between factors this means that they are implicitly weighted, because the range of scores available will be greater in the factors with more levels.

The total score for a factor is divided between the levels to produce the numerical factor scale. Progression may be arithmetic, eg 50, 100, 150, 200, or geometric, eg 40, 90, 150, 220. In the latter case, more scope is given to recognize senior jobs with higher scores.

The complete scheme consists of the factor and level definitions and the scoring system (the total score available for each factor and distributed to the factor levels). This comprises the factor plan.

Jobs are scored (ie allocated points) under each factor heading on the basis of the level of the factor in the job. This is done by comparing the features of the job with regard to that factor with the factor level definitions to find out which definition provides the best fit. The separate factor scores are then added together to give a total score that indicates the relative value for each job and can be used to place the jobs in rank order.

Evaluators, often formed into a panel consisting of management and staff representatives, have to interpret the definitions when comparing them with the job. But there are limits to the precision with which levels can be defined and the extent to which information about the job indicates which level is appropriate. Judgement is therefore required in making a 'best fit' decision and this is why point-factor evaluation, like any other form of valuing jobs, can never be wholly objective.

The members of a job evaluation panel often disagree initially about an evaluation and consensus may only be obtained after a prolonged discussion. The role of the panel facilitator is crucial in obtaining agreement without too many compromises. However, as evaluators become more experienced, possibly during the development and testing phases of a scheme, they become more skilled at interpreting the factor plan and the job information. They establish conventions that, on the basis of past decisions and precedents, expand and clarify the meaning of level definitions and indicate how the information about a job can be interpreted in order to make a judgement.

A weighted factor plan is illustrated in Figure 14.1. In this example, the evaluations are asterisked and the total score would be 450 points. Examples of factor level definitions are given in Figure 14.2.

FIGURE 14.1   Outline weighted factor plan

Knowledge and skills	20	50	90*	140	200
Interpersonal skills	15	40*	70	110	160
Planning and organizing	15	40	70*	110	160
Judgement and decision making	15	40	70*	110	160
Complexity	15	40	70*	110	160
Responsibility for resources	15	40	70	110*	160

FIGURE 14.2   Example of factor level definitions

Judgement and decision making: The requirement to exercise judgement in making decisions and solving problems, including the degree to which the work involves choice of action or creativity.

1 The work is well defined and relatively few new situations are encountered. The causes of problems are readily identifiable and can be dealt with easily.

2 Evaluation of information is required to deal with occasional new problems and situations and to decide on a course of action from known alternatives. Occasionally required to participate in the modification of existing procedures and practices.

3 Exercises discriminating judgement in dealing with relatively new or unusual problems where a wide range of information has to be considered and the courses of action are not obvious. May fairly often be involved in devising new solutions.

4 Frequently exercises independent judgement when faced with unusual problems and situations where no policy guidelines or precedents are available. May also frequently be responsible for devising new strategies and approaches which require the use of imagination and ingenuity.

5 Deals with widely differing problems calling for extreme clarity of thought in assessing conflicting information and balancing the risks associated with possible solutions. Additionally, one of the main requirements of the role may be to develop fundamentally new strategies and approaches.

A point-factor scheme can be operated manually – a paper scheme – or computers can be used to aid the evaluation process. Methods of designing a scheme are described at the end of the chapter.

Analytical job matching

Analytical job matching, like point-factor job evaluation, is based on the analysis of a number of defined factors. There are two forms of analytical matching. One matches role profiles of the jobs to be evaluated to grade/level profiles; the other matches role profiles to benchmark role profiles.

Role-to-grade analytical matching

Profiles of roles to be evaluated that have been analysed and described in terms of a number of job evaluation factors are compared with grade, band or level profiles that have been analysed and described in terms of the same job evaluation factors. The role profiles are then matched with the range of grade or level profiles to establish the best fit and thus grade the job.

Role-to-role analytical matching

Role profiles for jobs to be evaluated, analysed and described in terms of a number of job evaluation factors are matched analytically with benchmark role profiles that have been defined under the same factor headings. A benchmark role is one that has already been graded as a result of an initial job evaluation exercise. If there is a good fit between a role to be evaluated and a benchmark role that has already been graded, then the role being evaluated will be placed in that grade. Generic role profiles, that is, those covering a number of like roles, will be used for any class or cluster of roles with essentially the same range of responsibilities, such as team leaders or personal assistants. Role-to-role matching may be combined with role-to-grade matching.

Use of analytical matching

Analytical matching may be underpinned by a point-factor job evaluation exercise, which is used to grade roles or place them in levels. This takes the form of an initial evaluation of a representative and sufficiently large sample of benchmark jobs. It enables evaluation to take place without going through the laborious process of using a point-factor scheme for ever job, especially where 'generic' roles are concerned. Analytical matching factors may be the same as those used in the underpinning point-factor scheme. But in some matching schemes the number of factors is simplified; for example, the HERA scheme for higher education institutions clusters related factors together, reducing the number of factors from seven to four. The point-factor scheme can be invoked to deal with difficult cases or appeals.

However, analytical matching may not necessarily be underpinned by a point-factor evaluation scheme. To save time and trouble, each grade or level in the structure is defined in terms of no more than five or six factors and all the jobs to be evaluated are matched factor by factor to these grade definitions.

Factor comparison

The original factor comparison method compared jobs factor by factor, using a scale of money values to provide a direct indication of the rate for the job. It was developed in the United States but is not used in the UK. The only form of factor comparison used in the UK is graduated factor comparison, which compares jobs factor by factor with a graduated scale. The scale may have only three value levels – for example lower, equal, higher – and no factor scores are used. This is a method often used by the independent experts engaged by employment tribunals to advise on an equal pay claim. Their job is simply to compare one job with one or two others, not to review internal relativities over the whole spectrum of jobs in order to produce a rank order. In these circumstances a fairly simple method is appropriate.

Tailor-made, ready-made and hybrid schemes

Any of the schemes referred to above can be tailor-made or 'home-grown' in the sense that they are developed specifically by or for an organization, a group of organizations or a sector, such as further education establishments. The 2007 e-reward survey showed that only 20 per cent of the schemes were tailor-made. A number of management consultants offer their own ready-made schemes or 'proprietary brands'. Consultants' schemes tend to be analytical (point-factor, levelling or matching) and may be linked to a market rate database. As many as 60 per cent of the respondents to the e-reward survey used these schemes.

Hybrid schemes are consultants' schemes that have been modified to fit the particular needs of an organization; 20 per cent of the e-reward respondents had such schemes. Typically, the modification consists of amendments to the factor plan.

Non-analytical schemes

Non-analytical job evaluation schemes enable whole jobs to be compared in order to place them in a grade or a rank order – they are not analysed by reference to their elements or factors. Non-analytical schemes do not attempt to quantify judgements as do analytical schemes. They can stand alone or be used to help in the development of an analytical scheme. For example, the paired comparison technique described later can produce a rank order of jobs that can be used to test the outcomes of an evaluation using an analytical scheme. It is therefore helpful to know how non-analytical schemes function even if they are not used as the main scheme.

Non-analytical schemes can operate on a job-to-job basis in which one job is compared with another to decide whether it should be valued more, or less, or the same (ranking and 'internal benchmarking' processes). Alternatively, they may function on a job-to-grade basis in which judgements are made by comparing a whole job with a defined hierarchy of job grades (job classification). The e-reward 2007 survey showed that only 14 per cent of respondents' schemes were non-analytical.

Non-analytical schemes are relatively simple but rely on more subjective judgements than analytical schemes. Such judgements will not be guided by a factor plan and do not take account of the complexity of jobs. There is a danger therefore of leaping to conclusions about job values based on a priori assumptions that could be prejudiced. For this reason, non-analytical schemes do not provide a defence in a UK equal pay case.

There are four main types of non-analytical schemes: job classification, job ranking, paired comparison (a statistical version of ranking) and internal benchmarking.

Job classification

This approach is based on a definition of the number and characteristics of the levels or grades in a grade and pay structure into which jobs will be placed. It is akin to levelling. The level or grade definitions may refer to such job characteristics as skill, decision making and responsibility but these are not analysed separately. Evaluation takes place by a process of non-analytical matching or job slotting. This involves comparing a whole job description (ie one not analysed into factors), with the level or grade definitions to establish the level grade with which the job most closely corresponds. The difference between job classification and role-to-grade analytical matching as described above is that in the latter case the grade definitions or profiles are defined analytically, that is in terms of job evaluation factors, and analytically defined role profiles are matched with them factor by factor. However, the distinction between analytical and non-analytical matching can be blurred when the comparison is made between formal job descriptions or role profiles that have been prepared in a standard format that includes common headings for such aspects of jobs as levels of responsibility or knowledge and skill requirements. These factors may not be compared specifically but will be taken into account when forming a judgement. But this may not satisfy the UK legal requirement that a scheme must be analytical to provide a defence in an equal pay claim.

Job ranking

Whole-job ranking is the most primitive form of job evaluation. The process involves comparing whole jobs with one another and arranging them in order of their perceived value to the organization. In a sense, all evaluation schemes are ranking exercises because they place jobs in a hierarchy. Job ranking or paired comparison ranking schemes as described below are sometimes used as a check on the rank order obtained by point-factor rating.

Paired comparison ranking

Paired comparison ranking is a statistical technique that is used to provide a more sophisticated method of whole-job ranking. It is based on the assumption that it is always easier to compare one job with another than to consider a number of jobs and attempt to build up a rank order by multiple comparisons.

The technique requires the comparison of each job as a whole separately with every other job. If a job is considered to be of a higher value than the one with which it is being compared, it receives two points; if it is thought to be equally important, it receives one point; if it is regarded as less important, no points are awarded. The scores are added for each job and a rank order is obtained.

Paired comparisons can be done factor by factor and in this case can be classified as analytical. A simplified example of a paired comparison ranking is shown in Figure 14.3.

The advantage of paired comparison ranking over normal ranking is that it makes comparisons easier. But it cannot overcome the fundamental objections to any form

FIGURE 14.3   A paired comparison ranking

Job reference	a	b	c	d	e	f	Total score	Ranking
A	–	0	1	0	1	0	2	5=
B	2	–	2	2	2	0	8	2
C	1	0	–	1	1	0	3	4
D	2	0	1	–	2	0	5	3
E	1	0	1	0	–	0	2	5=
F	2	2	2	2	2	–	10	1

of whole-job ranking – that no defined standards for judging relative worth are provided and it is not an acceptable method of assessing equal value or comparable worth. There is also a limit to the number of jobs that can be compared using this method – to evaluate 50 jobs requires 1,225 comparisons. Paired comparisons are occasionally used analytically to compare jobs on a factor-by-factor basis.

Internal benchmarking

Internal benchmarking means comparing the job under review with any internal job that is believed to be properly graded and paid (a benchmark job) and placing the job under consideration into the same grade as that job. It is what people often do intuitively when they are deciding on the value of jobs, although it is not usually dignified in job evaluation circles as a formal method of job evaluation. The comparison is made on a whole-job basis without analysing the jobs factor by factor. It can be classified as a formal method if there are specific procedures for preparing and setting out role profiles and for comparing profiles for the role to be evaluated with standard benchmark role profiles.

Market pricing

Market pricing is the process of obtaining information on market rates (market rate analysis) to inform decisions on pay structures and individual rates of pay. It is called extreme market pricing when market rates are the sole means of deciding on internal rates of pay and relativities and conventional job evaluation is not used. An organization that adopts this method is said to be market driven. Techniques of collecting and analysing market rate data were described in Chapter 13. This approach has been widely adopted in the United States. It is associated with a belief that 'the market rules, OK', disillusionment with what was regarded as bureaucratic job evaluation, and the enthusiasm for broad-banded pay structures (structures with a limited number of grades or bands, as described in Chapter 15). It is a method that often has appeal at board level because of the focus on the need to compete in the marketplace for talent.

However, conventional market pricing, as distinct from extreme market pricing, may be associated with formal job evaluation. The latter establishes internal relativities and the grade structure, and market pricing is used to develop the pay structure – the pay ranges attached to grades. Information on market rates may lead to the introduction of market supplements for individual jobs or the creation of separate pay structures (market groups) to cater for particular market rate pressures.

The acceptability of either form of market pricing is dependent on the availability of robust market data (not always easy) and, when looking at external rates, the quality of the job-to-job matching process (ie comparing like with like). It can therefore vary from analysis of data by job titles to detailed matched analysis collected through bespoke surveys focused on real market equivalence. Extreme market pricing can provide guidance on internal relativities even if these are market driven. But it can lead to pay discrimination against women where the market has traditionally been discriminatory, and it does not satisfy UK equal pay legislation. To avoid a successful equal pay claim in the UK, any difference in pay between men and women carrying out work of equal value based on market rate considerations has to be objectively justified; in other words, the employment tribunal will need to be convinced that this was not simply a matter of opinion and that adequate evidence from a number of sources was available. In such cases, the tribunal will also require proof that there is a business case for the market premium to the effect that the recruitment and retention of essential people for the organization was difficult because pay levels were uncompetitive.

Levelling

Levelling is an approach to job evaluation that is akin to job classification and focuses on defining the levels of work in an organization and fitting jobs into those levels. The levels may be defined in terms of one factor such as decision making. Levelling may serve as the basis for a pay structure but, increasingly, it contributes to organizational analysis, provides guidance on career mapping and the development and description of international organization structures, and acts as a link to an information technology system such as PeopleSoft or SAP.

The levelling concept

The concept of defining levels of work was a feature of the work of Elliott Jaques (1956) on the measurement of responsibility. His research at Glacier Metal led to the conclusion that: 'It appeared as though there existed in people's minds a pattern of rates expected for levels of work done, and that this pattern was made manifest by stating level of work in maximum time-span terms.' This was his notion of the time span of discretion, which he defined as 'the maximum period of time that would elapse under the particular conditions of review, during which the member was

FIGURE 14.4   Nationwide's five job family levels

Job family level	Level title	Nature of job
Level 1	Service and support	This level contains those roles in which decision making extends over a few days or weeks and the work is fairly well patterned, involving people working individually.
Level 2	Advice and team leading	For technical and professional employees where work cannot always be specified in advance. Decision making tends to involve tasks with a time span of between three months and one year.
Level 3	Senior management	Decision making tends to involve tasks with a time span of between one and two years. These managers are often responsible for other managers and may include senior specialists who refine professional practices.
Level 4	Executive management	This level contains general managers whose work involves designing and developing new systems, services and products with strategic direction and turning corporate strategies into action. The decision making would tend to involve tasks with a time span of between two and five years.
Level 5	Director	Decision making tends to involve tasks with a time span of between one and five years.

authorized and expected to exercise discretion on his own account to discharge the responsibilities allocated to him'. He proposed that levels of work should be defined in terms of time span. This had some appeal as seemingly providing a single significant criterion for measuring responsibility, but it has not been widely adopted because of measurement difficulties, especially at higher levels. One example of a firm using time span as the main criterion is Nationwide, as illustrated in Figure 14.4.

An alternative criterion for defining levels of work, called the decision band method (DBM), was evolved by Paterson (1974). He claimed that there are six levels or bands of decision making in organizations. They range from simple defined decisions 'made within the limits of a prescribed operation', to corporate policy-making decisions that 'determine the scope, direction and goal of the whole enterprise'. These definitions are used as the basis for assigning jobs to levels. The DBM method was adopted extensively in Africa but did not take hold in the UK.

A later approach that acknowledged the influence of Jaques but not Paterson was developed at Unilever. As described by Dive (2004), the notion of broad-banding was rejected and a 'work level' structure was introduced. The process was called 'The decision-making accountability solution set' (DMA). There are eight work levels, each defined in terms of seven separate elements, namely: expected work, resources, problem solving, change, lateral teams, environment and task horizon. As Dive explained, DMA 'concentrates on the added value of decisions taken'. Its key premise is that 'Job holders must take decisions that cannot be taken at a lower level and which need not be taken at a higher level.' He emphasized that using DMA is a way of developing a healthy organization. It is not just a method of grading jobs.

Applications of levelling

When it is used simply as a means of defining pay structures, levelling is just another name for job evaluation. But it is more meaningful when the focus is on the organizational, career mapping and IT applications mentioned above. Defining an organization structure in levels may express the philosophy of a business about how it should be organized and the career steps that are available to its people.

In practice, levelling uses established job evaluation techniques such as analytical matching or job classification and may be underpinned by point-factor rating. It makes a decision on the number of levels required, which could be based on a ranking exercise using either point-factor scheme scores or whole-job ranking. Alternatively, an a priori decision may be made on the number of levels needed by a study of the organization structure, which may be supported by a role profiling exercise. This decision may be amended later after the level structure has been tested.

Levels may be defined in terms of job evaluation factors or a selection of them. Sometimes only a single descriptor is used such as time span or decision levels. In cases where the focus is on career mapping as well as or instead of pay determination, the level definitions or profiles may be defined in ways that clearly establish the career ladder, often in a job family (ie a group of jobs in which the nature of the work will be similar but it is carried out at different levels). The definition may express what people are expected to know and be able to do at each level (technical competencies) and may refer to behavioural competencies. The aim is to produce a clear hierarchy of levels that will ease the process of allocating roles to levels and define career progression steps in and between families.

Job analysis for job evaluation

The reliability and validity of job evaluation depend largely on the quality of the analysis of jobs that provides the factual information in the form of job descriptions or role profiles upon which the evaluation is based.

Existing job descriptions are seldom any use for job evaluation because they are generally limited simply to listing tasks or duties and do not cover the demands made on people in their roles. Further analysis is almost always necessary and there is a choice of methods as described below, namely: written questionnaires, structured interviews or computer-aided interviews. When developing a scheme, it may be worth trialling more than one method.

Written questionnaires

Embarking on a complete rewrite of the organization's job descriptions could be a formidable and time-consuming task. Instead a questionnaire may be used, with a commitment to review the design of job descriptions or role profiles on completion of the job evaluation project, using the information drawn from the questionnaires.

Questionnaires ask for narrative responses to questions that relate to each factor in the scheme. They may be given to employees for completion on the basis that they know best how the job is done, or to the line manager, or, ideally, to both as a shared task.

Structured interviews

Alternatively, questionnaires can be used as the basis for a structured interview with job holders – either directly sharing the questionnaire with the job holders, or using an interview guide based on the questionnaire, administered by job analysts. The results of the interview are then written up in full after the interview. Sharing a questionnaire with job holders can increase the transparency of the process if it is given to job holders either before or during the interview.

Computer-aided analysis

Interactive computer-aided systems, as described later, use a set of online questions. The answers are converted into a job profile.

Job descriptions

The job descriptions resulting from the analysis contain information about the job's place in the organization structure followed by a definition of its overall purpose, a list of key result areas and an analysis of the job demands in terms of each of the factors in the scheme. An example is given in Figure 14.5.

Computer-aided job evaluation

Computer-aided job evaluation uses computer software to convert information about jobs into a job evaluation score or grade. It is generally underpinned by a conventional point-factor scheme. The 'proprietary brands' offered by consultants are often computer aided. Computers may be used simply to maintain a database that records evaluations and their rationale. In the design stage they can provide guidance on weighting factors through multiple regression analysis, although this technique has been largely discredited and is little used now.

FIGURE 14.5 Example of role profile prepared for job evaluation

Job title	Office Manager
Responsible to	HR Director
Responsible to job holder	• Administrative assistant • Receptionist • Security guards (2) • Maintenance fitter
Overall purpose of job	To ensure that the office building is maintained as a cost-effective, safe and secure environment, and provide office services
Key activities	1 Conduct or arrange for the periodic inspection and maintenance of offices 2 Negotiate agreements with building, office equipment maintenance and cleaning contractors and monitor their performance 3 Maintain reception and security procedures 4 Conduct or arrange for health and safety inspections 5 Liaise with fire service on fire precautions 6 Purchase office equipment and stationery and other office supplies 7 Provide petty cash facilities
Factor analysis	Knowledge and skills (general)	• Knowledge of maintenance methods • Knowledge of health, safety and fire precautions • Knowledge of office systems • Maintenance skills
	Interpersonal skills	• Negotiating skills • Keeping internal customers satisfied
	Judgement and decision making	• Within budget, negotiate standard terms with contractors and suppliers • Obtain approval for the engagement of new contractors and suppliers or for major variations in contractual terms • Deal with health, safety, fire and security issues on own initiative
	Complexity	• The work is diverse, involving many different elements, often unconnected
	Responsibility for resources	• Five staff • Controls a large budget for maintenance and purchasing • Controls petty cash float

Methodology

The software used in a fully computer-aided scheme essentially replicates in digital form the thought processes followed by evaluators when conducting a 'manual' evaluation. It is based on defined evaluation decision rules built into the system shell. The software typically provides a facility for consistency checks by, for example, highlighting scoring differences between the job being evaluated and other benchmark jobs.

The two types of computer-aided evaluation are:

1 Schemes in which the job analysis data is either entered direct into the computer or transferred to it from a paper questionnaire. The computer software applies predetermined rules to convert the data into scores for each factor and produce a total score. This is the most common approach.

2 Interactive computer-aided schemes in which the job holder and their manager sit in front of a computer and are presented with a series of logically interrelated questions, the answers to which lead to a score for each of the built-in factors in turn and a total score.

Choice of approach to job evaluation

The fundamental choice is between using formal or informal methods of valuing jobs. This may not be a conscious decision. A company may use informal methods simply because that's what it has always done and because it never occurs to its management that there is an alternative. But it may decide deliberately that an informal approach fits its circumstances best, especially when it uses 'spot rates' rather than a graded structure as described in Chapter 15.

If it is decided that a formal approach is required, the advantages and disadvantages of each approach as summarized in Table 14.1 need to be considered, examined in the light of criteria for choice (such as those set out below) and compared with the objectives of the scheme and the context in which it will be used.

Criteria for choice

The criteria to be used in making a choice are that the scheme should be:

- Thorough in analysis and capable of impartial application: it should have been carefully constructed to ensure that its methodology is sound and appropriate in terms of all the jobs it has to cater for. It should also have been tested and trialled to check that it can be applied impartially to those jobs.

- Appropriate: it should cater for the particular demands made on all the jobs to be covered by the scheme.

- Comprehensive: it should be applicable to all the jobs in the organization covering all categories of staff, and if factors are used they should be common to all those jobs. There should therefore be a single scheme that can be used

TABLE 14.1 Comparison of different job evaluation methods

Scheme	Brief description	Advantages	Disadvantages
Point-factor rating	An analytical approach in which separate factors are scored and added together to produce a total score for the job that can be used for comparison and grading purposes.	As long as they are based on proper job analysis, point-factor schemes provide evaluators with defined yardsticks that help to increase the objectivity and consistency of judgements and reduce the over-simplified judgement made in non-analytical job evaluation. They provide a defence against equal value claims as long as they are not in themselves discriminatory.	Can be complex and give a spurious impression of scientific accuracy – judgement is still needed in scoring jobs. Not easy to amend the scheme as circumstances, priorities or values change.
Analytical matching	Grade profiles are produced that define the characteristics of jobs in each grade in a grade structure in terms of a selection of defined factors. Role profiles are produced for the jobs to be evaluated, set out on the basis of analysis under the same factor headings as the grade profiles. Role profiles are matched with the range of grade profiles to establish the best fit and thus grade the job.	If the matching process is truly analytical and carried out with great care, this approach saves time by enabling the evaluation of a large number of jobs, especially generic ones, to be conducted quickly and in a way which should satisfy equal value requirements.	The matching process could be more superficial and therefore suspect than evaluation through a point-factor scheme. In the latter approach there are factor level definitions to guide judgements and the resulting scores provide a basis for ranking and grade design which is not the case with analytical matching. Although matching on this basis may be claimed to be analytical, it might be difficult to prove this in an equal value case.

TABLE 14.1 *continued*

Scheme	Brief description	Advantages	Disadvantages
Ranking	Non-analytical – whole job comparisons are made to place them in rank order.	Easy to apply and understand.	No defined standards of judgement; differences between jobs not measured; does not provide a defence in an equal value case.
Internal benchmarking	Jobs or roles are compared with benchmark jobs that have been allocated into grades on the basis of ranking or job classification, and placed in whatever grade provides the closest match of jobs. The job descriptions may be analytical in the sense that they cover a number of standard and defined elements.	Simple to operate; facilitates direct comparisons, especially when the jobs have been analysed in terms of a set of common criteria.	Relies on a considerable amount of judgement and may simply perpetuate existing relativities; dependent on accurate job/role analysis; may not provide a defence in an equal value case.

to assess relativities across different occupations or job families and to enable benchmarking to take place as required.

- Transparent: the processes used in the scheme from the initial role analysis through to the grading decision should be clear to all concerned. If computers are used, information should not be perceived as being processed in a 'black box'.
- Non-discriminatory: it should meet requirements relating to equal pay for work of equal value.
- Easy to administer: it should not be too complex or time-consuming to design or implement.

The decision may be to use one approach, for example point-factor rating or analytical matching. But an increasing number of organizations are combining the two: using point-factor rating to evaluate a representative sample of benchmark jobs and, to save time and trouble, evaluating the remaining jobs by means of analytical matching.

Making the choice

The overwhelming preference for analytical schemes shown by the e-reward 2007 survey suggests that the choice is fairly obvious. The advantages of using a recognized analytical approach that satisfies equal value requirements appear to be overwhelming. There is much to be said for adopting point-factor methodology as the main scheme but using analytical matching in a supporting role to deal with large numbers of generic roles not covered in the original benchmarking exercise. Analytical matching can be used to allocate generic roles to grades as part of the normal job evaluation procedure to avoid having to resort to job evaluation in every case. The tendency in many organizations is to assign to job evaluation a supporting role of this nature rather than allowing it to dominate all grading decisions and thus involve the expenditure of much time and energy.

Developing a point-factor job evaluation scheme

Point-factor job evaluation schemes are the most popular type of scheme. The sequence of activities required to develop one is shown in Figure 14.6.

Set up the project

Establish project team

It is highly desirable to set up a project team to oversee and take part in the project. The team should include line manager and staff representatives. Technical support can be provided by HR, possibly with the help of outside consultants. The support will include the detailed work of job analysis and developing and testing factor plans.

FIGURE 14.6 Developing and implementing a point-factor job evaluation scheme

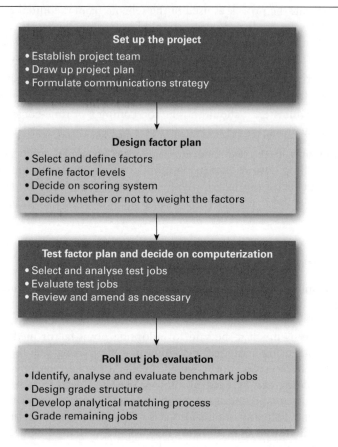

Draw up project plan

A project plan should be prepared in as much detail as possible. This will provide the basis for managing the project. A plan set out as a bar chart is illustrated in Figure 14.7.

Job evaluation schemes can arouse intense suspicion, even fear. It is essential to have a strategy for communicating information about the job evaluation to allay inevitable suspicions and fears.

Design factor plan

Identify and define factors

Guidelines on the selection of factors are given in Table 14.2.

Guidelines on defining factor levels are given in Table 14.3.

FIGURE 14.7   Project plan bar chart

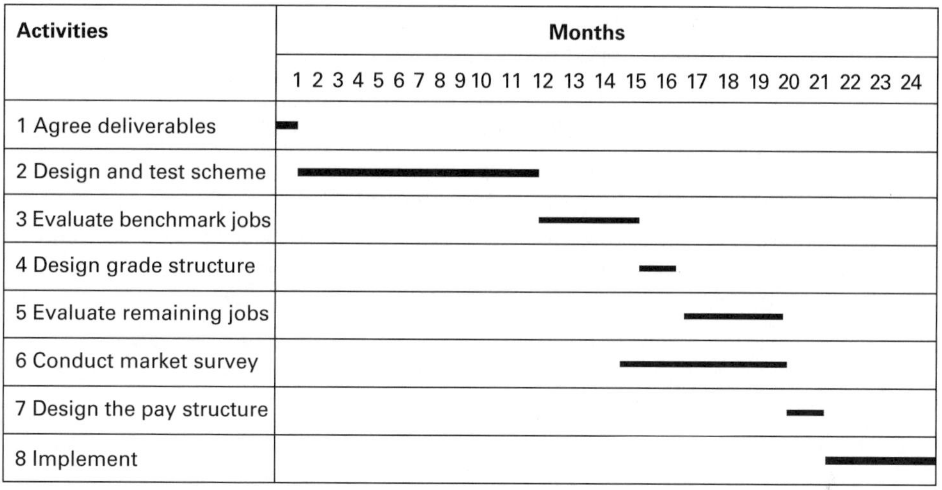

Activities	Months
	1 2 3 4 5 6 7 8 9 10 11 12 13 14 15 16 17 18 19 20 21 22 23 24
1 Agree deliverables	▬
2 Design and test scheme	▬▬▬▬▬▬▬▬▬▬
3 Evaluate benchmark jobs	▬▬▬
4 Design grade structure	▬
5 Evaluate remaining jobs	▬▬
6 Conduct market survey	▬▬▬▬
7 Design the pay structure	▬
8 Implement	▬▬

Decide on scoring system

The next step is to decide on the scoring system. Each level in the factor plan has to be allocated a points value so that there is a scoring progression from the lowest to the highest level. A decision needs to be made on how to set the scoring progression within each factor.

There are two methods. First, the arithmetic or linear approach assumes that there are consistent step differences between factor levels – eg a five-level factor might be scored 10, 20, 30, 40 and 50. Alternatively, geometric scoring assumes that there are larger score differences at each successive level in the hierarchy to reflect progressive increases in responsibility. Thus the levels may be scored 10, 20, 35, 55 and 80, rather than 10, 20, 30, 40 and 50. This increases the scoring differentiation between higher-level jobs. The e-reward 2007 job evaluation survey found that 73 per cent of respondents used the geometric model in their schemes. An example of a geometrically scored outline unweighted factor plan is given in Table 14.4.

Decide whether or not to weight

Weighting recognizes that there are differences in the importance of factors by allocating more or fewer points to them. An example of an explicitly weighted factor plan was given in Figure 14.1. The choice is first between weighting or not weighting factors. Only 19 per cent of the schemes of the e-reward 2007 survey respondents were unweighted. This reflects the view of the majority of people that some factors must be more important than others.

TABLE 14.2 Guidelines for selecting factors

1 The factors must be capable of identifying relevant and important differences between jobs that will support the creation of a rank order of the jobs to be covered by the scheme.

2 The factors should between them measure all significant job features and should be of broadly comparable scope.

3 The factors should reflect the values of the organization.

4 They should apply equally well to different types of work including specialists and generalists, lower-level and higher-level jobs, and not be biased in favour of one gender or group.

5 The whole range of jobs to be evaluated at all levels should be covered without favouring men or women, people belonging to a particular racial group, different age groups or any particular job or occupation.

6 The scheme should fairly measure features of female-dominated jobs as well as male-dominated jobs.

7 The choice should not lead to discrimination on the grounds of gender, race, disability, religion, age or for any other reason. Experience should not be included as a factor because it could be discriminatory either on the grounds of gender or age. The same principle applies to education or qualifications as stand-alone factors.

8 Job features frequently found in jobs carried out mainly by one gender should not be omitted, for example manual dexterity, interpersonal skills and 'caring' responsibilities. However, if such features are included, it is important that the scheme captures the range of skills across all jobs, including those that might be dominated by another gender.

9 Double counting should be avoided, ie each factor must be independent of every other factor. The more factors (or sub-factors) in the plan, the higher the probability that double counting will take place.

10 Elision or compression of more than one significant job feature under a single factor heading should be avoided. If important factors are compressed with others it means that they could be undervalued.

11 The factor definitions should be clear, relevant and understandable and written in a way that is meaningful to those who will use the scheme.

12 The factors should be acceptable to those who will be covered by the scheme.

TABLE 14.3   Guidelines on defining factor levels

1. Consider the number of levels (often four, five, six or seven), which may be needed to reflect the range of responsibilities and demands in the jobs covered by the scheme.

2. Analyse what would characterize the highest or lowest level for each factor and how these should be described.

3. Decide provisionally on the number of levels (say three) between the highest and lowest level so that the level structure reflects the graduation in responsibilities or demands. (This decision could be amended following the process of defining levels, which might reveal that more, or fewer levels are required.)

4. Define each level as clearly as possible to help evaluators make 'best fit' decisions when they compare role data with level definitions.

5. Ensure that the levels should cover the whole range of demands in this factor, which are likely to arise in the jobs with which the evaluation scheme is concerned.

6. Relate the content of level definitions to the definition of the factor concerned and ensure that it does not overlap with other factors.

7. Ensure that the factor levels represent clear and recognizable steps in demand.

8. Provide for uniform progression in the definitions level by level from the lowest to the highest level. There should be no gaps or undefined intermediate levels which might lead to evaluators finding it difficult to be confident about the allocation of a level of demand.

9. Define levels in absolute, not relative terms. So far as possible any dimensions should be defined. They should not rely upon a succession of undefined comparatives, eg small, medium, large.

10. Ensure that each level definition stands on its own. Level definitions should not be defined by reference to a lower or higher level, ie it is insufficient to define a level in words to the effect that it is a higher (or lower) version of an adjacent level.

TABLE 14.4   Outline unweighted factor plan

Knowledge and skills	15	40	70	110	160
Interpersonal skills	15	40	70	110	160
Planning and organizing	15	40	70	110	160
Judgement and decision making	15	40	70	110	160
Complexity	15	40	70	110	160
Responsibility for resources	15	40*	70	116	160

The most common but highly judgemental approach to decide on weighting is for the project team to discuss and agree subjective views on which factors are more important and arbitrarily allocate additional points or extra levels to them. A typical method of deciding on explicit weighting, ie extra points, is to get each member of the team to distribute 100 points amongst the factors which are then revealed to the whole team, which reaches an agreement on the most acceptable distribution. This discussion may be expected to take account of guiding principles such as that no factor will have a weighting of less than 5 per cent or more than 30 per cent.

It is common practice to defer the final weighting decision until the unweighted factor plan has been tested. This test may reveal whether or not weighting is required.

The factor plan should not discriminate on the grounds of gender, race or disability. Guidelines on avoiding bias are given at the end of this chapter.

Test factor plan

To test the factor plan it is necessary first to select, analyse and describe a representative sample of test jobs and then to evaluate the jobs using the draft factor plan. The aims of the test are to check on the extent to which the factor plan is appropriate and establish as far as possible that the evaluation produces a valid result. Following the test the factor plan can be revised.

Decide on computerization

At this stage a decision on whether or not to computerize can be made. The advantages and disadvantages of computer-aided evaluation are set out in Table 14.5.

TABLE 14.5   Advantages and disadvantages of computer-based job evaluation

Advantages	Disadvantages
• Greater consistency can be achieved – the same input information gives the same output result. • The speed of evaluations can be increased. • Facilities are provided for sorting, analysing, reporting on the input information and system outputs and for record keeping on a database. • The resources required are reduced.	• Expensive. • Elaborate. • Lack of transparency. • Means abandoning the involvement of employees and their representatives in the traditional panel approach.

Implement job evaluation

Identify, analyse and evaluate benchmark jobs

The final paper or computer-aided scheme is used to evaluate benchmark jobs. These are typical jobs, which represent the different occupations and levels of work in an organization and are used as points of reference with which other jobs can be compared and evaluated. The evaluated benchmark jobs provide the basis for designing a grade structure and are used in analytical matching as described below. They will include the test jobs but it may be necessary to select additional ones to provide a sufficient number for designing a grade structure.

Design grade structure

The information on the benchmark job evaluation can be used to design a grade structure as described in Chapter 15.

Develop analytical matching approach

Analytical matching involves matching jobs to be evaluated on a factor-by-factor basis either with analytical grade definitions (grade profiles) or analytical job descriptions for benchmark posts (role profiles). It will be necessary to ensure that the grade profiles are defined in terms of the job evaluation factors. It will also be necessary to define a protocol for analytical matching which specifies:

- what constitutes a perfect match, ie where all the elements in the role profile match all the elements in the grade or benchmark role profile;
- the number of matches required of individual elements to indicate that a profile match is justified, for example six out of 10; but it is usual to restrict the mismatches allowed to fairly small variations – if there are any large ones, the match would be invalidated;
- any elements which must match for there to be a profile match; for example, it may be decided that there must be a match for an element covering knowledge and skills;
- the procedure for grading if there has been a mismatch; this may specify a full evaluation of the role if the matching process used the point-factor analytical scheme.

Develop operating procedures

These will cover how jobs should be analysed and evaluated, including who is responsible, the basis upon which requests for re-evaluation can be made and the appeals procedure. The procedures should be set out and operated to ensure that there is no bias or discrimination on the grounds of gender, race or disability. Guidelines on avoiding discrimination are given below.

Grade remaining jobs

The analytical matching procedure is used to grade the jobs not covered in the benchmark evaluation exercise.

Ensuring that the scheme is unbiased

The approaches required to ensure that a job evaluation scheme is free of gender bias in both design and application are set out below. The aim is to create and use job evaluation schemes to ensure that work of equal value is paid equally.

Avoiding bias in design

The factors should not be biased in favour of one gender or group:

- The whole range of jobs to be evaluated at all levels should be covered without favouring men or women, people belonging to a particular racial group, different age groups or any particular job or occupation.
- The scheme should fairly measure features of female-dominated jobs as well as male-dominated jobs.
- Experience should not be included as a factor because it could be discriminatory on the grounds of gender or age. The same principle applies to education or qualifications as stand-alone factors.
- Job features frequently found in jobs carried out mainly by one gender should not be omitted, for example manual dexterity, interpersonal skills and 'caring' responsibilities.
- Double counting should be avoided, ie each factor must be independent of every other factor – the more factors (or sub-factors) in the plan, the higher the probability that double counting will take place.
- Elision or compression of more than one significant job feature under a single factor heading should be avoided. If important factors are compressed with others it means that they could be undervalued.
- The factor definitions should be clear, relevant and understandable and written in a way that is meaningful to those who will use the scheme.

Avoiding bias in operation

- The scheme should be transparent; everyone concerned should know how it works – the basis upon which the evaluations are produced.
- Appropriate proportions of women, those from ethnic minorities and people with disabilities should be involved in the process of applying job evaluation.

- The quality of role analysis should be monitored to ensure that analyses produce accurate and relevant information, which will inform the job evaluation process and will not be biased.
- Consistency checks should be built into operating procedures.
- The outcomes of evaluations should be examined to ensure that gender bias or any other form of bias has not occurred.
- Particular care is necessary to ensure that the outcomes of job evaluation do not simply replicate the existing hierarchy – it is to be expected that a job evaluation exercise will challenge present relativities.
- All those involved in role analysis and job evaluation should be thoroughly trained in the operation of the scheme and in how to avoid bias.

Developing job evaluation: six tips

1   Keep it simple: minimize paperwork and avoid bureaucracy.

2   Involve managers, other employees and employee representatives in the choice of scheme and its design and operation.

3   Use an analytical approach: analytical job matching underpinned by a point-factor scheme.

4   Ensure it fits the context of the business: culture, type of work and people.

5   Keep everyone informed on how it works and how it affects them.

6   Ensure that the design of the scheme and the process of operating it do not involve any form of discrimination or bias.

References

Armstrong, M and Cummins, A (2008) *Valuing Roles*, Kogan Page, London

Dive, B (2004) *The Healthy Organization*, Kogan Page, London

Equality and Human Rights Commission (2011) Job Evaluations Schemes Free of Bias [online] http://www.equalityhumanrights.com/advice-and-guidance/guidance-for-employers/tools-equal-pay/step-2-additional-information [accessed 27 December 2011]

e-reward (2007) Survey of Job Evaluation, e-reward [online] www.e-reward.co.uk [accessed 13 May 2015]

Gupta, N and Jenkins, D G (1991) Practical problems in using job evaluation to determine compensation, *Human Resource Management Review*, 1 (2), pp 133–44

Jaques, E (1956) *Measurement of Responsibility*, Harvard University Press, Cambridge, MA

Nielsen, N (2002) Job Content Evaluation Techniques Based on Marxian Economics, *WorldatWork Journal*, 11 (2), pp 52–62

Paterson, T T (1974) *Job Evaluation*, Business Books, London

15
Grade and pay structures

LEARNING OUTCOMES

On completing this chapter you should be able to define these key concepts. You should also know about:

- The nature of grade and pay structures
- Guiding principles for grade and pay structures
- Types of grade and pay structures
- Choice of grade and pay structure
- Developing a grade and pay structure
- Minimizing bias in grade and pay structure design

Introduction

This chapter is mainly concerned with formal grade and pay structures the purpose of which is to provide a framework within which an organization's base pay management policies are implemented. But reference will also be made to the other less formal pay arrangements of spot rates and individual job grades, which, while they cannot be described as structures, are frequently used by organizations to indicate how much a job or a person is paid.

The chapter starts with definitions of grade and pay structures. This is followed by a list of guiding principles and descriptions of each type of structure, namely: multi-graded, broad-graded and broad-banded structures, job families and pay spines. Unstructured systems (spot rates and individual job grades) are then examined. The factors affecting the choice of structure are considered next and the chapter concludes with a description of the process of developing a grade and pay structure and, importantly, how bias should be minimized in doing this.

Grade structures

A grade structure consists of a sequence or hierarchy of grades (also called bands or levels) into which groups of jobs that are broadly comparable in size are placed. There may be a single structure that is defined by the number of grades it contains. These can vary in different structures. Alternatively the structure may be divided into a number of job families consisting of groups of jobs where the essential nature and purpose of the work are similar but the work is carried out at different levels.

Grade and pay structures

A grade structure becomes a grade and pay structure when pay ranges, brackets or scales are attached to each grade, band or level. In some broad-banded structures reference points and pay zones may be placed within the bands and these indicate the range of pay for jobs allocated to each band.

Graded pay structures are defined by the number of grades they contain and the span or width of the pay ranges attached to each grade, ie the difference between the lowest and highest points in the grade. The structures define the different levels of pay for jobs or groups of jobs by reference to external relativities as established by market rate surveys and relative internal value as determined by job evaluation. They provide scope for pay progression in accordance with merit or service.

There may be a single grade and pay structure covering the whole organization. Sometimes segmentation takes place, which involves the use of separate pay arrangements for different categories of staff so that special requirements can be catered for, eg executive directors or sales staff. The traditional form of segmentation is to have one structure for staff and another for manual workers, but this is becoming less common. The trend is to harmonize terms and conditions between different groups of staff as part of a move towards single status. This has been particularly evident in many public sector organizations in the UK, supported by national agreements.

Guiding principles

Grade and pay structures should:

- be appropriate to the culture, characteristics and needs of the organization and its employees;
- facilitate the management of relativities and the achievement of equity, fairness, consistency and transparency in managing gradings and pay;
- enable jobs to be graded appropriately and not be subject to grade drift (unnecessary upgradings);
- be flexible enough to adapt to pressures arising from market rate changes and skill shortages;
- facilitate operational flexibility and continuous development;
- provide scope as required for rewarding merit and increases in skill and competence;
- clarify reward, development and career opportunities;
- be constructed logically and clearly so that the basis upon which they operate can readily be communicated to employees;
- enable the organization to exercise control over the implementation of pay policies and budgets.

Formal grade and pay structures

The main types of formal structures described in this section are illustrated in Figure 15.1.

The CIPD 2013 reward survey found that 37 per cent of respondents had multi- or narrow-graded structures, 31 per cent had pay spines, 29 per cent had broad-banded structures (this includes broad-graded structures) and 30 per cent had job-family structures. It is interesting to note than nearly half the respondents (49 per cent) adopted the informal approach of spot rates and individual job grades as described later.

Multi-graded structures

A multi-graded, sometimes called a narrow-graded or traditional, structure consists of a sequence of job grades into which jobs of broadly equivalent value are placed. There may be 10 or more grades, and long-established structures, especially in government

FIGURE 15.1   Types of pay structures

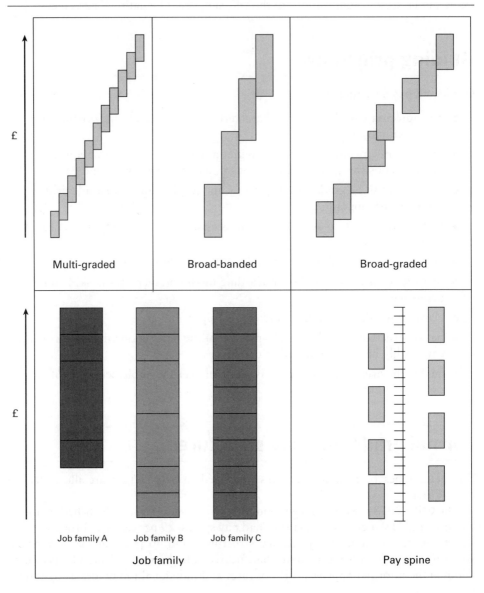

organizations, can have as many as 18 or even more. Grades may be defined by a range of job evaluation points so that any job for which the job evaluation score falls within the points bracket for a grade would be allocated to that grade. Alternatively, they may be defined by grade or level definitions that, if analytical factor comparison or job classification is used as described in Chapter 14, provide the information required to match jobs.

Pay ranges are attached to each grade to allow scope for pay progression. They are usually described in terms of their range spreads (the percentage by which the highest point exceeds the lowest point). This is typically between 20 per cent and 40 per cent. The centre of the range is called the mid-point and this can be aligned to market rates in accordance with pay policy.

Mid-point management techniques can help to control the structure. They use compa-ratios that express the actual rate of pay as a percentage of the mid-point when the latter is regarded as the policy rate of pay or the reference point. The analysis of compa-ratios indicates what action may have to be taken to slow down or accelerate increases if compa-ratios are too high or too low compared with the policy level. Compa-ratios can also be used to measure where an individual is placed in a salary range, and therefore provide information on the size of pay increases.

Differentials between pay ranges – the percentage by which the mid-point of a range is higher than the mid-point of the range below – are typically between 5 per cent and 15 per cent but they can be as high as 25 per cent. Too low a differential means that the scope for pay progression on upgrading is limited. Too high a differential means that a decision to upgrade may mean that the increase in pay is disproportionate to the increase in responsibility.

There is usually an overlap between ranges. This is the difference between the highest point of the range below and the lowest point of the range above. The argument in favour of overlaps is that they provide more flexibility by enabling recognition to be given to the fact that a highly experienced individual at the top of a range may be contributing more than someone who is still in the learning curve portion of the next higher grade. But if overlaps are too high they can cause confusion.

Advantages

The advantages claimed for multi-graded structures are that they provide a framework for managing relativities and for ensuring that jobs of equal value are paid equally. They are supposed to be easy to manage because the large number of grades enables fine distinctions to be made between different levels of responsibility. Theoretically, they also enable better control of costs because the range for progression is restricted. Staff may favour them because they appear to offer plenty of opportunities for increasing pay by upgrading.

Disadvantages

But there are major disadvantages. The main problem is that of grade drift. If there are too many grades, there will be constant pressure for upgrading, leading to inappropriate gradings and overpayments.

The other problems are: (1) the structure may be aligned to a traditional extended hierarchy which no longer exists, (2) it can function rigidly, which is at odds with the requirement of flexibility in team- and process-based organizations and (3) the structure may reinforce the importance of promotion as a means of progression, which may run counter to the need for organizations to be more flexible and grow capability by moving people within grades to broaden their experience and competencies.

Broad-banded structures

The concept of broad-banded structures emerged in the 1990s in the United States as a means of overcoming the deficiencies of the traditional narrow-graded structures. In its original version, as described by Leblanc (1992) and Gilbert and Abosch (1996), a broad-banded structure contained no more than five or six bands, each with a span of 70 per cent to 100 per cent. Bands were unstructured and pay was managed much more flexibly than in a conventional graded structure (no limits are defined for progression) and much more attention was paid to market rates, which governed what were in effect the spot rates for jobs within bands. Progression in bands depended on competency and the assumption of wider role responsibilities. Bands were described verbally, not by reference to the results of analytical job evaluation. More authority was devolved to line managers to make pay decisions within a looser framework.

The original notion of unstructured broad bands is now no longer commonly practised. It created expectations of the scope for progression that could not be met. This had to stop somewhere if costs were going to be controlled, and no rationale was available for deciding when and why to stop. Line managers felt adrift without adequate guidance and staff missed the structure they were used to.

Inevitably, therefore, structure crept in. It started with reference points aligned to market rates around which similar roles could be clustered. These were then extended into zones for individual jobs or groups of jobs. Reference points were frequently placed in zones so that they increasingly resembled conventional structure grades. Armstrong and Brown (2001) established that in the UK 80 per cent of the organizations they surveyed had introduced some controls in the form of zones (43 per cent) and zones with reference points (37 per cent). Job evaluation was used not only to define the boundaries of the band but to size jobs as a basis for deciding where reference points should be placed in conjunction with market pricing.

Progressively, therefore, the original concept of broad-banding was eroded as more structure was introduced, and in the UK job evaluation became more prominent to define the structure and meet equal pay requirements. Zones within broad bands began to look very like conventional grades and so-called broad-banded structures became in effect broad-graded structures as described below.

Perceived advantages

The main advantage originally claimed for broad-banding was that it appeared to provide for more flexibility by catering for broader roles rather than tightly defined jobs, by adopting less rigid approaches to the allocation of roles to bands and how people progress within them, and by being able to respond more quickly to market rate pressures. The advantages of doing without formal job evaluation and using market pricing were also powerful arguments in favour of broad-banding. Moreover, broad-banding was in accord with the drive for de-layering. The reduction in the number of grades meant that the pressure for upgrading was reduced, there was less likelihood of grade drift and it was thought that grades would be easier to manage.

Reservations

The two reservations that emerged from the experience of developing broad bands in the 1990s and early 2000s were: (1) What's the point of unstructured broad bands if they simply consist of spot rates? and (2) What's the difference between, say, a four-banded structure with three zones in each band and a 12-graded structure? The answer given by broad band devotees to the first question was that at least there was some overall structure within which spot rates could be managed. In reply to the second question, the usual answer was that as roles develop, movements between zones within bands could be dealt with more flexibly. Neither of these responses is particularly convincing.

Apart from such fundamental reservations, there are a number of other objections to broad-banding. In general, it has been found that broad-banded structures are harder to manage than narrower graded structures in spite of the original claim that they would be easier – they make considerable demands on line managers as well as HR. Pay can spin out of control unless steps are taken to prevent that happening. As a reward manager in an engineering company told Armstrong (2000): 'Broad bands offer huge scope for flexibility, but equally huge scope for getting it wrong.'

Broad-banding can build employee expectations of significant pay opportunities, which are doomed in many cases if proper control of the system is maintained. It can be difficult to explain to people how broad-banding works and how they will be affected, and they may be concerned by the apparent lack of structure and precision. Decisions on movements within bands can be harder to justify objectively than in other types of grade and pay structures.

Broad-banded structures may be more costly to operate than more conventional structures because there is less control over pay progression. Research conducted in the United States by Fay *et al* (2004) found that both base pay and total cash compensation were significantly higher in the companies with broad-banded structures than in those with more conventional structures. They estimated that broad-banding increased payroll costs by 7 per cent-plus.

Broad-graded structures

The aim of broad-graded structures is to achieve the best of the two worlds of multi-graded and broad-banded structures. They do this by reducing the number of grades from the 12 or more in multi-graded structures to six or seven and, as established by a WorldatWork survey in 2013 (Stoskopf *et al*), adopting wider range spreads – 30 per cent to 80 per cent compared with 20 per cent to 40 per cent. The grades and pay ranges in broad-graded structures are defined and managed in the same way as multi-graded structures, except that wider pay spans mean that organizations sometimes introduce mechanisms to control progression in the grade so that staff do not inevitably reach its upper pay limit. Close attention is paid to market rates in establishing pay ranges and fixing salary levels.

Broad-graded structures are used to overcome or at least alleviate the grade drift problem which is endemic in multi-graded structures. If the grades are defined as in the example in Figure 15.1 it is easier to differentiate them, and matching (comparing role profiles with grade definitions or profiles to find the best fit) becomes more accurate. But it may be difficult to control progression and this would increase the costs of operating such systems, although these costs could be offset by better control of grade drift. They usually cost less to implement than multi-graded structures because fewer people are likely to fall below the pay limits of a broader grade. They also overcome the main disadvantage of broad bands – that it is difficult to control progression and therefore costs.

Broad-graded structures are described by WorldatWork as market-based structures to emphasize the link to market rates. But, as defined by WorldatWork, a market-based structure exhibits the typical features of a broad-graded structure. Their 2013 US survey found that market-based structures were by far the most popular structure (64 per cent compared with the 23 per cent who had traditional or narrow-graded structures and with the mere 12 per cent with broad bands).

Example of broad grading at Bristol-Myers Squibb

Pay is determined in relation to the market, and is pitched at the median, though the total reward package is upper quartile. There are eight overlapping bands, each with a span of between 80 per cent and 100 per cent, covering everyone, apart from the UK's dozen or so senior executives. The bands are:

D 1   basic clerical, factory semi-skilled;

D 2   clerical and factory semi-skilled;

D 3   clerical and factory supervisor;

D 4   senior supervisor, entry level for professionals (eg scientists), customer-facing sales staff;

D 5   customer-facing sales staff;

D 6   first-level manager, head of department;

D 7   function heads;

D 8   business heads, eg oncology, finance.

These eight bands are used in all the countries in which Bristol-Myers Squibb operates, though the salaries attached to them are locally determined. But the bands are seen as more of a safety net than anything else and something that the US parent is keen to retain, although the market is more important in the UK. The company says the bands are helpful if there is an intention to recruit someone at a salary way over or under the band, which signals that the job may need to be regraded.

Example of broad grading at Camelot

The broad-graded structure at Camelot is market driven – its focus is on paying the market rate for each job. Every salary is benchmarked against the market to ensure

TABLE 15.1   Grade definitions in a broad-graded structure

1 Support workers	• Provide basic support services
	• Work wholly prescribed, freedom to act very limited
	• Role requirements specified in detail
2 Administration workers	• Provide routine administrative services
	• Work largely prescribed, freedom to act fairly limited
	• Role requirements clearly defined
3 Senior administrators and support workers	• Provide fairly complex administrative and support services
	• Work generally standardized
	• Limited freedom to decide on methods and priorities
4 Team leaders and specialists	• Lead a small team of administrators or support workers; or provide specialist/basic professional services
	• Some diversity in role requirements
	• Act within specified policy and procedural guidelines
5 Middle managers	• Manage a function or department within an operational or technical area, or provide professional advice and services in an important aspect of the organization's activities
	• The work is diverse
	• Freedom to act within broad policy frameworks
6 Senior managers	• Head of a major function or department, making a major and strategic impact on the performance of the organization or is the main provider of professional advice and services in a key aspect of the organization's activities
	• The work is complex and involves making a broad range of highly diverse decisions
	• A considerable amount of independent action is required within the framework of organizational strategies and plans and subject only to general guidance

that jobholders are being 'paid fairly for the job that they do', with base pay set at the median market rate. The following six-level banding structure, covering everyone except the chief executive, is used:

Bands A and B cover administrative support and IT roles.

Band C includes supervisors, professionals and specialists.

Band D is for middle management.

Band E is for heads of department.

Band F covers functional directors.

Bands have some overlap, and each job has its own pay range within a band. The range is 85 per cent to 115 per cent, with 100 per cent being the rate for the job. The ranges are benchmarked against the market twice a year.

Job-family structures

Job families consist of jobs in a function or occupation such as marketing, operations and finance that are related through the activities carried out and the basic knowledge and skills required, but in which the levels of responsibility, knowledge, skill or competency needed differ. In a job-family structure the successive levels in each family are defined by reference to the key activities carried out and the knowledge and skills or competencies required to perform them effectively. They therefore define career paths – what people have to know and be able to do to advance their career within a family and to develop career opportunities in other families. Typically, job families have between six and eight levels, as in broad-graded structures. Some families may have more levels than others. The job families may be treated as market groups in which pay levels differ between families in accordance with market rate levels.

Job-family structures provide the foundation for personal development planning by defining the knowledge, skills and competencies required at higher levels or in different functions, and describing what needs to be learnt through experience, education or training. They are therefore sometimes called career-family structures.

Level definitions in a family can be more accurate than in a conventional structure because they concentrate on roles within the family with common characteristics and do not attempt to cover a wide and in some ways unconnected set of skills across the whole organization. However, they can be more difficult to develop, explain and manage than single-grade structures. They are popular in the UK where the CIPD 2013 survey found that they were used by 30 per cent of the respondents.

An example of a job-family structure developed for the NHS in the UK as part of its 'Agenda for Change' project is illustrated in Figure 15.2.

Pay spines

Pay spines are found in the public sector or in agencies and charities that have adopted a public sector approach to reward management, which includes the use of service-related pay. Pay spines consist of a series of incremental pay points extending from the lowest- to the highest-paid jobs covered by the structure, as was illustrated in Figure 15.1. Each increment usually represents one year's service. Typically, pay spine increments are between 2.5 per cent and 3 per cent. They may be standardized from the top to the bottom of the spine, or the increments may vary at different

FIGURE 15.2   The NHS skills ladder

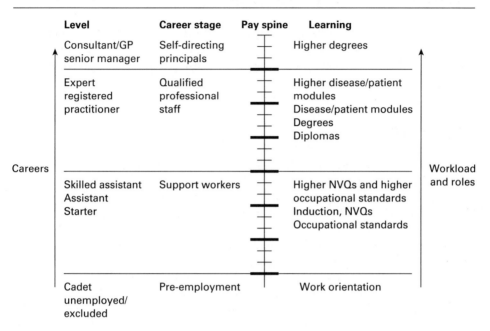

Level	Career stage	Pay spine	Learning
Consultant/GP senior manager	Self-directing principals		Higher degrees
Expert registered practitioner	Qualified professional staff		Higher disease/patient modules
			Disease/patient modules
			Degrees
			Diplomas
Skilled assistant Assistant Starter	Support workers		Higher NVQs and higher occupational standards
			Induction, NVQs
			Occupational standards
Cadet unemployed/ excluded	Pre-employment		Work orientation

Careers ... Workload and roles

levels, sometimes widening towards the top. Job grades are aligned to the pay spine, and the pay ranges for the grades are defined by the relevant scale of pay points. The width of grades can vary and job families may have different pay spines. Some organizations provide scope for accelerating increments or providing additional increments above the top of the scale for the grade to reward contribution or merit.

Pay spines almost manage themselves. Either no decisions on pay progression have to be made by management and line managers, or decisions on extra increments, if they are provided for, are made within an explicit framework. Additionally, because the need for managers to make possibly biased or inconsistent judgements on pay increases does not exist or is severely limited, they give the impression of being fairer than structures where progression is governed by managerial decisions on performance or contribution. For this reason they are favoured by trade unions and many managements in the public sector.

The disadvantages of pay spines are that: (1) relating pay progression to service means that people are rewarded for being there and not for the value of their contribution, (2) pay spines can be costly in organizations with low staff turnover where everyone drifts to the top of the scale, and (3) where there are a large number of incremental points in the scale, equal value complications can arise as men progress to the top while the progress of women is delayed because of career breaks. For this reason the Local Government Pay Commission recommended a move away from service-related increments to pay for contribution, restricting increments to the first few years in a job.

Unstructured pay systems

Many small and medium-sized organizations do not have a graded structure at all for any jobs, or for certain jobs such as directors. Instead they use spot rates or individual job grades. These arrangements are also common for manual workers irrespective of the organization's size.

Spot rates

A spot rate is a rate for a job, which does not define or prescribe any scope for the progression of base pay. This means that there are no pay ranges or salary brackets, although bonuses or other forms of incentive payment may be provided on top of the base rate. There will be scope for moving on to higher spot rates as skill, competence or contribution increases.

Spot rates for jobs may be increased to ensure that they are competitive in the marketplace. They may be attached to a person rather than a job (person-based pay) and thus reflect the perceived value of the individual to the organization. They will be increased on the basis of judgements about that value which will be affected by the assumed market worth of the individual – the rate he or she commands in the marketplace. Rates of pay and therefore relativities are governed by managerial judgement and market rates.

Spot rates may be used by organizations that want the maximum amount of scope to pay what they like and are therefore frequently found in businesses such as investment banks. They often exist in small or start-up firms that do not want to be constrained by a formal grade structure and in organizations seeking the maximum scope for flexibility in base pay management. They may be used when a simple and well-defined hierarchy of jobs exists, for example in manufacturing where there is an established negotiated or market rate for manual occupations. They are frequently adopted by retail firms for customer service staff. But they can result in serious inequities that may be difficult to justify.

Individual job grades

Individual job grades are spot rates to which a defined pay range of, say, 20 per cent on either side of the rate has been attached to provide scope for pay progression based on performance, competency or contribution. The mid-point of the range may be fixed by reference to market rates or, less often, by means of job evaluation.

Individual grades are usually attached to jobs, not persons, but there may be more flexibility for movement between grades than in a conventional grade structure. This can arise when people have expanded their role and it is considered that this growth in the level of responsibility needs to be recognized without having to upgrade the job. Individual job grades may be restricted to certain jobs, for example more senior managers, where freedom in determining increasing rates of pay is felt to be desirable. They provide for greater flexibility than more conventional structures but can be difficult to manage and justify and can result in pay inequities. The 'zones' that are often established in broad-banded structures have some of the characteristics of individual job grades.

Choice of approach

It may be decided that a formal structure is required which will define where jobs should be placed in a grade and pay hierarchy, set out the scope for pay progression, facilitate the management of pay relativities and enable pay practices to be monitored and controlled.

Alternatively it may be thought that the flexibility provided by spot rates or individual job ranges is the most important consideration. The organization may be too small or volatile to justify the installation of what might be felt to be a rigid and bureaucratic system. In some cases it may be felt that there is no reason to abandon the tradition of spot rates for manual or retail workers.

However, although an informal approach may be preferred, it is still necessary to pay attention to the principles of reward management as set out in Chapter 1 in order to achieve the prime objectives of any method of rewarding people, ie to ensure that the process helps to recruit, retain and motivate high-quality people.

If a formal approach is adopted it should be remembered that one size does not fit all. The choice between the various formal structures described above will depend on the type, needs and values of the organization concerned. The criteria for choice are given in Table 15.2.

Developing formal grade and pay structures

The process of developing a formal grade and pay structure will of course vary according to the type of structure. But in general the steps required are as follows:

1 Determine the number of grades, bands or levels. Point-factor job evaluation can be used first to produce a rank order of jobs according to their job evaluation scores and then to analyse the rank order to establish where jobs might be grouped into grades and how many grades emerge from this procedure. Alternatively an *a priori* decision may be made on the number of grades, bands or levels required based on an analysis of the value-adding tiers in the organization.

2 Define the grades, bands or levels. This can be a range of job evaluation points for each grade or a verbal description. To enable job matching with grades the latter may refer to a number of factors such as problem solving, level of responsibility and resource complexity.

3 Conduct a market rate survey of benchmark jobs (a typical job which represents the different occupations and levels of work in the organization and can be used as a point of reference with which other jobs can be compared and evaluated).

TABLE 15.2   Grade and pay structures: criteria for choice

Type of structure	The structure may be considered more appropriate when:
Multi-graded	• The organization is large and bureaucratic with well-defined and extended hierarchies. • Pay progression is expected to occur in small but relatively frequent steps. • The culture is one in which much significance is attached to status as indicated by gradings. • Some but not too much scope for pay progression is wanted. • The values of the organization favour the achievement of internal equity as well as external competitiveness.
Broad-banded	• Greater flexibility in pay determination and management is required. • It is believed that job evaluation should no longer drive grading decisions. • The focus is on rewarding people for lateral development. • The organization has been de-layered. • Pay policy in the organization is market-driven.
Broad-graded	• It is believed that if there are a relatively limited number of grades it will be possible to define and therefore differentiate them more accurately as an aid to better precision when grading jobs. • An existing multi-graded structure is the main cause of grade drift. • It is considered that pay progression through grades can be related to contribution and that it is possible to introduce effective control mechanisms. • The values of the organization emphasize the need for pay to be competitive if necessary at the expense of internal equity.
Job family	• There are distinct market groups that need to be rewarded differently. • The range of responsibility and the basis upon which levels exist vary between families. • The value of defining career paths in terms of competency requirements is recognized.
Pay spine	• When it is important to have a system that is easy to manage, and, because there is little or no scope for flexibility, appears to provide equal treatment for all. • Where strong trade unions oppose any change.

4 Decide the policy on how the organization's pay levels should relate to market rates – its 'market stance'. This could be at the median, or above the median if it is believed that pay levels should be more competitive.

5 For a narrow or broad-graded structure calculate the average market rates for the benchmark jobs in each grade according to market stance policy. This produces the target rate for each grade, which can act as the midpoint. In a broad-banded structure the benchmark rates can be used to determine individual reference points or zones.

6 Ensure that bias in favour of men or women is minimized by following the steps set out below.

Minimizing bias in grade and pay structure design

Grade and pay structures should be designed in a way which minimizes bias in favour of men or women. The following guidelines should be adopted:

● Grade boundaries should not be placed between jobs which have been evaluated as virtually indistinguishable, bearing in mind that the problem will be most acute if grade boundaries are placed between traditionally male and female jobs.

● Read-across mechanisms should exist between different job families and occupational groups if they are not all covered by the same plan.

● Market rate comparisons should be treated with caution to ensure that differentials arising from market forces can be objectively justified.

● Male and female employees, those who are disabled or those from different ethnic groups should not be disadvantaged by the methods used to adjust their pay following regrading.

● A non-discriminatory analytical job evaluation system should be used to define grade boundaries and grade jobs.

● Discriminatory job descriptions should not be used as a basis for designing and managing the structure.

● Women's or men's jobs should not cluster respectively at the higher and lower levels in the grade of the hierarchy.

● Any variation between pay levels for men and women in similarly evaluated jobs (for example for market rate reasons) should be objectively justified.

● Red-circling (the process of identifying when a person's salary is retained at a higher level than the size of the job and internal relativities justifies, usually associated with the introduction of a new grade and pay structure) should be free of sex bias.

● Objectively justifiable reasons should exist for any inconsistency in the relation of the grading of jobs in the structure to job evaluation results.

Grade and pay structure design: six tips

1 Involve stakeholders (top management, line managers and staff) in drawing up guiding principles on the design and operation of the structure.

2 Analyse the options available and select one that meets the guiding principles and fits the values and methods of work in the business.

3 Keep it as simple as possible.

4 Ensure that good data is available on which to base the design (job evaluation and market rates).

5 Obtain the buy-in of stakeholders.

6 Communicate very widely and very often what is being done and why.

References

Armstrong, M (2000) Feel the Width, *People Management*, 3 February, pp 34–38

Armstrong, M and Brown, D (2006) *New Dimensions in Pay Management*, CIPD, London

Chartered Institute of Personnel and Development (2012) *Reward Management Survey*, CIPD, London

Fay, C H, Schulz, E, Gross, S E and Van De Voort, D (2004) Broadbanding, Pay Ranges and Labour Costs: An empirical test, *WorldatWork Journal*, **19** (2), pp 21–29

Gilbert, D and Abosch, K S (1996) *Improving Organizational Effectiveness Through Broad-banding*, American Compensation Association, Scottdale, AZ

Leblanc, P V (1992) Banding: The new pay structure for the transformed organization, *Journal of Compensation and Benefits*, January–February, pp 34–38

Stoskopf, G, Sever, S, Nguyen, M and Mueller, W (2013) The Evolution of Salary Structures over the Past 10 Years: Are market-based salaries the new normal? *WorldatWork Journal*, First quarter, pp 29–39

16
Equal pay

KEY CONCEPTS AND TERMS

- Equivalent work
- Gender pay gap
- Genuine material factor

- Like work
- Market supplement
- Work of equal value

LEARNING OUTCOMES

On completing this chapter you should be able to define these key concepts. You should also know about:

- The reasons for unequal pay
- The Equality Act 2010
- Applying equal pay legislation
- How to achieve equal pay
- Defending an equal pay claim
- Assessing the risk of an equal pay claim

Introduction

In 1970 the difference between the earnings of men and women in the UK (the gender pay gap) was 37.9 per cent. Pay inequality between men and women in the UK is not so blatant now since the 1970 Equal Pay Act, the efforts of the Equal Opportunities Commission (now the Equality and Human Rights Commission) and a proliferation of reports – the 2001 Kingsmill *Review of Women's Employment and Pay*, the National Institute of Economic and Social Research (NIESR) (2001), the Equal Pay Task Force (Just Pay) (2001) and the Women and Work Commission (2006). But in spite of all this effort there is still a gender gap even though it is considerably smaller. The *Annual Survey of Hours and Earnings* produced by the Office of National Statistics revealed that in 2012 the gap between the hourly earnings of full-time men and women excluding overtime was 10 per cent.

As Robert Elliott (1991) commented: 'Discrimination arises when equals are treated unequally.' Historically, it has been generally accepted by men in a man's world that women's place was in the home, unless they were needed to carry out menial and therefore underpaid jobs. Women's work has been undervalued because of the low rates of pay. It has been a vicious circle. Prior to the Equal Pay Act, collective agreements tended to have only one rate of pay for women workers, with no differentiation between grades of work or levels of skill.

The entry of women into the professions in the 19th century and pressures for women's rights in the 20th heralded a very gradual change in this climate of discrimination. But it needed the Treaty of Rome (1957), Article 179 of which enshrined the principle of equal pay for equal work, to stimulate anti-discriminatory law in the United Kingdom. The first British legislation was the Equal Pay Act of 1970, amended by the Equal Pay Amendment Regulations in 1983.

Any steps to deal with this situation must be based on an understanding of the causes of pay discrimination and these are analysed in the first section of this chapter. The major, but not hugely successful, instrument for dealing with it in the UK has been the UK legislation on equal pay, which is described in the second section of the chapter. The final sections cover the steps that can be taken to achieve equality, manage the risks of successful equal pay claims and defend claims.

Reasons for unequal pay

In an analysis of the economics of equal pay for work of equal value, Rubery (1992) suggested that the undervaluation of women's employment is caused by three inter-related factors: (1) gender discrimination in the ways in which jobs are graded and paid, (2) widespread occupational segregation by gender, and (3) differences in the labour supply and labour market conditions that allow the differences to be perpetuated. A further reason was given in the report of the Equal Pay Task Force (Just Pay) (2001), namely, the unequal impact of women's family responsibilities.

Comprehensive research conducted by the NIESR (2001) into the causes of the gender pay gap identified the following five key factors:

1 Human capital differences: differences in educational levels and work experience. Historical differences in the levels of qualifications held by men and women have contributed to the pay gap. Women are still more likely than men to have breaks from paid work to care for children and other dependants. These breaks impact on women's level of work experience, which in turn impacts on their pay rates.

2 Part-time working: the pay gap between women's part-time hourly earnings and men's full-time hourly earnings is particularly large and, because so many women work part time, this is a major contributor to the gender pay gap.

Some of this gap is due to part-time workers having lower levels of qualifications and less work experience. However, it is also due to part-time work being concentrated in less well-paid occupations.

3 Occupational segregation: women's work is highly concentrated in certain occupations (60 per cent of working women work in just 10 occupations). And the occupations that are female dominated are often the lowest paid. In addition, women are still underrepresented in the higher-paid jobs within occupations – the 'glass ceiling' effect.

4 Workplace segregation: at the level of individual workplaces, high concentrations of female employees are associated with relatively low rates of pay. And higher levels of part-time working are associated with lower rates of pay, even after other factors have been taken into account.

5 Travel patterns: on average women spend less time commuting than men. This may be because of time constraints due to balancing work and caring responsibilities. This can impact on women's work in two ways: a smaller range of jobs to choose from and/or lots of women wanting work in the same location (ie near to where they live), which leads to lower wages for these jobs.

Other factors that affect the gender pay gap include: job grading practices, appraisal systems, reward systems, retention measures, career breaks, poor union representation and wage-setting practices. In the last case, wage levels set entirely on the basis of external comparisons (market rates) can lead to unequal pay for women within the organization simply because external rates reflect the pay inequities already existing in the labour market.

The design and operation of pay structures can contribute to maintaining or even enlarging the pay gap. For example, experienced men with skills that, because of unequal opportunities, women do not have to the same extent may be started at higher rates of pay within a pay range for the job. It is said that men are better at negotiating higher rates of pay for themselves, although there is no supporting evidence for this.

Extended pay ranges, especially where progression is based on length of service, will favour men, who are much less likely than women to have career breaks and may therefore progress further and faster. The assimilation of men on their present higher rates of pay in the upper reaches of new pay ranges may leave women behind and they may take a long time to catch up, if they ever do. Broad-banded pay structures, as described in Chapter 15, can also lead to discrimination.

It is noteworthy that none of the key factors identified by the NIESR research refers specifically to pay inequities as a cause of the gender pay gap. Indeed, Diana Kingsmill (2001) commented that: 'Unlawful wage inequality – the occurrence of unequal pay... does not appear to be as commonplace as the 18 per cent headline gap would suggest.' This opinion seems to be backed up in part by the 2001 report of the Equal Pay Task Force (Just Pay), which stated that in their view, pay discrimination contributed to 25 per cent to 50 per cent of the pay gap – a wide range that seems to be a matter of opinion rather than evidence.

The Kingsmill Review focused mainly on the other factors creating the pay gap and Diana Kingsmill commented that: 'Time and time again I have been confronted with data demonstrating that women are clustered towards the bottom of organizational hierarchies while men are clustered towards the top. This distribution clearly has a profound impact on the pay gap.'

The pay gap may have decreased in recent years but it is still unacceptable. But dealing with it is difficult. The equal pay legislation described below has had some effect although it cannot deal with reasons for the pay gap that are not associated with unequal base rates of pay such as part-time working, occupational segregation, workplace segregation or career breaks resulting in gaps in pay progression, and lower starting rates for women. These are complex issues and they are more difficult to cope with than relatively straightforward unequal base rates for like work. But this does not detract from the need to deal with pay inequities.

The rest of this chapter covers (1) the basic legal requirements set out in the Equality Act 2010, (2) how the legal requirements set out in the Act and case law are applied, (3) how to achieve equal pay, (4) how to defend an equal pay claim and (5) managing equal pay risks.

The Equality Act 2010

The Equality Act 2010 gives women (and men) a right to equal pay for equal work. It replaces previous legislation, including the Equal Pay Act 1970 and its amendments. The Act's provisions on equal pay and sex discrimination are intended to ensure that pay and other employment terms are determined without sex discrimination or bias.

Basic provisions

- A woman doing equal work with a man in the same employment is entitled to equality in pay and other contractual terms, unless the employer can show that there is a material reason for the difference which does not discriminate on the basis of her sex.

- Where there is equal work, the Act implies a sex equality clause automatically into the woman's contract of employment, modifying it where necessary to ensure her pay and all other contractual terms are no less favourable than the man's.

- Where a woman doing equal work shows that she is receiving less pay or other less favourable terms in her contract, or identifies a contract term from which her comparator benefits and she does not, the employer will have to show why this is. If the employer is unable to show that the difference is due to a material factor which has nothing to do with her sex, then the equality clause takes effect.

- These equal pay provisions apply to all contractual terms including wages and salaries, non-discretionary bonuses, holiday pay, sick pay, overtime, shift payments, and occupational pension benefits, and to non-monetary terms such as leave entitlements or access to sports and social benefits.

Definition of equal work

A woman can claim equal pay and other contract terms with a male comparator when her work can be placed in any of the following three categories:

- *Like work* – work that is the same or broadly similar, provided that where there are any differences in the work these are not of practical importance.
- *Equivalent work* – work which is different, but which is rated under the same job evaluation scheme as being work of equal value.
- *Work of equal value* – work that is different but of equal value in terms of factors such as effort, skill and decision making.

A claim can be made by a woman for equal pay for equal work with a man or men in the same employment and it is for her to select the man or men with whom she wishes to be compared.

Applying the equal pay legislation

The application of the Equality Act is affected by the provisions of the Equality and Human Rights Commission (2011) Statutory Code of Practice. This is not legally binding but employment tribunals considering an equal pay claim are obliged to take into account any part of the code that appears relevant to the proceedings. A considerable amount of case law also affects the interpretation and application of the legislation. The main areas affected are dealt with below.

Determining like work

The two questions to be answered in determining like work are:

1 Whether the woman and her male comparator are employed in work that is the same or of a broadly similar nature. This involves a general consideration of the work and the knowledge and skills needed to do it.

2 If the work is broadly similar, whether any differences between her work and that done by her comparator are of practical importance having regard to the frequency with which any differences occur in practice, and the nature and extent of those differences.

It is for the employer to show that there are differences of practical importance in the work actually performed. Differences such as additional duties, level of responsibility, skills, the time at which work is done, qualifications, training and physical effort could be of practical importance. A difference in workload only counts if the increased workload represents a difference in responsibility or other difference of practical importance.

Determining work rated as equivalent

Work is rated as equivalent if the jobs have been assessed by a job evaluation scheme as scoring the same number of points and/or as falling within the same job evaluation grade. A small difference may or may not reflect a material difference in the value of the jobs, depending on the nature of the job evaluation exercise. Because the focus is on the demands of the job rather than the nature of the job overall, jobs, which may seem to be of a very different type may be rated as equivalent.

To be valid, a job evaluation study must:

- encompass both the woman's job and her comparator's;
- be thorough in its analysis and capable of impartial application (Eaton v Nuttall, 1977);
- take into account factors connected only with the requirements of the job rather than the person doing the job (so, for example, how well someone is doing the job is not relevant);
- be analytical in assessing the component parts of particular jobs, rather than their overall content on a 'whole job' basis (Bromley v Quick, 1988).

The definition of pay

In Barber v Guardian Royal Exchange Assurance Group (1990) the European Court of Justice held that occupational pensions under a contracted-out pensions scheme constitute 'pay' under Article 119 and so must be offered to men and women on equal terms.

Extended pay scales

In Crossley v ACAS (1999) the applicant claimed that she was doing work of equal value to the comparator but earned significantly less due to the fact that the ACAS pay scales required many years' experience to reach the top of the pay band. This, it was argued, discriminated against women, who are more likely to have shorter periods of service. Although the Tribunal accepted that there was a period during which the job was being learnt, it agreed the period in this case was too long.

In Cadman v the Health and Safety Executive (2006) the European Court ruled that pay could be related to service but might have to be objectively justified by demonstrating that longer service results in skills necessary to do a higher job. This means that employers can be challenged by women if the latter can provide evidence that longer service does not lead to better performance.

Market forces

In Enderby v Frenchay Health Authority (1993) the European Court of Justice ruled that the state of the employment market, which may lead an employer to increase the pay of a particular job in order to attract candidates, may constitute an objectively justified ground for a difference in pay. But tribunals will want clear evidence that a market forces material factor defence is based on objectively justified grounds, bearing in mind that the labour market generally discriminates against women. They may view with suspicion evidence gleaned only from published surveys that they may hold to be inherently discriminatory because they simply represent the status quo.

Red-circling

In Snoxell v Vauxhall Motors Ltd (1977) it was held that if an employee's pay is not reduced, ie is 'protected', following a regrading exercise when their pay falls above the maximum for their new grade (red-circling), the protection should not last indefinitely.

Transparency

In what is usually referred to in abbreviated form as the 'Danfoss' case, the European Court of Justice in 1989 ruled that:

> The Equal Pay Directive must be interpreted as meaning that when an undertaking applies a pay system which is characterized by a total lack of transparency, the burden of proof is on the employer to show that his [sic] pay practice is not discriminating where a female worker has established, by comparison with a relatively large number of employees, that the average pay of female workers is lower than that of male workers.

Protection

A process to phase out historical disparity in pay and benefits between men and women, which involves a period of pay protection for men to cushion the impact on them of the new arrangements, has the long-term objective of reducing inequality between the sexes. This is a legitimate aim. However, the employer will have to prove on the facts of the case that the approach to achieving that aim is proportionate. It may be difficult to prove that protecting the men's higher pay for any length of time is a proportionate means of achieving the aim where the reason for the original pay disparity is sex discrimination.

Defending an equal pay claim

The two most common grounds for defending a claim are: (1) that the work is not equal (this is known as 'the job evaluation defence' when the results of a job evaluation are used to justify the inequality) and (2) that even if they are equal, there is a genuine material factor that justifies the difference in pay as long as the justification is objective. Objective justification has to demonstrate that:

1 The purpose of the provision or practice is to meet a real business need.
2 The provision or practice is appropriate and necessary as a means of meeting that need.

Employers cannot defend equal value cases on the grounds of the cost of implementation or the effect a decision could have on industrial relations, and part-time working per se cannot provide a defence to a claim. A tribunal can ask an independent expert to analyse the jobs and report on whether or not they are of equal value.

Note that it is not a defence to a claim to say that a lower hourly rate of pay for one person is compensated for by, for example, a better annual holiday entitlement. The contracts of the applicant and the comparator have to be compared clause by clause. The applicant can pick any part of the contract that provides more favourable terms to the comparator.

Proving that the work is not equal – the job evaluation defence

The onus is on the employer to prove that the complainant is not carrying out like work, work rated as equivalent or work of equal value when compared with the comparator. If the employer uses the job evaluation defence to support a claim that the jobs are not equal, the scheme must be analytical. This means it must analyse and compare jobs by reference to factors such as effort, skill and decisions. Slotting jobs on a whole-job comparison basis is not acceptable as a defence. The legislation and case law do not specify that a point-factor or a scored factor comparison scheme should be used, but even if an analytical matching process is followed (see Chapter 14) a tribunal may need to be convinced that this is analytical within the meaning of the Act. The employer will also have to demonstrate that the scheme is unbiased both in design and application. Methods of eliminating bias are listed in Chapter 14.

Genuine material factor

The legislation provides for a case to be made by the employer that there is a genuine material factor creating and justifying the difference between the pay of the applicant and the comparator. A genuine material factor could be the level of performance or length of service of the comparator, which means that she or he is paid at a higher level than the applicant in the pay range for a job. But this only applies if the basis for deciding on additions to pay and the process of doing so are not discriminatory. The Crossley case referred to above is an example of where a tribunal found that length of service criteria could be discriminatory if they meant that women are paid less than men and find it hard to catch up.

Pay differences because of market supplements (additions to pay to bring it in line with market rates) can be treated as genuine material factors as long as they are objectively justified. In the case of a claim that market pressures justify unequal pay, the tribunal will need to be convinced that this was not simply a matter of opinion and that adequate evidence from a number of sources was available when the decision was made. In such cases, the tribunal will also require proof that the recruitment and retention of the people required by the organization were difficult because pay levels were uncompetitive.

However, The Employment Appeals Tribunal in the case of Sharp v Caledonia Group Services (2006) ruled that employers using the genuine material factor defence must 'objectively justify' it in all cases. This means showing that the pay disparity:

- is unrelated to sex;
- relates to a real need of the employer;
- is appropriate to achieving the objective pursued;
- is necessary to that end and is proportionate.

In other words, the difference must be sensible and necessary rather than merely due to a material factor.

Independent experts

If there is any doubt as to whether or not work is of equal value, employment tribunals will require an independent expert to prepare a report. The expert must:

- evaluate the jobs concerned analytically;
- take account of all information supplied and representations that have a bearing on the question;
- before reporting, send the parties a written summary of the information and invite representations;
- include the representations in the report, together with the conclusion reached on the case and the reason for that conclusion;
- take no account of the difference in sex, and at all times act fairly.

The independent expert's task differs in a number of ways from that of someone carrying out a conventional job evaluation within an organization. This is because the aim in the latter case is to establish relative value by ranking a number of jobs, while an independent expert will be concerned with comparative value – comparing the value of a fairly narrow range of jobs.

Achieving equal pay

The achievement of equal pay is a matter of eliminating discrimination or bias in fixing rates of pay. Bear in mind that discrimination can occur on grounds of race, disability, age, sexual orientation or religious belief as well as between men and women.

The following actions are required to ensure that equal pay is achieved:

1 Use an analytical job evaluation scheme that is free of bias (see Chapter 14).
2 Ensure that discrimination or bias does not occur in operating the job evaluation scheme (see Chapter 14).
3 Design a grade and pay structure that is free of bias. This will cover such issues as discrimination in placing grade boundaries in the structure and over-extended pay scales (see Chapter 15).
4 Ensure that the processes used for grading jobs in the structure are free of bias.
5 Check the policy and practice on positioning employees within a pay range in a graded pay structure or on a pay point in a pay spine to ensure that bias does not occur (for example, if men are consistently placed at a higher point in the scale than women on appointment or promotion without justification in terms of qualifications or experience, or women returning from maternity

leave are not re-entering their pay scale at the position they would have attained had they not been on leave).

6 Check the policy and practice on assimilating staff into a new grade and pay structure to ensure that one category of staff is not favoured over another.

7 Check the policy and practice on progressing the pay of staff within a pay structure to ensure that no category of staff is progressing faster up a grade or to higher points in a grade without good reason.

8 Review policy and practice on upgradings and promotions to ensure that discrimination is not taking place, for example between white and Asian employees.

9 Conduct an equal pay review to establish the extent to which there is inequality in rates of pay for work of equal value (eg part-time female workers paid less pro rata than full-time male workers carrying out like work or work of equal value), identify the causes of the inequality and take action as necessary to deal with any problem (see below).

10 Ensure that line managers are aware of their responsibility for avoiding pay discrimination.

The Equality and Human Rights Commission (2011), in its Code of Practice on equal pay, also recommends that there should be only one pay system, which should be transparent and simple and that any change in the system should be evaluated to ensure that it will not be discriminatory.

Risk assessment

Some organizations in low-risk situations may be convinced that they are doing enough about ensuring equal pay without introducing job evaluation. Others have decided that because their business imperatives are pressing they are prepared to accept a measure of risk in their policy on equal pay. Some, regrettably, may not care. But if there is medium or high risk then action needs to be taken to minimize it. Successful equal pay claims can be hugely expensive, especially in UK public sector organizations with powerful and active trade unions. It is advisable to carry out a risk assessment so that the organization is aware of the scale of the risk, if any. It can then decide whether or not to take steps to minimize the risk, such as introducing a non-discriminatory analytical job evaluation scheme.

The best way to make this assessment is to conduct a formal equal pay review as described below. If an organization is unwilling or unable to take this step, it should at least analyse the pay of men and women carrying out like work to identify the existence and cause of any unjustified differences.

Assessing the risk of a claim also means considering the possibility of individuals initiating action on their own or trade unions taking action on behalf of their members. Individual actions may come out of the blue but the person may have raised an equal pay grievance formally or informally, and line managers should understand that they must report this immediately to HR or senior management. A clear indication of trouble brewing in the UK is when an employee submits an equal pay questionnaire to request information about whether his or her remuneration is equal to that of colleagues. Although trade unions are most likely to lodge questionnaires on behalf of their members, individuals can still do so independently. The likelihood of trade union action will clearly be higher when there is a strong union with high penetration in the organization, which is often the case in the public sector. But any union member can seek help from her or his union. Even if the union is not recognized for negotiating purposes it can still provide support.

Equal pay review

The purpose of an equal pay review is to:

- establish whether any gender-related pay inequities exist;
- analyse the nature of any inequities and diagnose the cause or causes;
- determine what action is required to deal with any inequities that are revealed.

The three main stages to an equal pay review are:

1 Analysis: the collection and analysis of relevant data to identify any gender gaps.
2 Diagnosis: the process of reviewing gender gaps, understanding why they have occurred and what remedial action might be required if the differences cannot be objectively justified.
3 Action: agreeing and enacting an action plan that eliminates any inequalities.

References

Elliott, R F (1991) *Labor Economics*, McGraw-Hill, Maidenhead

Equality and Human Rights Commission (2011) Statutory Code of Practice, Equal Pay, *Equality and Human Rights Commission* [online] www.equalityhumanrights.com/uploaded_files/EqualityAct/equalpaycode.pdf [accessed 27 December 2011]

Just Pay (2001) *Report of the Equal Pay Task Force to the Equal Opportunities Commission*, Equal Opportunities Commission, Manchester

Kingsmill, D (2001) *Review of Women's Employment and Pay*, Department of Trade and Industry, London

National Institute of Economic and Social Research (NIESR) (2001) *The Gender Pay Gap, Women and Equality Unit*, Department of Trade and Industry

Office for National Statistics (2011) Annual Survey of Hours and Earnings, *Office for National Statistics* [online] www.ons.gov.uk/ons/rel/mro/news-release/annual-survey-of-hours-and-earnings-2011/ashe-2011-nr.html [accessed 27 December 2011]

Rubery, J (1992) *The Economics of Equal Value*, Equal Opportunities Commission, London

Women and Work Commission (2006) *Shaping a Better Future*, Communities and Local Government, London

PART THREE
Rewarding and recognizing performance and merit

17
Merit pay

KEY CONCEPTS AND TERMS

- Bonus
- Competency-related pay
- Contingent pay
- Contribution-related pay
- Expectancy theory
- Incentives

- Line of sight
- Merit pay
- Performance-related pay
- Rewards
- Skills-based pay
- Variable pay

LEARNING OUTCOMES

On completing this chapter you should be able to define these key concepts. You should also know about:

- Objectives of merit pay
- Criteria for success
- Types of individual merit pay

Introduction

This chapter describes the main types of merit pay schemes, which are defined as formal contingent pay arrangements that link pay increases to merit in the shape of performance, competency or contribution. Skills-based pay, which in the UK is mainly provided for manual workers, is dealt with in Chapter 25. In the United States, paying for skill can also mean paying for competency while in the UK skill-based pay is quite different from competency-related pay.

Bonus schemes, which pay non-consolidated lump sums based on performance (variable pay), are covered in Chapter 18. Pay schemes providing rewards for team or organizational performance are described in Chapters 19 and 20 respectively. In addition, rewards can be provided by recognition schemes as discussed in Chapter 21.

The chapter should be read in conjunction with Chapter 9 which dealt generally with financial incentives. The first section of this chapter consists of an overall review of the characteristics of merit pay and the next four sections describe the main merit pay schemes. A summary of these schemes with an analysis of their strengths and weaknesses is set out in the next section and the chapter concludes with notes on the choice of whether or not to have merit pay and, if it is decided to introduce it, how this should be done.

Characteristics of merit pay

Merit pay provides payments to individuals in addition to their base rate related to their performance, competency or contribution. It is sometimes known as contingent pay although the latter also covers bonuses and service-related pay.

Average merit payments are typically about 3 per cent of the base rate; the maximum seldom exceeds 10 per cent. A notable characteristic of merit pay is that while pay goes up as a reward for better performance it does not come down if performance declines. It can therefore be described as a gift that goes on giving. This is one of the reasons why bonuses in the shape of re-earnable sums of money paid in addition to base pay are favoured in many organizations, although even bonus schemes tend to reward success but neglect to penalize failure. To remedy this situation there is some support for the use of earn-back pay as described in the next chapter.

However, merit pay is the most typical method of rewarding individuals financially – 56 per cent of the respondents to the 2013 CIPD reward survey used it.

Objectives of merit pay

The objectives of using merit pay given by respondents to the e-reward 2009 survey are set out in Table 17.1.

It is noticeable that by far the most important objective was to recognize and reward better performance. Much less significance was attached to motivating people and changing their behaviour. This is in accord with the conclusion reached in Chapter 9 that the main argument in favour of financial rewards is that it is right and proper to recognize higher levels of performance. It also corresponds with the view expressed in that chapter that financial rewards in the shape of merit pay are not necessarily effective as motivators.

Method of operation

Merit pay schemes are based on measurements or assessments of performance, competency or contribution. These may be expressed as ratings that are converted by

TABLE 17.1   Objectives of merit pay

Recognize and reward better performance	88
Improve organizational performance	50
Attract and retain high-quality people	42
Focus attention on key results and values	29
Motivate people	26
Deliver a message about the importance of performance	25
Influence behaviour	22
Support cultural change	12

means of a formula to a payment. Use may be made of what is called a 'pay matrix' which indicates the percentage increase payable for different ratings according to the position of the individual's pay in the pay range. The operation of a pay matrix is described in more detail later in this chapter.

Alternatively, there may be no formal ratings and pay decisions are based on broad assessments rather than a formula.

Effectiveness of merit pay

The effectiveness of merit pay in achieving the first five objectives listed by respondents to the 2009 e-reward survey is examined in Table 17.2

Types of merit pay

The three main types of merit pay are described below.

Performance-related pay

While performance-related pay (PRP) is the most popular merit pay scheme it is also controversial, largely because, especially in its early days, it was introduced and managed badly and the high expectations of its impact on performance and its ability to change cultures were not fulfilled.

Methods of operating PRP vary considerably but its typical main features are modelled in Figure 17.1 and described below.

TABLE 17.2   The effectiveness of merit pay in achieving its objectives

Objective	Effectiveness of merit pay in achieving the objective
Recognize and reward better performance	Merit pay can be used retrospectively to recognize and reward better performance and therefore demonstrate that people are valued. And this is perhaps its most important function as is shown by the fact that it was by far the most popular objective mentioned by the respondents to the e-reward survey. But its effectiveness depends on the accuracy and fairness with which merit is assessed through formal ratings or by other means, and too often assessments are neither accurate nor fair.
Improve organizational performance	A worthy objective but the evidence that merit pay improves performance is mixed. The summary of research on the impact of performance pay on performance in Chapter 8 includes some studies which indicated that there was little or no impact and that performance pay could have negative effects on morale if badly managed, and it is hard to manage it well. On the other hand, a number of studies did show that individual performance improved. But only two studies – Thompson (1998) and West *et al* (2005) found a connection between performance pay and organizational performance. However, although these projects established a correlation between organizational performance and the use of performance pay they did not demonstrate a causal relationship. It is, in fact very difficult to do this and this is why a belief that performance pay improves organizational performance is usually based more on an act of faith than on convincing evidence.
Attract and retain high-quality people	The attraction and retention of high-quality staff depends on a number of factors besides the level of pay and the existence of merit pay or bonus schemes. But some people will attach a lot of importance to what they earn and welcome the existence of opportunities to enhance their earnings by large amounts. This applies in sectors such as finance and those involved in sales and marketing. Generous bonus or incentives in such sectors may be necessary to get and to keep good people.
Focus attention on key results and values	Focusing on key results and values is important but it is one of the prime roles of a performance management system. Merit payments can only reinforce the messages from goal setting and review processes, they cannot do it alone.
Motivate people	Some people believe that motivation is the prime purpose of merit pay but the relatively small proportion of the respondents to the e-reward 2009 survey who listed this as an objective suggests that many people do not share that view. The reason for this is simple. The effectiveness of PRP as an incentive is highly questionable. As normally operated it fails to meet the requirements of expectancy theory (see Chapter 6) in two critical ways. First, people are too often unclear about what they have to do to get a reward; a 'line of sight' does not exist between the effort they make and what they might or might not get for doing it. Second, they do not expect that the reward will be worthwhile. It was established by the 2009 e-reward survey that the average merit increase was 3.5 per cent and it is unlikely that any amount below 10 per cent would act as a motivator.

FIGURE 17.1   Performance-related pay model

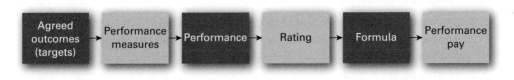

The basis of the scheme is that pay increases are related to the achievement of agreed results defined as targets or outcomes. Scope is provided for consolidated pay progression within pay brackets attached to grades or levels in a graded or career-/job-family structure or zones in a broad-banded structure. Such increases are permanent.

A formula in the shape of a pay matrix as illustrated in Figure 17.2 is often used to decide on the size of increases. This indicates the percentage increase payable for different performance ratings according to the position of the individual's pay in the pay range. It is sometimes referred to as an individual 'compa-ratio' (short for comparison ratio) and expresses pay as a percentage of the mid-point in a range. A compa-ratio of 100 per cent means that the salary would be at the mid-point.

Alternatively, or additionally, high levels of performance or special achievements may be rewarded by cash bonuses that are not consolidated and have to be re-earned. Individuals may be eligible for such bonuses when they have reached the top of the pay bracket for their grade, or when they are assessed as being fully competent, having completely progressed along their learning curve. The rate of pay for someone who reaches the required level of competence can be aligned to market rates according to the organization's pay policy.

Another approach is to define performance zones in a pay range as in the following examples.

FIGURE 17.2   PRP pay matrix

Rating	Percentage pay increase according to performance rating and position in pay range (compa-ratio)			
	Position in pay range			
	80%–90%	91%–100%	101%–110%	111%–120%
Excellent	12%	10%	8%	6%
Very effective	10%	8%	6%	4%
Effective	6%	4%	3%	0
Developing	4%	3%	0	0
Ineligible	0	0	0	0

XANSA

Salary ranges are divided into three levels:

1 Entry level typically represents employees who are new to the job, meeting some objectives and demonstrating some of the skills and competencies at the required level.

2 Market average typically represents employees who either consistently meet their objectives and demonstrate many of the skills and competencies at the required level, or who meet most but not all objectives and consistently demonstrate all of the skills and competencies at the required level.

3 High level typically represents employees who meet all objectives and exceed some, and who demonstrate all of the skills and competencies at the required level and some at a higher level.

Nationwide

The majority of ranges consist of a target rate (100 per cent of the median market rate), a minimum (80 per cent), and a maximum (120 per cent). People tend to enter the range at the minimum. Progression thereafter is solely by means of performance. Each year, pay scales are uplifted by the percentage paid to 'good' performers. The percentage increases paid to individuals are applied to the target, rather than their own salaries, ensuring that everyone on a particular range with the same performance rating receives the same amount of money; that is, the same effort is guaranteed the same reward.

Employees who start on the minimum of a range are guaranteed progression to the target in three years if they receive consistently 'good' performance ratings. Those rated higher receive enhanced progression. Once the target has been reached, employees get the percentage increase resulting from their performance rating based on their target salary. This means that 'good' performers will stay at the target, since this (and the rest of the scales) is uprated by the percentage given to good performers, while better performers will move beyond the target towards the maximum.

Conclusions on PRP

PRP has all the advantages and disadvantages listed in Chapter 9 for any form of financial reward. Many people feel the latter outweigh the former. It has attracted a lot of adverse comment, primarily because of the difficulties organizations have met in managing it but also because it is uni-dimensional in that it is only concerned with results and not how the results are achieved. Contribution-related pay schemes, as described later in this chapter, aim to overcome the latter problem.

Competency-related pay

Competency-related pay rewards people wholly or partly by reference to the level of competency they demonstrate in carrying out their roles. It is a method of paying people for the ability to perform. But the key word is 'demonstrate'. It is not just a matter of having competencies; they have to be used effectively.

Competency is defined as an underlying characteristic of a person that results in effective or superior performance. There are two types of competencies: behavioural competencies are the personal characteristics that individuals bring to their work roles, and technical competencies consist of what people have to know and be able to do (knowledge and skills) to carry out their roles effectively (the latter may be known as competences). The main features of competency-related pay schemes are illustrated in Figure 17.3 and described below.

FIGURE 17.3   Competency-related pay model

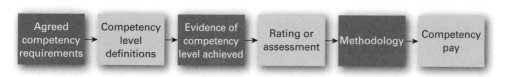

As in all merit pay schemes, competency-related pay provides scope for consolidated pay progression within pay brackets attached to grades or levels in a graded or job family structure, or zones in a broad-banded structure (competency pay is often regarded as a feature of such structures). The rate and limits of progression through the pay brackets can be based on ratings of competency using a PRP type matrix, but they may be governed by more general assessments of competency development.

Competency-related pay is superficially attractive because it can be part of an integrated competency-based approach to HRM. It fits with the concept of human capital management, which emphasizes the skills and competencies people bring with them to the workplace. It is all about paying for the person. As Brown and Armstrong (1999) comment: 'Increasingly, organizations are finding that success depends on a competent workforce. Paying for competency means that an organization is looking forward, not back.' Pay based on competency avoids the overemphasis in PRP schemes on quantitative and often unrealistic targets. It is appealing because it rewards people for what they are capable of doing, not for results over which they might have little control. However, it is much less popular than performance-related pay – competency-related pay was used by 33 per cent of the respondents to the 2009 e-reward survey compared with the 84 per cent who had performance-related pay.

There are three reasons for this. First, there is the problem of measurement. As Sparrow (1996) suggested, difficulties arise because of deciding the performance criteria on which competencies are based, the complex nature of what is being measured and the relevance of the results to the organization. He concluded that 'we should avoid over-egging our ability to test, measure and reward competencies'.

Second, there is the problem raised by Sparrow of answering the question, 'What are we paying for?' Are we paying for behavioural competencies, or technical competencies (competences) or both? If we are just rewarding for behaviour then this increases the measurement difficulties. The third reason was explained by Lawler (1993). He expresses concern about schemes that pay for an individual's personality traits and emphasizes that such plans work best 'when they are tied to the ability of an individual to perform a particular task and when there are valid measures available of how well an individual can perform a task'. He also points out that 'generic competencies are not only hard to measure, they are not necessarily related to successful task performance in a particular work assignment or work role'.

This raises another question: 'Are we paying for the possession of competency or the use of competency?' Clearly it must be the latter. But we can only assess the effective use of competency by reference to performance. The focus is therefore on results and if that is the case, competency-related pay begins to look suspiciously like performance-related pay. Perhaps the difference between the two is all 'smoke and mirrors'. Competency-related pay could be regarded as no more than a more acceptable name for PRP.

It was claimed by Zingheim and Schuster (2002) that pay systems built round competencies are:

- complex and over-designed;
- vague and ambiguous;
- laborious and time-consuming;
- disconnected from the labour market;
- tentatively championed and communicated.

And Giancola (2011) commented that: 'Its underlying assumptions have not yet been proven, and no evidence has been provided that the changes it promises cannot be achieved by other means.'

There may be a case for rewarding the possession of competency but there is an even stronger one for linking the reward to outputs (performance) as well as inputs (competency). This is the basis of the notion of contribution-related pay as described below.

Contribution-related pay

Contribution-related pay as modelled in Figure 17.4 provides a basis for making pay decisions that are related to assessments of both the outcomes of the work carried out by individuals and their inputs in terms of the levels of competency that have influenced these outcomes. It focuses on what people in organizations are there to do: to contribute by their skill and efforts to the achievement of the purpose of their organization or team. In some schemes the rewards are related to contributions both to achieving results and to upholding corporate core values.

Contribution-related pay is a holistic process that takes into account all aspects of a person's performance in accordance with Brumbach's (1988) view that performance means both behaviours and results.

The case for contribution-related pay was made by Brown and Armstrong (1999) as follows:

> Contribution captures the full scope of what people do, the level of skill and competence they apply and the results they achieve, which all contribute to the organization achieving its long-term goals. Contribution pay works by applying the mixed model of performance

FIGURE 17.4   Contribution-related pay model

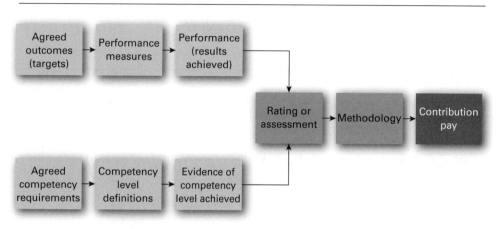

management: assessing inputs and outputs and coming to a conclusion on the level of pay for people in their roles and their work; both in the organization and in the market; taking into account both past performance and future potential.

However, there is still the difficulty of measurement. It is hard enough to measure performance when outputs cannot be quantified, and it is even more difficult objectively to measure the level of competency as pointed out above.

The most typical method of deciding contribution awards is to use a pay matrix as illustrated in Figure 17.5.

FIGURE 17.5   Contribution pay matrix

Performance rating	Percentage pay increase according to performance rating and competence assessment		
	Competence assessment		
	Developing – does not yet meet all competence standards	Fully competent – meets all competence standards	Highly competent – exceeds most competence standards
Exceptional	–	8%	10%
Very effective	–	6%	7%
Effective	–	4%	5%
Developing	3%	–	–
Ineligible	0	–	–

A more sophisticated approach was developed by the Shaw Trust as illustrated in Figure 17.6.

FIGURE 17.6   Contribution-related pay model: The Shaw Trust

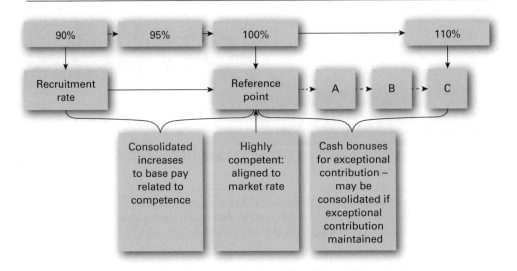

The main features of this method are:

1   A 'reference point' rate of pay is determined within each grade, band or level, which includes jobs of broadly equal size.

2   The reference point is defined as the rate of pay for a person in a job who is highly competent, ie fully competent in all aspects of the job and therefore achieving high levels of performance.

3   The reference point takes account of both internal relativities and market rates.

4   The level of comparison for market rates is in accordance with the pay policy of the organization – this might be set at above the median, eg at the upper quartile, to ensure that the high quality of staff required can be attracted and retained.

5   The reference point is the maximum level of consolidated pay a high performer can expect to attain.

6   A minimum level of pay for each grade is determined and progression to the reference point depends upon achieving defined levels of competence – there may be three or four levels.

7   There is scope to reward those who perform exceptionally well with a re-earnable cash bonus, which could be consolidated if the level of exceptional performance is sustained over two to three years up to a maximum level defined for the grade.

Conclusions on contribution pay

Contribution-related pay provides a broader basis for pay decisions than performance-related pay, and the concept of contribution is an attractive one in that it refers to the fundamental reason why people are employed in organizations – to contribute to organizational success. But contribution pay decisions depend on the measurement of both performance and competency. Measuring performance is bad enough. Measuring competency is even worse. The requirements for success are demanding and organizations should never rush into contribution pay – more time than is usually thought necessary is needed to plan and implement it.

Overall conclusions on merit pay

There are strong arguments against merit pay, especially those referring to the problems of measurement and assessment and therefore perceived fairness that exist in each of the varieties described in this chapter. Steps can be taken to reduce the problems through extensive consultation and communications, effective performance management processes, providing training and guidance to line managers, and monitoring the operation and impact of the merit pay scheme carefully. However, it is very difficult to overcome them completely.

But what is the alternative? One answer is to rely more on non-financial motivators, although it is still necessary to consider what should be done about pay. The traditional alternative is service-related pay. This certainly treats everyone equally (and therefore appeals to trade unions) but pays people simply for being there and this could be regarded as inequitable in that rewards take no account of relative levels of performance. Two other alternatives are team-based pay and pay based on organizational performance. But the former still has measurement difficulties and other problems, as described in Chapter 19, and has never become really popular, while the rewards provided by the latter, although they may increase commitment to the organization, are too remote from the day-to-day activities of most employees to make any real impact on performance.

Another alternative is a spot rate job-based system. However, many people want and expect a range of base pay progression or some other method of payment for results such as cash bonuses.

It is because none of these alternatives adequately satisfies the natural inclination of people to believe that individuals who contribute more should be paid more that merit pay schemes are common in the private sector (according to the CIPD 2013 survey, 88 per cent of manufacturing organizations and 86 per cent of private sector service organizations have them), although they are less used in the public and voluntary sectors (45 and 55 per cent respectively).

Merit pay schemes, whatever their faults, are here to stay. What is evident is that they are difficult to manage and considerable care and effort are therefore required when designing and operating them. Notes on developing merit pay schemes are set out below.

Developing merit pay schemes

The design and development sequence for merit pay is described in Figure 17.7. Involvement and communication activities play a prominent part in the sequence, and in addition to the normal project planning, design and implementation activities

FIGURE 17.7   The merit pay design and development sequence

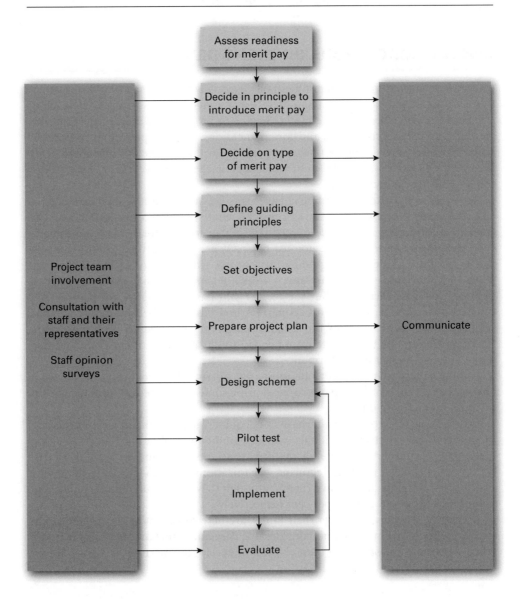

pilot testing and evaluation are essential. The key decisions to be made as discussed below are on:

- readiness for merit pay;
- choice of scheme:
- definition of guiding principles;
- definition of objectives.

Readiness for merit pay

Merit pay too often fails because the organization is not ready for it. The degree of readiness will depend on the extent to which:

- it is believed that linking pay to performance, competence or contribution is right for the business;
- it is believed by all concerned that it is right and proper to reward people according to their performance, competence or contribution;
- merit pay would both fit and support the organization's culture;
- managers are capable of making fair and justifiable judgements on performance competence or contribution;
- employees believe that current performance management processes are fair;
- established performance management systems provide for expectations to be agreed and outcomes to be assessed jointly;
- criteria or measures are available to assess performance, competence or contribution;
- it is believed by managers and other employees that pay decisions can be fairly and equitably related to performance, competence or contribution;
- it is believed that people will understand and accept the merit pay decisions that affect them;
- the organization can afford to make meaningful merit payments.

It is likely that readiness will be incomplete in a number of the above areas. Judgement will have to be exercised on the extent to which on balance conditions are sufficiently favourable to introduce merit pay. But if it is decided to go ahead, this analysis will at least identify any weaknesses which can be dealt with during the design and development process.

Choice of scheme

The simplest choice is a straightforward performance-related pay scheme, but there are alternatives. Details of the possible schemes, their advantages and disadvantages and the circumstances in which they may be appropriate are set out in Table 17.3.

TABLE 17.3 Summary of merit pay schemes

Type of scheme	Main features	Advantages	Disadvantages	When appropriate
Performance-related pay	Increases to basic pay or bonuses are related to assessment of performance.	• May motivate (but this is uncertain). • Links rewards to objectives. • Meets the need to be rewarded for achievement. • Delivers message that good performance is important and will be rewarded.	• May *not* motivate. • Relies on judgements of performance which may be subjective. • Prejudicial to teamwork. • Focuses on outputs, not quality. • Relies on good performance management processes. • Difficult to manage well.	• For people who are likely to be motivated by money. • In organizations with a performance-orientated culture. • When performance can be measured objectively.
Competency-related pay	Pay increases are related to the level of competence.	• Focuses attention on need to achieve higher levels of competence. • Encourages competence development. • Can be integrated with other applications of competency-based HR management.	• Assessment of competence levels may be difficult. • Ignores outputs – danger of paying for competences that will not be used. • Relies on well-trained and committed line managers.	• As part of an integrated approach to HRM where competencies are used across a number of activities. • Where competence is a key factor and it may be inappropriate or hard to measure outputs. • Where well-established competency frameworks exist.
Contribution-related pay	Increases in pay or bonuses are related both to inputs (competence) and outputs (performance).	Rewards people not only for what they do but how they do it.	As for both PRP and competence-related pay – it may be hard to measure contribution and it is difficult to manage well.	When it is believed that a well-rounded approach covering both inputs and outputs is appropriate.

Guiding principles

Guiding principles should be defined; for example:

- Ensure that people are valued and rewarded fairly according to what they achieve and how they achieve it.
- Adopt a fair, consistent and transparent approach to measuring and assessing performance which is based on agreed expectations and success criteria.
- Communicate details to staff so that they understand the operation of the process, the part they and their managers play, and its impact on them.
- The scheme should be developed in consultation with those concerned – managers, employees and union representatives.
- Devolve the maximum amount of responsibility to managers in operating the system but provide safeguards to ensure that fair and consistent decisions are made within the framework of policies and guidelines, including budgets.

Objectives

Objectives such as those listed below should be defined in order to guide the development programme and to provide criteria for evaluating the success of the scheme:

- recognize and reward better performance;
- improve organizational performance;
- deliver a message about the importance of performance;
- attract and retain high-quality people;
- increase employee engagement;
- support cultural change;
- focus attention on key results and values.

Developing merit pay: six tips

1. Check on readiness for merit pay – stakeholders' views, effective performance management, competent line managers.

2. Define guiding principles and objectives.

3. Identify alternatives and evaluate them in terms of relevance to objectives and context.

4. Involve stakeholders in scheme design (keep it simple and relevant).

5. Pilot test scheme.

6. Communicate details of scheme to all concerned.

References

Brown, D and Armstrong, M (1999) *Paying for Contribution*, Kogan Page, London

Brumbach, G B (1988) Some Ideas, Issues and Predictions about Performance Management, *Public Personnel Management*, Winter, pp 387–402

CIPD (2013) *Annual Reward Survey*, CIPD, London

e-reward (2009) Survey of Contingent Pay, *e-reward* [online] www.e-reward.co.uk [accessed 23 July 2015]

Giancola, F L (2011) Skill Based Pay: Fad or classic? *Compensation & Benefits Review*, **43** (5), pp 273–81

Lawler, E E (1993) Who Uses Skill-Based Pay, and Why? *Compensation & Benefits Review*, March/April, pp 9–14

Sparrow, P A (1996) Too Good to be True, *People Management*, December, pp 22–29

Zingheim, P K and Schuster, J R (2002) Pay Changes Going Forward, *Compensation & Benefits Review*, **34** (4), pp 48–53

18
Bonus schemes

LEARNING OUTCOMES

On completing this chapter you should be able to define these key concepts. You should also know about:

- The nature and aims of bonus schemes and their rationale
- The criteria for a bonus scheme
- The main types of bonus scheme
- Who benefits from bonus schemes
- How they should be designed and introduced

Introduction

Bonus schemes in the form of cash payments are an increasingly important part of the remuneration package. The 2013 CIPD reward survey established that 60 per cent of the respondents have them. The 2012 CIPD survey found that the highest bonuses go to the more senior employees – for executives and directors the most common maximum bonus amounts available were 59 per cent of base pay, for senior and middle managers they were 19 per cent of base pay and for technical, professional, clerical and manual employees they were less than 10 per cent.

The so-called bonus culture in banks has produced in some cases excessive rewards for failure, and high payouts to some people have received a bad press. The danger is that the attraction of astronomic bonuses in banks could lead to extreme risk taking with other people's money (proprietary trading).

Bonus schemes can go wrong, especially when the 'moral hazard' is present of striving to obtain higher rewards by manipulating results or focusing on easy short-term gains rather than the tougher long-term goals. Will Hutton (2012) criticized excessive bonuses because of their lack of proportionality, their dependence on sheer good luck, and the lack of rigour in their design and operation.

This chapter starts with definitions of what bonus schemes aim to achieve and their justification. It then lists the criteria for bonus schemes, which leads to an analysis of the different types of bonus schemes and who can be covered by them. The chapter continues with a summary of how conventional bonus schemes can be designed and introduced. A feature of conventional bonus arrangements is that they purport to reward for success, but do not usually provide for any penalty for failure. It was argued in the Hutton Review of Fair Pay in the Public Sector Final Report (2011) that this problem should be remedied by the use of a payback mechanism as discussed in the penultimate section of the chapter, which concludes with a discussion of the impact bonuses make on performance.

Bonus schemes defined

Bonus schemes provide cash payments to employees that are related to the performance of their organization, their team or themselves, or a combination of two or more of these. Cash bonuses may be the sole method of providing people with rewards in addition to their base pay, or they may be paid on top of individual merit pay. A defining characteristic of a bonus is that it has to be re-earned, unlike increases arising from merit pay schemes.

Bonuses are sometimes described as variable pay. They may also be referred to as pay-at-risk, although this is something of a misnomer when applied to a conventional scheme rather than the payback arrangement described later in this chapter. In a conventional scheme the only risk is that someone does not get a bonus; their basic pay is not at risk. Bonuses may be paid solely in cash or wholly or partly in shares. Bonuses for directors and senior executives may be deferred.

Aims of bonus schemes

The aims of bonus schemes may differ, but typically they include one or more of the following:

- to provide a reward that recognizes past performance or achievements and encourages individuals or teams to perform well in the future;
- to provide a direct incentive that increases motivation and engagement and generates higher future levels of individual and team performance;

- to provide rewards related to business performance so as to increase motivation, commitment and engagement;
- to ensure that pay levels are competitive and will attract and retain good-quality people;
- to enable people to share in the success of the organization and therefore increase their commitment to it.

Rationale for bonus schemes

Bonuses can provide a reward for a special achievement and can be used to provide financial recognition to people who are at the top of the salary range for their grade and are continuing to perform well. Lump-sum payments can sometimes make a bigger impact on people (they can go out and spend them) than incremental increases spread thinly out over a year. Overall they can contribute to the creation of a high-performance culture and make a positive impact on bottom-line results.

The business cases made by a number of respondents to the 2006 e-reward survey of bonus schemes are given below:

> 'The bonus structures are such that they are self-financing when people are over the 100 per cent to target levels. As the 100 per cent target level is set at the budget level, everything over this is of added benefit. The structure of the schemes also has a higher weighting of the products with more margin, which again helps to self-finance the schemes.'

> 'The industry is driven by margins and total operating profit at branch and regional levels, so the bonus schemes reflect this requirement to deliver. The schemes are rigorously enforced and tested by Finance.'

> 'We have a pay-for-performance culture and in turn recognize and award high achievers. This is a key driver in motivating employees and organizational performance.'

> 'The bonus scheme is a key to attaining scorecard performance at levels necessary to achieve the flexibility to manage costs finely in line with varying volumes of production and the lowest-margin products to ensure that the site can make a positive profit before tax contribution.'

When considering the rationale it is necessary to evaluate the case for having a bonus scheme either as an alternative to a more conventional merit pay scheme (ie only providing cash bonuses), or as an addition to merit pay (ie providing both cash bonuses and the opportunity to earn merit pay that is consolidated in base pay). The advantages and disadvantages of these alternatives are summarized in Table 18.1.

TABLE 18.1   Advantages and disadvantages of alternative bonus arrangements

Arrangement	Advantages	Disadvantages
Bonus only	• Can be related to corporate or team performance as well as individual performance, thereby increasing commitment and enhancing teamwork. • Cash sums, as long as they are sizeable, can have a more immediate impact on motivation and engagement. • Has to be re-earned.	• May be perceived as arbitrary. • May not be pensionable. • Many people may prefer the opportunity to increase their base pay rather than rely on potentially unpredictable bonus payments. • If unconsolidated, the payment will not be pensionable. • If not designed and operated with care they may reward senior executives for failure or present a moral hazard.
Bonus and merit pay	Get best of both worlds – consolidated increases and cash payments.	• Potentially complex. • The impact made by either bonuses or consolidated payments might be dissipated, especially when the sums available are divided into two parts.

Criteria for a bonus scheme

An effective bonus scheme must:

- be based on realistic, significant and measurable key performance indicators;
- operate fairly, equitably, consistently and transparently;
- not create a moral hazard, ie an incentive to act inappropriately in pursuit of a high bonus;
- not encourage the pursuit of short-term gains or engagement in unduly risky enterprises at the expense of longer-term and sustained success;
- never reward failure;
- only pay out if a demanding threshold of performance is achieved;
- provide a clear line of sight between effort or contribution and the reward;
- be appropriate for the type of people to whom it applies;

- contain arrangements to restrict (cap) the maximum payment to an acceptable sum;
- provide for review at regular intervals to decide whether the scheme needs to be amended, replaced or cancelled;
- provide scope to moderate corporate bonuses by reference to personal performance.

Types of scheme

Table 18.2 summarizes the features of the different types of bonus schemes and their advantages and disadvantages.

Bonuses based on organizational performance may be made available to all staff to provide a general reward and encourage identification with the business. Such bonuses can be in addition to merit pay. They are sometimes provided in organizations that have team pay for certain categories of staff, for example branch staff in a financial services company, but are unable to extend team payments to other categories of staff who do not work in such well-defined teams. Combination plans may also be applied to all staff, although they are sometimes restricted to senior managers. Bonuses based on individual performance may also be paid to all categories of staff or restricted to certain categories, such as directors or sales staff.

Designing a bonus scheme

The considerations affecting the design of a bonus scheme are set out below.

Formula

Every bonus scheme is different. In an individual scheme a single criterion such as profit before tax may be used for directors, with a threshold performance level to generate a bonus and a sliding scale up to a maximum that determines the size of the bonus. Alternatively, in a scheme applying to all staff, ratings may be used that determine the size of the bonus for individuals or teams by reference to the extent to which objectives have been achieved.

The formula for a combined scheme as set out below may be more complex:

- Individual or team payments may only be made if a threshold level of organizational performance is reached.
- The level of bonus related to organizational performance may be modified in accordance with the level of individual performance achieved.
- There are many variations on the split between corporate and individual bonuses, although a 50/50 division is quite common.
- The split may vary at different levels, providing a greater proportion of bonus for corporate performance at higher levels.

TABLE 18.2 Features and advantages and disadvantages of different bonus schemes

Type of scheme	Main features	Advantages	Disadvantages
Business performance schemes	• Bonus payments related to the performance of the whole business or a major function such as a division, store or site. • Performance is measured by key performance indicators (KPIs), eg profit, contribution, shareholder value, earnings per share or economic value added.	• Enable employees to share in the organization's success, thus increasing commitment. • Can focus on a range of key factors affecting organizational performance. • Can readily be added to other forms of contingent pay to recognize collective as distinct from individual effort.	• Do not provide an individual incentive.
Individual bonus or incentive plans	Bonus payments related to individual performance.	• Provide a direct reward related to individual performance. • Cash, if sufficiently high, can make an immediate impact on motivation and engagement.	• May not be pensionable. • Some people may prefer consolidated increases to their base pay rather than rely on possibly unpredictable bonus payments, which may be perceived as arbitrary.
Team pay*	Payments to members of a formally established team are linked to the performance of that team. The rewards are shared among the members of the team in accordance with a published formula or on an ad hoc basis in the case of exceptional achievements.	• Encourage team working. • Enhance flexible working and multiskilling. • Clarify team goals. • Encourage less effective performance to improve by meeting team standards.	• May be difficult to identify well-defined teams with clear and measurable goals. • Individuals may resent the fact that their own performance is not recognized.

TABLE 18.2 *continued*

Type of scheme	Main features	Advantages	Disadvantages
Combination plans	Bonuses are related to a combination of plans measuring performance across several levels, for example: corporate and individual performance; business, team and individual; team and individual.	Combine the advantages of different types of bonus arrangements, eg business and individual (the most common form of combination scheme).	• May be over-complex. • Could disperse the impact of either the collective or the individual elements.
Cash-based profit sharing**	The payment of sums in cash related to the profits of the business. Such schemes operate on a corporate basis and usually make profit shares available to all employees, except possibly directors or senior managers. They do not require Inland Revenue approval and are fully liable for income tax and national insurance.	• Increases identification with the firm. • Recognizes that everyone contributes to creating profit.	• Does not provide an individual incentive. • Amounts distributed are taken for granted.
Gain-sharing**	A formula-based company- or factory-wide bonus plan which provides for employees to share in the financial gains made by a company as a result of its improved performance as measured, for example, by added value.	• Recognizes that everyone working in a plant contributes to creating added value and should benefit accordingly. • Provides a platform for the joint analysis of methods of improving productivity.	• Does not provide an individual incentive. • Can be complex. • Ineffective if too high a proportion of added value is retained by the company.

NOTES: * See Chapter 19
** See Chapter 20

Examples of the formulas used by the e-reward survey respondents are given in Table 18.3.

TABLE 18.3   Bonus scheme formulas

Business performance	Earnings per share, revenue growth and R&D re-investment.
	Budgeted profit.
	Target set for financial performance: earnings before interest, tax, depreciation and amortization. If first target is not met, no pool is generated. Three further targets are set, each generating a higher level of bonus.
	Key performance indicators and profit.
	Customer satisfaction levels, unique customer interactions and low-cost interventions.
Individual performance	Determined by performance rating indicator – the top three performance ratings receive a bonus.
	Individual performance is judged against pre-agreed objectives.
	Balanced scorecard – typically sales, customer service, call-handling time and a development objective for call handling.
	Individual criteria linked to the area of responsibility – eg to achieve budget target, a particular level of growth etc.
	Demonstrable achievement over and above normal performance in one of six core competencies.
Combined	50% business performance, 50% individual performance.
	20% company-wide performance, 30% business performance, 50% individual performance.
	30% business performance, 70% individual performance.
	Group-wide business performance. Individual element 'flexes' the maximum business performance downward for bad performance – eg if rating '1' to '3', get the full bonus; rating '4', the business performance bonus is reduced by 25%; a '5' rating by 50%; a '6' rating gets zero award.
	Business performance creates a bonus opportunity for an individual, which is then flexed according to a personal performance factor.

Introducing a bonus scheme

The actions required when introducing a scheme are:

1 Consult with those concerned on the purpose and features of the scheme.

2 Define responsibilities for introducing, maintaining and evaluating the scheme.

3 Pilot test it if at all possible in a department or division or a representative sample of employees to obtain information on how well the formula works, the appropriateness of the measures, the cost of the scheme, its impact, the effectiveness of the process of making decisions on bonuses (eg the application of performance management) and the reactions of staff.

4 Make amendments as necessary in the light of the test.

5 Prepare a description for communication to staff of the purpose of the scheme, how it works and how staff will be affected.

6 Ensure that the scheme is bedded down in the organization's day-to-day operating processes, including management reports and performance reviews.

7 Draw up a budget for the costs of the scheme.

8 Define operating and control processes including responsibilities, the achievement of fairness and consistency and cost control.

9 Prepare a plan for introducing the scheme, covering the agreement of performance indicators and targets, methods of reviewing performance, the process of deciding on bonus payments and communications.

Earn-back pay

The description of bonus schemes so far in this chapter has referred to conventional schemes, which provide rewards for successful performance in addition to base pay. This is sometimes called variable pay or pay-at-risk. But in the typical scheme, pay only varies upwards, and the only risk involved is that the additional pay may not be forthcoming. There is no risk to basic pay. Success, rightly, is rewarded, but failure is not penalized. In the Hutton Review of Fair Pay in the Public Sector Final Report (2011) the following comment was made:

> The majority of performance pay schemes entail upside opportunities to earn more for performance that is better than average, but do not feature equivalent downside risks: employees do not lose pay for performance that is poorer than average. This situation is inconsistent with the findings of behavioural economics, which state that individuals are motivated more by a loss than by a gain of equivalent size.

Earn-back pay schemes as recommended by the Hutton Review aim to remedy this situation. In such schemes, those involved, who are most likely to be executives, are required to meet agreed objectives in order to earn back an element of base pay placed at risk. If they do not succeed against the objectives, some or all of the earn-back pay will be lost. There would still be the possibility of awarding bonuses for performance that is genuinely beyond expectations. Splitting the scheme in this way introduces the possibility that pay will run in both directions – downwards as well as upwards.

Perhaps because of the understandable hostility of those who might be affected, earn-back pay schemes have not proved popular in the UK private sector.

Bonus schemes and performance

The comments on merit pay made in the last chapter could be applied to bonuses. But there are two differences. First, because bonuses are one-off payments made soon after the performance that generated them, they can make more impact than the delayed and spread-out effect of merit pay. Second, the amounts can be more significant than those awarded in merit pay schemes. Potentially, therefore, they can provide a better incentive for improved performance because they overcome two significant defects of merit pay, ie that it is delayed and insufficient.

However there is a downside. The very size and immediacy of bonuses can present a moral hazard, encouraging people to adopt unacceptable approaches to earning bonuses such as overselling, focusing too much on short-term results and going for easy gains rather than tackling fundamental problems. All these will be detrimental to effective performance.

Bonus schemes: six tips

1 Base the scheme on realistic, significant and measurable key performance indicators.

2 Do not create a moral hazard, ie an incentive to act inappropriately in pursuit of a high bonus.

3 Do not encourage the pursuit of short-term gains or engage in unduly risky enterprises at the expense of longer-term and sustained success.

4 Never reward failure.

5 Only pay out if a demanding threshold of performance is achieved.

6 Provide a clear line of sight between effort or contribution and the reward.

References

CIPD (2012) *Annual Reward Survey*, CIPD, London
CIPD (2013) *Annual Reward Survey*, CIPD, London
e-reward (2006) *Survey of Bonus Schemes, e-reward* [online] www.e-reward.co.uk
    [accessed 13 June 2015]
Hutton Review of Fair Pay in the Public Sector (2011) *Final Report*, HM Treasury, London
Hutton, W (2012) Commentary, *Observer*, 29 January, p 5

19
Team pay

KEY CONCEPTS AND TERMS

- Bonus formula
- Team
- Team pay

LEARNING OUTCOMES

On completing this chapter you should be able to define these key concepts. You should also know about:

- The nature of team pay
- The nature of a team
- The aim of team pay
- The rationale for team pay
- How team pay works
- Advantages and disadvantages
- Developing team pay

Introduction

Two factors have combined to create interest in rewarding teams rather than individuals. The first is the significance attached to good teamwork and the belief that team pay would enhance it, and the second is dissatisfaction with the individual nature of performance-related pay, which is believed to be prejudicial to teamwork. The notion of team pay appeals to many people but the number of organizations using it is relatively small. The CIPD 2012 survey found that only 18 per cent of respondents had team pay.

Team pay is an attractive idea but one difficult to put into practice. The reason for the limited number of schemes may be that organizations find it hard to meet the quite exacting conditions for team pay set out later in this chapter. Others may believe that they have to focus their incentive schemes on individual rather than group effort.

This chapter starts with a definition of team pay and its aims and rationale, and continues with a description of how team pay works, an analysis of the arguments for and against team pay and suggestions on how team pay can be introduced. It ends with a summary of the outcomes of research into a team project in the NHS with mixed results that illustrates some of the difficulties with team rewards.

Team pay defined

Team pay links payments to members of a formally established team to the performance of that team. The rewards are usually provided in the form of a cash bonus and are shared among the members of the team in accordance with a published formula. Rewards for individuals may also be influenced by assessments of their contribution to team results.

Rationale for team pay

There are six reasons for team pay:

1 Teams are the natural unit in organizations and it is appropriate to provide teams with incentives and reward their achievements financially.

2 Team pay encourages good teamwork while performance pay militates against it by focusing on individual effort

3 Team pay clarifies what teams are expected to achieve by relating rewards to the attainment of predetermined and agreed targets and standards of performance, or to the satisfactory completion of a project or a stage of a project.

4 Team pay conveys the message that one of the organization's core values is effective teamwork.

5 Team performance measures may be the only ones available; measuring output at an individual level can be difficult, especially in the public sector.

6 As noted by Prentice *et al* (2007) on the basis of their research, team incentives can help to promote peer monitoring in smaller teams, particularly when team members are mutually dependent on each other to achieve results.

How team pay works

The most common method of providing team pay is to distribute a cash sum related to team performance amongst team members. There are a number of formulas and ways of distributing team pay as described below.

The team pay formula

This establishes the relationship between team performance, as measured or assessed in quantitative or qualitative terms, and the reward. It also fixes the size of the bonus pool or fund earned by the team to be distributed among its members, or the scale of payments made to team members, in relation to team performance with regard to certain criteria. Bonuses may be related to performance in such specific areas as sales, throughput, achievement of targets in the form of the delivery of results for a project, levels of service, or an index of customer satisfaction. Targets are agreed and performance is measured against the targets.

Alternatively bonuses may be related to an overall criterion, which can be a more subjective assessment of the contribution of the team to organizational performance.

Method of distributing bonuses

Bonuses can be distributed to team members in the form of either a percentage of base salary or the same sum for each member, usually based on a scale of payments. Payment of bonus as a percentage of base salary is the most popular method. The assumption behind it is that base salary reflects the value of the individual's contribution to the team. The correctness of this assumption clearly depends on the extent to which base salary truly indicates the level of performance of individuals as team members.

Team pay and individual pay

Some organizations pay team bonuses only. A minority pay individual bonuses as well, which are often related to an assessment of the competence of the person, thus, it is thought, providing encouragement to develop skills and rewarding individuals for their particular contribution. Organizations that do not have formal team pay schemes but still want to reward good teamwork may include effective performance as a team member as an important criterion in their individual merit pay scheme.

Dealing with high and low individual performance in a team

It is sometimes assumed by advocates of team pay that all members of a team contribute equally and should therefore be rewarded equally. In practice the contribution of individual team members will vary and if this is the case, for example in shop floor groups, team pressure may be forcing everyone to work at the same rate so as to avoid 'rate busting'. This is an example of how a highly cohesive team can work against the interests of the organization.

When designing a team pay scheme, decisions have to be made on the likelihood that some people will perform better or worse than others. It may be decided that, even if this happens, it would be invidious and detrimental to single anyone out for different treatment. It could, however, be considered that 'special achievement' or 'sustained high performance' bonuses should be payable to individuals who make an exceptional contribution, while poor performers should receive a lower bonus or no bonus at all.

Project team bonuses

The design considerations described above apply to permanent work teams. Different arrangements are required for project teams specially set up to achieve a task and, usually, disbanded after the task has been completed. Project team bonuses should, wherever possible, be self-financing – they should be related to increases in income or productivity or cost savings arising from the project. Project teams can be set targets and their bonuses can be linked with achieving or surpassing targeted results. Alternatively, a fixed bonus can be promised if the project is on time, meets the specification and does not exceed the cost budget. The bonus could be increased for early completion or to reflect cost savings. For lengthy projects, interim payments may be made at defined 'milestones'.

Requirements for team pay

Team pay works best if teams:

- stand alone as performing units for which clear targets and standards can be agreed and outputs measured;
- have a considerable degree of autonomy: team pay is likely to be most effective in self-managed teams;
- are composed of people whose work is interdependent: it is acknowledged by members that the team will deliver the expected results only if they work well together and share the responsibility for success;
- are stable: members are used to working with one another, know what is expected of them by fellow team members and know where they stand in the regard of those members;
- are mature: teams are well established, used to working flexibly to meet targets and deadlines, and capable of making good use of the complementary skills of their members.

These are exacting requirements. If they can be met there may be a case for team pay. But the fact that they are so demanding explains why it has never taken off, in spite of the powerful arguments in favour of it.

Advantages and disadvantages of team pay

Conceptually, team pay can:

- encourage teamworking and co-operative behaviour;
- enhance flexible working within teams and encourage multiskilling, clarify team goals and priorities and provide for the integration of organizational and team objectives;

- encourage less effective performers to improve in order to meet team standards;
- serve as a means of developing self-managed or self-directed teams.

But:

1 The effectiveness of team pay depends on the existence of well-defined and mature teams, and they may be difficult to identify. Even if they can be identified, do they need to be motivated by a purely financial reward?

2 Team pay may seem unfair to individuals who could feel that their own efforts are unrewarded.

3 Pressure to conform, which is accentuated by team pay, could result in the team maintaining its output at lowest common denominator levels – sufficient to gain what is thought collectively to be a reasonable reward but no more.

4 It can be difficult to develop performance measures and methods of rating team performance that are seen to be fair. Team pay formulas may well be based on arbitrary assumptions about the correct relationship between effort and reward.

5 There may be pressure from employees to migrate from poorly performing teams to high-performing teams. If this is allowed, it could cause disruption and stigmatize the teams from which individuals transfer, while if it is refused, it could leave dissatisfied employees in the inadequate teams, making them even worse.

As Merriman (2009) observed, research has demonstrated that team incentives are often counterproductive because team members perceive that they are inequitable: 'To avoid inadvertent violations of equity expectations organizations must make certain that team rewards are applied consistently across team members and consistently across time. Reward must be differentiated for at least the extreme high and extreme low performers within the team.'

Developing team pay

If, in spite of the problems that may beset team pay, it is decided to introduce it, the development steps are as follows:

1 *Initial analysis*. This should identify whether there are teams that satisfy the requirements set out above.

2 *Select teams*. Decide on which teams will be eligible for team pay.

3 *Scheme design*. Decide the team bonus formula (the criteria to be used in judging performance, the amount available for team pay and the method of distributing team pay).

4 *Scheme introduction*. Team pay is likely to be unfamiliar and should therefore be introduced with care, especially if it is replacing an existing system of individual performance-related pay. The process will be easier if employees have been involved in developing the scheme, but it is still essential to communicate in detail to all employees the reasons for introducing team pay, how it will work and how it will affect them. It is advisable to conduct a pilot scheme initially in one or two well-established teams to test how well the proposed arrangements work. If the pilot scheme teams think it has been a success, other teams may be more willing to convert to team pay.

It is easier to introduce team pay into mature teams whose members are used to working together, trust one another and can recognize that team pay will work to their mutual advantage. Although it may seem an attractive proposition to use team pay as a means of welding new work teams together, there are dangers in forcing people who already have to adapt to a different situation to accept a radical change in their method of remuneration. It should be remembered that it might not be easy to get people in work teams to think of their performance in terms of how it impacts on others. It can take time for employees to adapt to a system in which a proportion of their pay is based on team achievement.

NHS case study

As reported by Reilly *et al* (2005), the UK Department of Health decided to trial team pay in NHS trusts. The 17 teams in the trial were based at a number of sites and were given targets aimed at improving the patient experience through faster response, better service or an improved environment. The team reward was a cash payment: money put into an 'improvement fund' for staff to spend on staff facilities/development or a mixture of the two.

Many positive results were achieved by the trials. These included improvements in the management of the trusts and benefits to patients and staff. The end-of-pilot survey results generally elicited positive responses to questions relating to the operation of team-based pay. But as the researchers involved in the survey observed: 'So far so good, but there are still question marks over the success of the scheme. First, not all sites met their targets... and not every participant was as keen about the benefits of the scheme. Second, even at the better-performing sites, did team-based pay drive service improvement, even if the staff thought it did?'

In the opinion of the researchers, the causes of relative failure in some trusts can be attributed to the following three factors:

1 Team structure: some people were excluded from teams, which they resented, and the teams sometimes cut across natural groupings. But the size of the team and the degree to which it was well established did not make much difference.

2 Targets: there were a number of difficulties with targets. Some administrators found it hard to specify output, let alone outcome measures. They felt happier with input metrics. It was confirmed that the poorer the line of sight between work actions and the target, the less likely there was to be employee

engagement and thereby effort to deliver. In particular, when targets were externally imposed, failure was more probable. The degree of stretch in the targets varied greatly, but it did not always seem easy at the outset to predict what would be hard to achieve and what would be easier.

3 Matters outside the team's control: these genuinely affected the teams' ability to deliver, producing understandable criticism.

The main conclusions reached by the researchers were that:

- Success depends on having a clear purpose, effective leadership, the trust of staff in the integrity and competence of management, good communications and efficient project management.

- The 'right' size of team depends on the objectives of the exercise; for example, bigger teams may be necessary to cope with complex processes and multiple targets.

- Targets need to be clear and simple, easy to communicate and evaluate, relate to the work people do and seen as achievable and within the team's control.

- Team-based pay, like individual performance pay schemes, will only operate successfully for a limited period. This is because employees fear that the performance bar will be continuously raised and the discretionary effort that schemes tap into may not always be there to exploit.

Team pay: six tips

1 Be clear about the objectives of team pay.

2 Ensure that there are clearly defined teams in the organization for which the results achieved by the joint efforts of team members can be measured.

3 Involve team leaders and team members in developing the team pay scheme, including methods of setting targets and measuring and monitoring performance, and the formula used for calculating team pay.

4 Provide training in team building and operating the scheme.

5 Pilot test the scheme.

6 Get teams involved in setting their own targets and monitoring their own performance.

References

CIPD (2012) *Annual Reward Survey*, CIPD, London

Merriman, K K (2009) On the Folly of Rewarding Team Performance While Hoping for Team Work, *Compensation & Benefits Review*, **41** (1), pp 61–66

Prentice, G, Burgess, S and Propper, C (2007) *Performance Pay in the Public Sector: A review of the issues and evidence*, Office of Manpower Economics, London

Reilly, P, Phillipson, J and Smith, P (2005) Team-Based Pay in the United Kingdom, *Compensation & Benefits Review*, July/August, pp 54–60

20
Rewarding for business performance

KEY CONCEPTS AND TERMS

- Employee share option plans (ESOPs)
- Gain sharing
- Profit sharing
- Save-as-you-earn plans (SAYE)

LEARNING OUTCOMES

On completing this chapter you should be able to define these key concepts. You should also know about:

- Aims of rewarding for business performance
- How profit-sharing schemes work
- How gain-sharing schemes work
- How share ownership schemes work

Introduction

Many organizations believe that their financial reward systems should extend beyond individual merit pay, which does not recognize collective effort, or team pay, which is difficult. They believe that their system should help to enhance engagement and commitment and convince employees that they have a stake in the business as well as providing them with additional pay. The response to this belief is to offer financial rewards that are related to business or organizational performance (sometimes known as company-wide or factory-wide schemes). This is a popular form of reward – the 2013 CIPD reward survey found that 50 per cent of respondents had what they called 'goal sharing schemes'.

Types of schemes

The three types of formal business performance schemes are:

1 Profit sharing: the payment of sums in cash or shares related to the profits of the business; 40 per cent of the respondents to the 2013 CIPD survey had such schemes.
2 Gain sharing: the payment of cash sums to employees related to the financial gains made by the company because of its improved performance; only 12 per cent of the CIPD 2013 respondents had such schemes.
3 Share ownership schemes: employees are given the opportunity to purchase shares in the company; 26 per cent of the respondents to the 2013 CIPD survey had such schemes.

Aims

The aims of relating rewards to business performance are to:

- increase the commitment of employees to the organization;
- enable employees to share in the success of the organization;
- stimulate more interest in the affairs of the organization;
- focus employees' attention on what they can contribute to organizational success and bring areas for improvement to their attention;
- obtain tax advantages for employees through approved share schemes – such 'tax-efficient' schemes enable the business to get better value for money from its expenditure on employee remuneration.

Perhaps the two most important reasons for organizational schemes are the beliefs that they increase the identification of employees with the company and that the company is morally bound to share its success with its employee stakeholders – those who collectively make a major contribution to it. However, it is generally recognized that they do not provide a direct incentive because the links between individual effort and the collective reward are too remote.

Profit sharing

Profit sharing is a plan under which an employer pays to eligible employees, as an addition to their normal remuneration, special sums related to the profits of the business. The amount shared is either determined by an established formula or entirely at the discretion of management. As a percentage of pay, the value of profit shares varies considerably between companies, and within companies from year to year. Between 2 per cent and 5 per cent is a fairly typical range of payments but it can be 20 per cent or more. It is unlikely that profit distributions of less than 5 per cent will make much impact on commitment, never mind motivation. Employees tend to take the smallish sums they receive for granted.

Profits can be distributed in the form of cash or shares, usually share options. The arrangements for profit sharing are concerned with eligibility, the basis for calculating profit shares and the method of distribution. They vary considerably between companies.

Eligibility

In most schemes all employees except directors are eligible. A period of time, often one year's service, is usually required before profit shares can be received.

Basis of calculation

There are three approaches to calculating profit shares:

1 A predetermined formula: a fixed percentage of profits is distributed. This clarifies the relationship of payout to profits and demonstrates the good faith of management, but it lacks flexibility and the amount available may fluctuate widely.

2 No predetermined formula: the board determines profit shares entirely at its own discretion in accordance with the directors' assessment of what the company can afford. This gives them complete control over the amount distributed but, because of the secrecy involved, is at odds with the principle of getting employees more involved with the organization. This is the most typical approach.

3 A threshold formula: a profit threshold is set below which no profits will be distributed and a maximum limit is defined. Between these, the board exercises discretion on the amount to be distributed.

Methods of distributing profit shares

There are four methods of distribution:

1 Percentage of pay with no allowance for service: this is a fairly common method that recognizes that profit shares should be related to the employee's basic contribution as measured by their level of pay, which takes into account service.

2 Percentage of pay with an allowance for service: this approach is also frequently used on the grounds that it rewards loyalty.

3 Percentage of pay with an allowance for individual performance: this method is fairly rare below board level because of the difficulty of measuring the relationship between individual performance and profit.

4 As a fixed sum irrespective of earnings, service or performance: this is an egalitarian approach but is fairly rare.

Gain sharing

Gain sharing is a formula-based company- or factory-wide bonus plan that provides for employees to share in the financial gains made by a company as a result of its improved performance. The formula determines the share by reference to a performance indicator such as added value or some other measure of productivity. In some schemes the formula also incorporates performance measures relating to quality, customer service, delivery or cost reduction.

The most popular performance indicator is value added, which is calculated by deducting expenditure on materials and other purchased services from the income derived from sales of the product. It is, in effect, the wealth created by the people in the business. A manufacturing business 'adds value' by the process of production as carried out by the combined contribution of management and employees.

Gain sharing differs from profit sharing in that the latter is based on more than improved productivity. A number of factors outside the individual employee's control contribute to profit, such as depreciation procedures, bad debt expenses, taxation and economic changes. Gain sharing aims to relate its payouts more specifically to productivity and performance improvements within the control of employees.

Although the financial element is obviously a key feature of gain sharing, its strength as a means of improving performance lies equally in its other important features – ownership, involvement and communication. The success of a gain-sharing plan depends on creating a feeling of ownership that first applies to the plan and then extends to the operation. When implementing gain sharing, companies enlist the support of employees in order to increase their commitment to the plan. The involvement aspect of gain sharing means that information generated on the company's results is used as a basis for enabling employees to make suggestions on ways of improving performance, and for giving them scope to make decisions concerning their implementation.

However, gain sharing has never been very popular in the UK, perhaps because its use is mainly limited to the manufacturing sector and it takes time to plan and operate if it is to work well. Conventional profit sharing and share ownership schemes are much easier to manage.

Share ownership schemes

There are two main forms of share ownership plans: share incentive plans and save-as-you-earn (SAYE) schemes. These can be Inland Revenue and Customs approved, and if so produce tax advantages as well as linking financial rewards in the longer term to the prosperity of the company.

Share incentive plans

Share incentive plans must be Inland Revenue and Customs approved. They provide employees with a tax-efficient way of purchasing shares in their organization, to which the employer can add 'free', 'partnership' or 'matching' shares. There is a limit to the amount of free shares that can be provided. Employees can use up a sum determined by the Inland Revenue and Customs out of pre-tax and pre-National Insurance contributions pay to buy partnership shares, and employers can give matching shares at a ratio of up to two matching shares for each partnership share.

Save-as-you-earn schemes

These are savings-related share scheme where employees can buy shares with their savings for a fixed price. Up to £500 a month can be saved. At the end of the savings contract (three or five years) the savings can be used to buy shares in the company. The tax advantages are:

- the interest and any bonus at the end of the scheme are tax-free;
- Income Tax or National Insurance is not payable on the difference between what is paid for the shares and what they're worth.

Employees may have to pay Capital Gains Tax if they sell the shares – but not if they put them into an Individual Savings Account (ISA) or pension as soon as they buy them.

SAYE schemes must be Inland Revenue and Customs approved.

Impact of share schemes

A study by Oxera (2007) examined the impact of tax-advantaged employee share schemes on company performance. The key findings were that the tax advantages of such schemes were not sufficient on their own to increase productivity. Other factors were important: namely, having non-tax-advantaged schemes, company size (only firms in the upper quartile experienced a statistically significant productivity effect) and being a listed company. In these circumstances productivity does increase; for example, companies with both tax-advantaged and non-tax-advantaged schemes achieved increases in productivity of around 5.2 per cent in the long run.

Rewarding for business performance: six tips

1 Produce a case for the scheme; this could be a business case but it could also be a case based on the moral obligation of employers to share their prosperity with employees.

2 Ensure that you get the maximum benefit in terms of engagement and commitment from whatever scheme you adopt.

3 Ensure that the scheme is given full publicity (as long, of course, as it is paying out).

4 Remember that a scheme may enhance engagement but will not directly motivate people.

5 Make the most of any opportunities the scheme presents to involve employees in discussing their contribution to the firm's prosperity.

6 Consider how a scheme could complement an individual or team bonus plan.

References

CIPD (2013) *Annual Reward Survey*, CIPD, London

Oxera (2007) *Tax-advantaged Employee Share Schemes: Analysis of productivity effects*, Report 37, HM Revenue & Customs, London

21
Recognition

LEARNING OUTCOMES

On completing this chapter you should know about:

- The nature of recognition schemes
- Principles of recognition
- The different types of non-cash recognition awards
- How to design a scheme
- You will also be able to learn from a number of examples

Introduction

Recognition schemes acknowledge success. They can form an important part of a total rewards approach, as described in Chapter 11, and as such complement direct financial rewards and enhance the reward system. They are based on the belief that taking steps to ensure that people's achievements and contribution are recognized is an effective way of motivating them.

Recognition schemes defined

Recognition schemes enable appreciation to be shown to individuals for their achievements either informally on a day-to day basis or through formal recognition arrangements. They can take place quietly between managers and individuals in their teams or be visible celebrations of success.

A formal recognition scheme can provide scope to recognize achievements by gifts or treats or public applause. Typically, the awards are non-financial but some organizations provide cash awards. Importantly, recognition is also given less formally when managers simply say 'Well done', 'Thank you' or 'Congratulations' face to face or in a brief note of appreciation.

Benefits of recognition schemes

Recognition schemes can:

- enable people's achievements and contributions to be publicly acknowledged and provide an effective way of motivating them;
- complement and reinforce financial rewards as part of a total reward process;
- increase engagement by demonstrating that the organization values its employees;
- provide rewards for the average performers who are the core contributors in a business and may not benefit much if at all from merit pay;
- provide ways of rewarding teams as well as individual effort and contribution;
- give line managers the means to provide their people with instant rewards for achievement or contribution rather than making them wait until the end of the year for a possible merit increase.

Principles of recognition

The principles that need to be borne in mind when developing recognition schemes are that recognition:

- should be given for specially valued behaviours and exceptional effort as well as for special achievements;
- should be personalized so that people appreciate that it applies to them;
- needs to be applied equitably, fairly and consistently throughout the organization;
- must be genuine, not used as a mechanistic motivating device;
- should not be given formally as part of a scheme if the achievement has been rewarded under another arrangement, for example a bonus scheme;

- needs to be given as soon as possible after the achievement;
- should be available to all – there should be no limits on the numbers who can be recognized;
- should not be predicated on the belief that such schemes are just about rewarding winners;
- should be available for teams as well as individuals to reward collective effort;
- should not be based on an over-elaborate scheme.

It is also necessary to bear in mind that awards above £100 are subject to income tax in the UK.

Types of recognition

Day-to-day recognition

The most effective form of recognition is that provided by managers to their staff on a day-to-day basis. This is an aspect of good management practice in the same way as getting to know people, monitoring performance (without being oppressive) and providing positive feedback. It is provided orally on the spot or in a short note (preferably handwritten) of appreciation, and should take place soon after the event (not delayed until an annual performance review). It must be genuine – people can easily spot insincerity, or someone simply going through the motions.

This type of recognition should be a natural part of the daily routine. The organization should aim to develop a recognition culture that is nurtured by the management style of senior managers and permeates the organization through each level of management so that it becomes 'the way we do things around here'. Managers can be encouraged to adopt this style, but this should be more by example than by precept, not the subject of a scheme, process or system.

Public recognition

Recognition for particular achievements or continuing effective contributions can be provided by public 'applause' through an 'employee of the month scheme' or some other announcement using an intranet, the house journal or noticeboards.

Formal recognition

Formal recognition schemes provide individuals (and importantly, through them, their partners) with tangible forms of recognition such as gifts, vouchers, holidays or trips in the UK or abroad, days or weekends away at hotels or health spas, or meals out. Some schemes also provide cash awards. Team awards may be through outings, parties and meals. Such schemes may be centrally driven, with formal award ceremonies. Managers and employees can nominate individuals for awards. If the awards

TABLE 21.1 Levels of recognition

Level	Examples
1 Below £25	• Volunteering to help others when the workload is heavy.
	• Providing extra help to a customer.
	• Working late or at weekends without extra pay to meet an important deadline.
	• Taking on a temporary extra task that is not part of normal duties.
	• Demonstrating valued behaviours.
2 £25 to £150	• Identifying improved work practices.
	• Providing a sustained level of customer service.
	• Making or recommending cost savings when not part of role.
	• Demonstrating valued behaviours that make a significant short-term impact.
3 £500 to £1,000	• Generating significant extra revenue when not part of role.
	• Reducing costs significantly when not part of role.
	• Successfully completing a major project that is not part of normal role.
	• Demonstrating valued behaviours that make a significant long-term impact.

are substantial, organizations can set up a recognition committee with employee representatives to agree on who should be eligible, thus ensuring that decisions are transparent.

Formal schemes can provide for different levels of recognition and rewards, as illustrated in the schedule shown in Table 21.1, which was developed for a large local authority. This provides for a graduated series of awards that can be made by managers within a budget. At the lowest level, managers may be given quite a lot of autonomy to make immediate small recognition awards. The next-highest level of rewards would have to be approved by a senior manager and the highest level would be reviewed by a recognition committee for final approval by top management.

Examples of non-cash awards

Some ideas for non-cash awards include:

• basket of fruit;
• books;

- bottle of champagne (with a personalized label);
- cinema or theatre vouchers;
- dinner out for two (include a taxi and a babysitter);
- experience days (eg hot air balloon ride, or a day at a health and beauty spa);
- flowers (delivered to the workplace or at home);
- food hamper;
- Friday off for one week or more;
- gift certificates;
- jewellery;
- personal letter from the chairman or chief executive;
- plaques or certificates;
- points-based catalogue gifts;
- retail shopping vouchers;
- tickets to a concert, theatre or sports event;
- trip for two to Amsterdam, Barcelona or Paris;
- trophy (passed from one person to another);
- weekend in a hotel for two.

Designing a recognition scheme

The principles set out earlier in this chapter should be borne in mind when designing and implementing a recognition scheme. Line managers and employees should be consulted, guidelines prepared and explained to managers, and the details of the scheme publicized.

The implementation of the scheme should be monitored and steps taken to maintain the impetus – managers can lose interest. Progress reports should be made to employees so that they know that the scheme is working well.

Examples of recognition schemes

British Gas

Recognition awards at British Gas are focused more on behaviours than financial results, say, which should be recognized by the bonus scheme. There are several levels of recognition, none of which involves cash awards. These are:

- everyday recognition from the line manager who says 'Thank you' either by means of a personal note or at a team meeting;
- site/directorate level;
- British Gas-wide and Centrica-wide recognition.

It is intended that a minimum of 20 per cent of staff should be recognized by their line manager; current rates are around 40 per cent. Three-hour workshops are being run to help line managers understand the benefits of recognition and how to do it.

Camelot

The company believes that it is important to reward staff as near to the event of exceptional performance as possible, so it has put in place a recognition scheme to provide instant rewards. Managers and the staff consultative forum were involved in designing the scheme.

The recognition scheme, called Above and Beyond, rewards 'one-off, exceptional performance that is not part of the normal job'. Managers make their nominations online and they are approved almost immediately. The employee is then informed and can spend the reward, in the form of points, straight away. Awards average £50, but range from £10 to £200. The company's recognition budget is £25 per quarter per employee, so there is an expectation that most staff will get at least one award each year.

Staff can 'spend' their awards on goods or retail vouchers or add them to their own money to buy big items such as holidays. Rather than train all the managers, the company used 'champions' to roll out the scheme. These could be employees at any level, who were trained and briefed to explain the scheme to everyone else.

Glenmorangie

Glenmorangie's scheme is called Heroes, which stands for Honouring Excellence and Rewarding Outstanding and Extended Service. It recognizes continuing professional development, improvement suggestions, long service and 'making a difference' – going the extra mile to get the job done. The scheme was developed by a working party consisting of a cross section of Glenmorangie employees. There are no cash awards; instead, there are certificates and gifts chosen from a catalogue, which are presented by the manager at a team meeting.

Lands' End

Lands' End prefers the term appreciation to recognition, since it thinks the latter suggests something tangible. It prefers to look for any and every opportunity to demonstrate its real appreciation of what staff do, and comments that when managers focus on how they can show their appreciation it improves their own motivation as much as that of the people they recognize.

London & Quadrant Housing Association

There are two schemes:

The Outstanding Achiever awards. These annual awards are designed to recognize and celebrate exceptional achievements that demonstrate the organization's values. They are awarded to around 5 per cent of staff, who each receive a lump sum payment worth 2.5 per cent of salary. The process is fairly formal. Anyone with at least one year's service can be put forward, by a fellow employee, customer or supplier, but the formal nomination must come from the responsible group director. The group director of human resources then checks attendance records, since 'exemplary attendance' is expected from an outstanding achiever. The chief executive considers all the recommendations and decides who is to get the awards.

Our People: individual awards. Nominations for this scheme can come from fellow employees, customers and suppliers, and must also be for behaviour that reflects the values of the organization. This scheme is less formal than the Outstanding Achiever scheme and rewards less exceptional but nonetheless praiseworthy behaviour. Nominations are considered by the individual's manager, and awards are made to staff who meet the criteria. These can take the form of chocolates, flowers, vouchers, or a meal or evening or day out for the family.

Recognition schemes: six tips

1 Whatever scheme you choose, make sure you can apply it fairly and consistently. Apply it to those who really deserve it.

2 For recognition to have any real value it must be genuine. Ensure that it is real, spontaneous and appropriate to what someone has done.

3 Involve everyone in recognition; empower the whole management team to recognize people formally, and encourage all colleagues to recognize each other.

4 Recognizing great behaviour as soon as it happens is the most powerful approach. Shout about great achievements and great behaviours.

5 Public recognition can let others in the business know what has been done, and make a colleague feel proud. Award schemes, newsletters and noticeboards are all great ways to publicly recognize achievement. But remember that not everyone likes public recognition.

6 A lot of genuine recognition is simple and costs nothing, such as a thank you, a letter, or a photo on the wall. But sometimes spending wisely to treat the team to a meal or a day out can go a long way.

PART FOUR
Rewarding special groups

22
Executive reward

LEARNING OUTCOMES

On completing this chapter you should be able to define these key concepts. You should also know about:

- The problem with executive pay levels
- The factors affecting the level and nature of executive rewards
- The role of remuneration committees
- The meaning and significance of corporate governance
- The Combined Code on Corporate Governance
- The Turner Review proposals on executive remuneration and risk
- The elements of executives' remuneration – base pay, bonuses and share schemes
- Executive benefits
- Directors' contracts

Introduction

Probably no aspect of remuneration has attracted as much attention recently as that of the pay of directors and senior executives. Searching questions are being asked about the level of remuneration, the basis upon which pay decisions are made, the conditions for earning bonuses, and pension arrangements.

This chapter starts with a review of the issues surrounding executive pay: What is the problem? What are the factors affecting executive pay? Why has it grown so much? Decisions on the pay of directors and, to a degree, senior executives are influenced by corporate governance considerations and the associated codes, as described in the next part of the chapter. The final section examines the different aspects of remuneration packages for directors and senior executives, namely base pay, incentives, benefits and service contracts.

Executive pay levels

Executives are well paid. According to a report by the High Pay Centre in 2014 (Croucher, 2014) the average pay of a FTSE100 chief executive in the previous year was £4.7m. The Centre also reported that the pay of chief executives had grown from 60 times that of the average worker in 1998 to 160 times in 2012.

PwC commented in 2012 that:

> There is an emerging consensus, at least in Western economies, that there is something deeply flawed about the current model of executive pay. Executive pay has risen dramatically over a period when, in hindsight, the Western economic model has not been at its most successful.

A non-executive director interviewed by Perkins and Hendry (2005) during their research on top pay remarked: 'There is neither a moral nor a market argument to justify the explosion in pay, but once started, it is hard to stop. You cannot be seen to be left out.'

It has been established by research (Conyon and Leech, 1994; Gomez-Mejia and Balkin, 1992; Gregg et al, 1993) that there is no evidence that the huge increases in pay have resulted in improved company performance.

Factors affecting the level of executive rewards

The level of executive rewards can be explained in general terms by agency theory and tournament theory. Agency theory states that the only way in which owners (principals) can get the performance they want from their managers (agents) is by paying them more. Shareholders must structure the CEO's pay arrangements to reward behaviours that increase shareholder value. Tournament theory explains that the remuneration of a chief executive is in effect a prize and executives expend effort to increase the likelihood of winning it.

High rewards for chief executives are sometimes justified by reference to beliefs in their value to the business as wealth creators – generators of shareholder value. But the High Pay Commission (2011a) found that at its worst, excessive high pay bears little relation to company success and is rewarding failure. The Commission established that between 1998 and 2009 chief executive remuneration quadrupled while share prices declined. The remuneration of chief executives of FTSE 100 companies rose by 6.7 per cent a year, while earnings per share fell by 1 per cent per year over the same period.

It may also be claimed that chief executives are worth more because they are overseeing larger, more complex operations. But it does not necessarily follow that larger firm size should be matched by proportionally larger executive remuneration. A firm that has grown in size by a certain percentage has not necessarily grown in complexity by the same proportion, nor has the contribution of the executive role grown by the same proportion. A firm that is double the size will not necessarily have double the strategic decisions to make.

But the major factor affecting the level of rewards is how companies react to market forces in order to recruit and retain the executives they want and need. The Hampel Report (1998) stated that British boardroom remuneration will be 'largely determined by the market'.

The way market forces work in executive pay is mainly based on benchmarking – finding out what other chief executives in relevant businesses are paid and responding accordingly.

The following comments on this approach were made by Elson and Ferrere (2013):

> In setting the pay of their CEO, boards invariably reference the pay of the executives at other enterprises in similar industries and of similar size and complexity. For this, compensation consultants are retained to construct a 'peer group' of such companies and survey the pay practices that are prevalent. Then, in what is described as 'competitive benchmarking', compensation levels are generally targeted to either the 50th, 75th, or 90th percentile. This process is alleged to provide an effective gauge of the 'market wage', which is necessary for executive retention. In essence, this process creates a model of a competitive market for executives where it otherwise does not exist. The model may, in this case, drive the empirical results rather than the other way around. As we describe, this conception of such a market was created purely by happenstance, and by its uniform application across companies, the effects of structural flaws in its design can have potentially compounding macro effects on the level of executive compensation. Both the academic and professional communities have observed that the practice of targeting the pay of executives to median or higher levels will naturally create an upward bias and movement in total compensation amounts.

In essence, what Elson and Ferrere are saying is that this benchmarking process produces an upward ratchet. Firms end up overpaying for executives in order to establish a short-lived advantage that is neutralized by rivals paying more as well.

Data collected by Perkins and Hendry (2005) over 10 years for 81 of the FTSE 100 companies tended to show a relative lack of intra-company movement among executive directors, in particular internationally. This, they commented, undermines the presumption of a market in executives and hence in executive pay. They went on to point out that: 'While the evidence for a market with price as a clearing mechanism remains questionable, therefore, there is certainly no widespread subjective sense of such a market among those who are closest to it. Rather, there are a series of localized bargains.' They quoted a remuneration committee member they interviewed who categorically denied the existence of a recognizable market for executives, 'certainly not like that for beef or shares'. Instead, he said, there are 'just key people in unique positions at a given moment in time, who are not readily interchangeable'.

Research conducted by the High Pay Commission (2011b) suggested that losing a CEO to a competitor remains very unlikely. In a survey of CEO departures over the last five years in the FTSE 100, it was found that the chance of a CEO being poached by a national competitor in any one year would be 0.2 per cent. The likelihood of a CEO being snatched by a global firm was zero. However, as the Commission commented, it remains the case that fear of poaching is encouraging generous rewards.

Corporate governance and executive remuneration

Corporate governance is the internal set of processes and policies that determine the way a corporation is directed and controlled, and serve the needs of shareholders and other stakeholders. It involves the board of a company and includes how members of that board are remunerated.

The Combined Code on Corporate Governance

Corporations may or may not pursue shareholder value at the expense of good corporate governance or stewardship, but their role in general and their specific role in deciding on remuneration arrangements for directors has been questioned regularly since 1992 when the Cadbury committee reported. This was followed by a report from the Greenbury Committee (1995) and the Hampel Report (1998). These led to The Combined Code on Corporate Governance produced by the Financial Reporting Council in 2008, which lays down general principles of governance and a number of specific principles relating to the remuneration of directors. These are:

- Levels of remuneration should be sufficient to attract, retain and motivate directors of the quality required to run the company successfully, but a company should avoid paying more than is necessary for this purpose. A significant proportion of executive directors' remuneration should be structured so as to link rewards to corporate and individual performance.

- The remuneration committee should judge where to position their company relative to other companies. But they should use such comparisons with caution, in view of the risk of an upward ratchet of remuneration levels with no corresponding improvement in performance. They should also be sensitive to pay and employment conditions elsewhere in the group, especially when determining annual salary increases.

- The performance-related elements of remuneration should form a significant proportion of the total remuneration package of executive directors and should be designed to align their interests with those of shareholders and to give these directors keen incentives to perform at the highest levels.
- The remuneration committee should consider whether the directors should be eligible for annual bonuses. If so, performance conditions should be relevant, stretching and designed to enhance shareholder value. Upper limits should be set and disclosed. There may be a case for part payment in shares to be held for a significant period.
- Payouts or grants under all incentive schemes, including new grants under existing share option schemes, should be subject to challenging performance criteria that reflect the company's objectives. The total rewards potentially available should not be excessive.
- The remuneration committee should consider the pension consequences and associated costs to the company of basic salary increases and any other changes in pensionable remuneration, especially for directors close to retirement.
- But it seems that these principles are frequently more honoured in the breach than in the observance.

The Turner Review

The banking crisis of 2008 prompted The Turner Review (2009), which proposed the following code of good practice:

- Firms must ensure that their remuneration policies are consistent with effective risk management.
- Remuneration should reflect an individual's record of compliance with risk management procedures, rules and appropriate culture, as well as financial measures of performance.
- Financial measures used in remuneration policies should entail the adjustment of profit measures to reflect the relative riskiness of different activities.
- The predominant share (two-thirds or more) of bonuses that exceed a significant level should be paid in a deferred form (deferred cash or shares), with a deferral period that is appropriate to the nature of the business and its risks.
- Payment of deferred bonuses should be linked to financial performance during the deferral period.

Recent developments

A firm's remuneration policy now requires the approval of over 50 per cent of shareholders and in October 2014, new rules came into effect forcing listed firms to give shareholders a binding vote on directors' pay.

The role of remuneration committees

The Committee on Corporate Governance (2000) of the Stock Exchange and other reports recommended the establishment of remuneration committees to provide an independent basis for setting the salary levels and the rules covering incentives, share options, benefit entitlements and contract provisions for executive directors. Such committees were to be accountable to shareholders for the decisions they take and the non-executive directors who sat on them would have no personal financial interests at stake. They would be constituted as subcommittees of company boards, and boards should elect both the chairman and the members. Their essential role would be to set broad policy for executive remuneration as a whole as well as the remuneration packages of executive directors and, sometimes, other senior executives. They should consist exclusively of non-executive directors and should determine remuneration policy and the reward packages of individual executive directors, which should appear as a section in the annual report. This report should include statements on remuneration policy and the methods used to form that policy and disclose details of the remuneration of individual directors. The Combined Code of Practice (see later in this chapter) laid down the principles they should take into account when considering pay levels.

Remuneration committees are now well established as bodies for making recommendations on directors' pay, often with the advice of remuneration consultants. The Combined Code states that they should avoid paying more than is necessary, and should also be sensitive to pay and employment conditions elsewhere in the group, especially when determining annual salary increases. But the extent to which they follow either of these precepts is often questionable. So is the degree to which they are independent; after all, members of the remuneration committee are also colleagues of the board members on whose remuneration they deliberate.

As Perkins and Hendry (2005) observed following their discussions with remuneration committee members, consultants engaged by managements to advise committees were felt to be encouraging a 'pernicious process of choosing comparators' that 'just leads to the ratcheting up of top pay... The problem becomes particularly acute when companies all strive to achieve the statistically impossible feat of setting reward levels to locate themselves in the upper quartile of their benchmark group.' They also noted the ambiguities and weaknesses of the non-executive directors and commented that: 'The workings of a market in executive pay are fatally undermined by the social realities.'

The elements of executive remuneration

The main elements of executive remuneration are basic pay, short- and long-term bonus or incentive schemes, share option and share ownership schemes, benefits and service contracts. The salary is usually a one-off, negotiated rate and commonly incorporates a golden hello or pay-off deal. It should be set through a remuneration committee that meets good practice guidelines.

Basic pay

Decisions on the base salary of directors and senior executives are usually founded on views about the market worth of the individuals concerned. Remuneration on joining the company is commonly settled by negotiation, often subject to the approval of a remuneration committee. Reviews of base salaries are then undertaken by reference to market movements and success as measured by company performance. Decisions on base salary are important not only in themselves but also because the level may influence decisions on the pay of both senior and middle managers. Bonuses are expressed as a percentage of base salary, share options may be allocated as a declared multiple of basic pay and, commonly, pension will be a generous proportion of final salary.

Bonus schemes

Virtually all major employers in the UK have incentive (bonus) schemes for senior executives. Bonus schemes provide directors and executives with cash sums or shares based on the measures of company and, frequently, individual performance. They are often paid annually but can be deferred for a longer period.

Typically, bonus payments are linked to achievement of profit and/or other financial targets and they are sometimes 'capped'; that is, a restriction is placed on the maximum amount payable. There may also be elements related to achieving specific goals and to individual performance. Bonuses tend to be high – 70 per cent of base salary or more. They are ostensibly intended to motivate directors to achieve performance improvements for the business. A more common although not always disclosed reason for bonuses is to ensure that what is believed to be a competitive remuneration package is available: 'Everyone else is doing it, so we must too.'

One of the problems with high bonus expectations is that of the 'moral hazard' involved. For example, directors might be tempted to manipulate reported profits to drive up the share price, frequently an important determinant of bonuses. Or they may go for high returns in risky short-term projects, ignoring the possible downside of longer-term losses.

Executives may benefit by receiving bonuses for performance which meets objectives, but they do not usually lose pay when their objectives are not achieved. They only gain, they never lose. It can be argued that they should get their base salary for doing their jobs, ie achieving their objectives, and only receive more in the shape of a bonus if they exceed expectations. It could also be argued that if they fail to meet their objectives they should be penalized by not receiving a portion of their base salary, which would then truly be pay-at-risk. Earn-back pay schemes as described in Chapter 18 aim to remedy this situation.

Long-term bonuses

Cash bonus schemes can be extended over periods of more than one year on the grounds that annual bonuses focus too much on short-term results. The most common approach to providing longer-term rewards is through share ownership schemes as described later.

Deferred bonus schemes

Some companies have adopted deferred bonus schemes under which part of the executive's annual bonus is deferred for, say, two years. The deferred element is converted into shares, each of which is matched with an extra, free share on condition the executive remains employed by the company at the end of the deferral period. Such a scheme is designed to reward performance and loyalty to the company.

Scheme effectiveness

In an effective bonus scheme:

- targets will be tough but achievable;
- the reward should be commensurate with the achievement;
- the targets will be quantified and agreed;
- the measures used will refer to the key factors that affect company performance, and these performance areas will be those that can be directly affected by the efforts of those eligible for bonus payments;
- the formula will be simple and clear.

On the evidence of recent bonus payouts to failing company directors, it does not seem that these criteria are being applied successfully.

Share option schemes

Many companies have share option schemes that give directors and executives the right to buy a block of shares on some future date at the share price ruling when the option was granted. They are a form of long-term incentive on the assumption that executives will be motivated to perform more effectively if they can anticipate a substantial capital gain when they sell their shares at a price above that prevailing when they took up the option.

Conditions may be laid down to the effect that the company's earnings per share (EPS) growth should exceed inflation by a set amount over a number of years (often three) and that the executive remains employed by the company at the exercise date.

The arguments advanced in favour of executive share options are that, first, it is right for executives to share in the success of their company to which, it is assumed, they have contributed and, second, they encourage executives to align their interests (incentive alignment) more closely in the longer term with those of the shareholders as a whole (the latter argument is based on agency theory although it is quite possible that those who advance it are unaware that such a thing as agency theory exists). The first point is valid as long as the reward for exercising share options is commensurate with the contribution of the executive to the improved performance of the business. The second point is dubious. The vast majority of shares acquired in this way are sold almost immediately and the gain is pocketed as extra income.

Share options have been severely criticized recently because of the enormous gains made by some executives. There is a strong feeling among the major investment institutions that share options do not achieve community of interest between executives and shareholders and are in effect no more than a form of cash bonus in which the payout has little or nothing to do with the executive's performance, and indeed can become a reward for failure.

Performance share schemes

Some companies have performance share schemes under which executives are provisionally awarded shares. The release of the shares is subject to the company's performance, typically determined on a sliding scale by reference to the company's total shareholder return (a combination of share price growth and dividend yield) ranking against its chosen peer companies over a three-year period. Release is also conditional on the executive remaining employed by the company at the vesting date. Such a scheme rewards loyalty to the company and the value delivered to shareholders in the form of share price performance and dividends but does not link directly to business performance.

Executive restricted share schemes

Under such schemes free shares are provisionally awarded to participants. These shares do not belong to the executive until they are released or vested; hence they are 'restricted'. The number of shares actually released to the executive at the end of a defined period (usually three or, less commonly, five years) will depend on performance over that period against specific targets. Thereafter there may be a further retention period when the shares must be held although no further performance conditions apply.

Benefits

Employee benefits for executives may amount to over 20 per cent of the total reward package. The most important element is the pension scheme, and directors may be provided with a much higher accrual rate than in a typical final salary scheme. This means that, typically, the maximum two-thirds pension can be achieved after 20 years' service or even less, rather than the 40 years it takes in a typical one-sixtieth scheme. Pensions are easily inflated, as in a recent notorious case, by presenting the departing director with a last-minute substantial increase in pensionable salary.

Service contracts

Long-term service contracts for directors have been fairly typical, but they are disliked in the City because of the high severance payments to departing chief executives and directors that are made if the contract is two or three years, even when it was suspected or actually the case that they had been voted off the board because of inadequate performance. Rolling contracts for directors are now more likely to be restricted to one year.

Executive reward: six tips

1 Follow the principles of corporate governance laid down by the Combined Code.

2 Make decisions on levels of remuneration by reference to objective evidence, not hearsay or assumptions.

3 Justify rates of pay on the basis of the performance of the chief executive or director as demonstrated by the performance of the business.

4 Ensure that members of the remuneration committee are properly briefed and supported in making their recommendations.

5 Subject all bonus plans to careful scrutiny to ensure that they conform to good practice.

6 Subject proposed bonus payments to rigorous scrutiny to ensure that they genuinely reflect the level of performance achieved and do not reward failure.

References

Bruce, A, Buck, T and Main, B G (2005) Top Executive Remuneration: A view from Europe, *Journal of Management Studies*, **42** (7), pp 1493–1506

Cadbury, A (1992) *Report of the Committee on the Financial Aspects of Corporate Governance*, Gee Publishing, London

Chartered Institute of Personnel and Development (2011) *Annual Reward Survey*, CIPD, London

Committee on Corporate Governance (2000) *The Combined Code: Principles of good governance and code of best practice*, London Stock Exchange, London

Conyon, M J and Leech, D (1994) Top Pay, Company Performance and Corporate Performance, *Oxford Bulletin of Economics and Statistics*, **56** (3), August, pp 229–47

Croucher, S (2014) High Pay Centre: Time to cap bosses' runaway salaries, *International Business Times* [online] www.ibtimes.co.uk/high-pay-centre-time-cap-top-bosses-runaway-salaries-1456569 [accessed 11 February 2015]

Elson, C M and Ferrere, C K (2013) Executive Superstars, Peer Groups and Overcompensation: Cause, effect and solution, *Journal of Corporation Law*, Spring, pp 98–131

Financial Reporting Council (2008) *The Combined Code on Corporate Governance*, The Financial Reporting Council, London

Gomez-Mejia, L R and Balkin, D B (1992) *Compensation, Organizational Strategy, and Firm Performance*, South Western, Cincinnati, OH

Greenbury, R (1995) *Report of the Study Group on Directors' Remuneration*, Gee Publishing, London

Gregg, P, Machin, S and Szymanski, S (1993) The Disappearing Relationship Between Directors' Pay and Corporate Performance, *British Journal of Industrial Relations*, 3 (1), pp 1–9

Hampel, R (1998) *Committee on Corporate Governance: Final report*, Gee Publishing, London

High Pay Commission (2011a) *More for Less: What has happened to pay at the top and does it matter?* High Pay Commission, London

High Pay Commission (2011b) *Final Report*, High Pay Commission, London

Hutton Review of Fair Pay in the Public Sector: Interim report (2010) HM Treasury, London

Perkins, S and Hendry, P (2005) Ordering Top Pay: Interpreting the signals, *Journal of Management Studies*, 42 (7), pp 1443–68

PwC (2012) Making Executive Pay Work: The psychology of incentives, *PwC* [online] www.pwc.co.uk/human-resource-services/publications/making-executive-pay-work.jhtml [accessed 12 February 2015]

Turner, A (2009) *The Turner Review: A regulatory response to the banking crisis*, Financial Services Authority, London

23
Rewarding sales and customer service staff

LEARNING OUTCOMES

On completing this chapter you should know about:

- Methods of rewarding sales staff
- Methods of rewarding customer service staff

Introduction

Sales and customer service staff make an immediate impact on business results. This has led to an emphasis on financial incentives, especially for sales representatives and sales staff in retailers, who are often treated quite differently from other employees. The reward system for sales and service staff also has to take account of the fact that they are the people who are in direct contact with customers, and this also applies to people in call centres.

Rewarding sales representatives

Sales representatives are more likely to be eligible for commission payments or bonuses than other staff on the grounds that their sales performance will depend on or at least be improved by financial incentives. Many companies believe that the special nature of selling and the type of person they need to attract to their salesforce requires some form of additional bonus or commission to be paid. The nature of the work of sales staff means that it is usually easy to specify targets and measure performance against them, and sales incentive schemes are therefore more likely to meet the line of sight requirement (ie that there should be a clear link between effort and performance) than schemes for other staff such as managers and administrators. Sales staff, including those in retail establishments, are often paid spot rates with a commission on sales.

Financial methods of rewarding sales staff

The approaches to rewarding sales staff described below are:

- salary only;
- basic salary plus commission;
- basic salary plus bonus;
- commission only.

Table 23.1 summarizes the different schemes, their advantages and disadvantages and when they may be appropriate.

Salary only

Companies may adopt a salary-only (no commission or bonus) approach when sales staff have little influence over sales volume, when representing the company and generally promoting its products or services is more important than direct selling, and when the company wants to encourage sales staff to build up good and long-term relationships with their customers, the emphasis being on customer service rather than on high-pressure selling.

Basic salary only may also be paid to sales staff who work in highly seasonal industries where sales fluctuate considerably, and businesses where regular orders for food and other consumer goods give little opportunity for creative selling.

However, companies that do not pay commission or bonus may have a pay-for-contribution scheme that provides for consolidated increases based on an assessment of performance and competence in such areas as teamwork, customer relations, interpersonal skills and communications. Where sales staff have to work together to achieve results or where it is difficult to apportion a successful sale to individuals, a team pay approach may be adopted. Additionally, salary-only sales representatives may be eligible for incentives in the form of prizes.

If no commission or bonus is offered, it is necessary for companies to ensure that the salaries paid to their sales staff are competitive. They have to take account of the total earnings of sales staff in markets from which they recruit people or where their own staff move. If they cannot or do not want to at least match these earnings they may have to offer other inducements to join or stay with the company. These can include opportunities for promotion, learning new skills, more stable pay and greater security.

Basic salary plus commission

Salary plus commission plans provide for a proportion of total earnings to be paid in commission, while the rest is paid in the form of a fixed salary. The commission is calculated as a percentage of the value of sales. The proportion of commission varies widely. As a general rule it is higher when results depend on the ability and effort of

TABLE 23.1 Summary of payment and incentive arrangements for sales staff

Method	Features	Advantages	Disadvantages	When appropriate
Salary only	Straight salary, no commission or bonus.	Encourages customer service rather than high-pressure selling; deals with the problem of staff who are working in a new or unproductive sales territory; protects income when sales fluctuate for reasons beyond the individual's control.	No direct motivation through money; may attract under-achieving people who are subsidized by high achievers; increases fixed costs of sales because pay costs are not flexed with sales results.	When representing the company is more important than direct selling; staff have little influence on sales volume (they may simply be 'order takers'); customer service is all-important.
Salary plus commission	Basic salary plus cash commission calculated as a percentage of sales volume or value.	Direct financial motivation is provided related to what sales staff are there to do, ie generate sales; but they are not entirely dependent on commission – they are cushioned by their base salary.	Relating pay to the volume or value of sales is too crude an approach and may result in staff going for volume by concentrating on the easier-to-sell products, not those generating high margins; may encourage high-pressure selling as in some financial services firms in the 1980s and 1990s.	When it is believed that the way to get more sales is to link extra money to results but a base salary is still needed to attract the many people who want to be assured of a reasonable basic salary which will not fluctuate but who still aspire to increase that salary by their own efforts.

TABLE 23.1 *continued*

Method	Features	Advantages	Disadvantages	When appropriate
Salary plus bonus	Basic salary plus cash bonus based on achieving and exceeding sales targets or quotas and meeting other selling objectives.	Provides financial motivation but targets or objectives can be flexed to ensure that particular sales goals are achieved, eg high-margin sales, customer service.	Does not have a clear line of sight between effort and reward; may be complex to administer; sales representative may find the system hard to understand and resent the use of subjective judgements on performance other than sales.	When flexibility in providing rewards is important; it is felt that sales staff need to be motivated to focus on aspects of their work other than simply maximizing sales volume.
Commission only	Only commission based on a percentage of sales volume or value is paid; there is no basic salary.	Provides a direct financial incentive; attracts high-performing sales staff; ensures that selling costs vary directly with sales; little direct supervision required.	Leads to high-pressure selling; may attract the wrong sort of people, who are interested only in money and not customer service; focuses attention on high volume rather than profitability.	When sales performance depends mainly on selling ability and can be measured by immediate sales results; staff are not involved in non-selling activities; continuing relationships with customers are relatively unimportant.
Additional non-cash rewards	Incentives, prizes, cars, recognition, opportunities to grow.	Utilizes powerful non-financial motivators.	May be difficult to administer; does not provide a direct incentive.	When it is believed that other methods of payment need to be enhanced by providing additional motivators.

individuals or when there is less emphasis on non-selling activities. As a rule of thumb, most sales managers believe that the commission element will not motivate their staff unless they have a reasonable opportunity to earn at least 20 per cent of base pay.

The commission may be a fixed percentage of all sales, possibly with a 'cap' or upper limit on earnings. Alternatively the commission rate can increase at higher levels of sales on a rising scale to encourage sales representatives to make even greater efforts.

Basic salary plus bonus

Cash bonuses may be paid on top of basic salary. They are based on the achievement of targets or quotas for sales volume, profit or sales contribution (sales revenue minus variable expenses). They differ from commission payments in that the latter are based simply on a percentage of whatever sales have been attained. In a bonus scheme, targets or objectives may be set just for sales volume but they can also focus on particular aspects of the results that can be achieved by sales staff that it is felt should be stimulated. These may include the sales of high-margin or more profitable products or services in order to encourage staff to concentrate on them rather than simply aiming to achieve sales volume with low-margin products that are easier to sell. They may also cover reviving moribund accounts, promoting new products and minimizing bad debt. Other criteria may include the level of customer service, the volume of repeat business, the number of productive calls made, product knowledge, teamwork and quality of administration.

There are many ways in which bonuses can be determined. The method used will take into account the following considerations:

- the formula for relating bonuses to sales: a bonus may be triggered when a sales threshold is reached, with additions related to increased sales directly or on an accelerated basis;
- the size of bonus payments available at different levels of performance;
- the maximum bonus that will be paid out;
- the bonus criteria: sales revenue is often used, but some companies use profit or contribution to encourage sales representatives to focus on selling high-margin products rather than going for volume.

Commission only

Sales staff who are at the hard end of selling (eg double glazing) may only receive a straight commission based on a percentage of the value of their sales. No basic salary is paid.

Other means of rewarding sales representatives

Financial rewards are usually important for members of the salesforce but there are other valuable means of recognizing achievement. These include prizes and non-financial forms of recognition (sales representative of the month, etc) and other items in the total reward package such as opportunities for growth. As pointed out by Gundy (2002):

In assessing how to motivate the salesforce, leading companies view commissions and bonuses as just one tool in the motivational toolbox... Performance management, career pathing and recognition programmes can be powerful ways of producing and managing sales results. Companies that consider the impact of all these programmes in the design process are generally more successful in driving both short- and long-term results.

Other forms of reward are described below.

Gifts and vouchers

Gifts and vouchers provide a tangible means of recognizing achievements. They may be linked to the achievement of specified targets but should not be restricted to exceptional sales representatives; the solid dependable salesperson also needs motivating through the recognition that such incentives provide. Gifts are subject to income tax.

Competitions

Prizes can be awarded to individuals or teams for notable sales achievements, such as bringing in new business. However, competitions can demotivate those who do not win prizes and they should be designed to ensure that all those who are doing well feel that they have a good chance of getting a prize.

Cars as perks

Sales representatives can be motivated by the opportunity to get a bigger and better car if they are particularly successful. The car may be retained for a defined period and made available again if the high performance is maintained.

Recognition schemes

Recognition schemes, as described in Chapter 21, are particularly appropriate for sales staff. Public applause and private thanks are both important.

Rewarding customer service staff

Customer service staff work mainly in retail establishments and in call or customer contact centres. Their rewards need to reflect the nature of their duties, ie enhancing levels of customer service as well as selling.

Reward practices

The CIPD in conjunction with the Institute of Customer Service commissioned Professor Michael West and a team from Aston University to investigate how customer service staff were employed and rewarded (West et al, 2005).

The 580 staff covered by the research illustrated that front-line customer service workers do not all conform to the young/female/fleeting image. While 70 per cent were women, their average age was 34 years and average length of service six years.

Eighty per cent were employed on a full-time basis and just 9 per cent on temporary contracts.

Nor did their typical working environment and conditions reflect the stereotypical sweatshop image. While the HR and reward practices varied, working conditions were generally good and staff rated their supervisors' skills, as well as their colleagues and the level of teamworking. Staff benefits such as company pension plans and sick pay schemes were the norm, as were various training courses.

The pattern of pay practices used by these 15 organizations for front-line staff and their first-line managers is shown in Table 23.2. Base pay levels were generally competitive for the location and sector, and a number mentioned the effect of the national minimum wage.

TABLE 23.2 The pattern of pay practices for customer service staff in the Aston research organizations

Pay structure	Managers	Customer service staff
Grades	6	6
Broad bands	3	3
Individual ranges	4	4
Pay spine	2	2
Pay progression and bonus		
Individual performance-related pay	4	5
Skills/competency pay	2	2
Contribution pay	3	3
Individual bonus	5	6
Team bonus	4	6
Commission	0	1
Profit sharing	2	2

Most employees in the researched organizations had the opportunity to progress their base pay on the basis of their performance or competence, either through a range or up a pay spine, or between grades/levels of job. Such arrangements have generally supplanted spot rates for service roles in call centres and retail shops.

At Boots the Chemists, for example, shop staff can progress up through a number of pay points according to their level of performance and skill – from entry level, to experienced, to advanced, to expert/specialist. At B&Q, customer advisers are paid on one of six different spot rates. Pay progression is based on the acquisition – and application on the shop floor – of skills and knowledge. There are four additional spot rates beyond the established rate designed to reward high performance. Each additional level represents an hourly increase up to a maximum rate. At House of Fraser, employees are allocated to one of four competency bands – training, bronze, silver and gold – with staff assessed for a 'promotion' every six months. At Lands' End, there is a six-grade pay structure for hourly paid staff, with spot rates for starters.

Low base pay/high commission arrangements were rare amongst the 15 organizations, but most of them operated variable performance-related pay schemes of some type, which again has become the norm for service staff. Tesco and John Lewis staff, for example, received company-wide profit-sharing payments. British Gas uses a company-wide balanced scorecard bonus scheme, while Homebase, Asda and Marks & Spencer use team, store-based schemes. A number of the organizations used multiple plans.

All forms of performance-related pay and recognition schemes were used more frequently and extensively by the highest-performing organizations in the research than amongst the other participants or amongst UK organizations as a whole. They were twice as likely as other UK organizations to use individual performance-related pay and various forms of individual and team non-financial recognition schemes, and five times as likely to use some form of team/collective bonus scheme as the remaining organizations in the study.

Reward policies in the research study organizations did not by themselves create high customer service performance. They operated through the medium of staff perceptions and in a general work and management context that encouraged high levels of staff commitment – see Figure 23.1. The best organizations recognize that when it comes to delivering outstanding service, staff perceptions and management practice, rather than fancy reward and HR strategy statements, plans and policies are what make the difference.

FIGURE 23.1   A summary of the relationships between HR and reward
practices, employee attitudes and customer service
performance

Culture/people management

- Supportive supervisors
- Regular open feedback/performance
  management
- Effective team working
- Communications and involvement
  methods
- Career development policies
- Work–life balance policies

Rewards

- Individual performance-related pay
- Team/collective variable pay
- Performance pay based on
  service/quality measures
- Single status benefits
- Individual/team recognition

Staff attitudes

Commitment based on:
- satisfaction with pay
  and recognition
- being treated fairly
- feeling involved, developed
  and looked after
- organization emphasizes
  customer service

Customer
service
performance

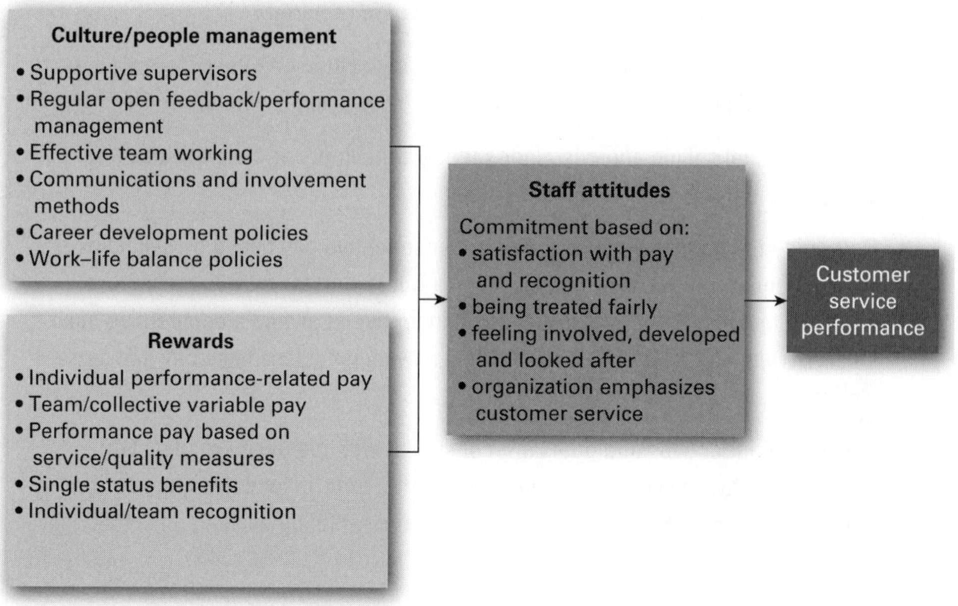

Sales and customer service staff reward: six tips

1   Analyse the business in terms of what is being sold or what customer services are provided to establish what types of people are required.

2   Select the approach to reward that is most likely to motivate the different types of people to deliver results in accordance with the business model.

3   Identify critical selling and customer service behaviours and capabilities and reinforce them through the reward package.

4   Determine the optimum mix of base pay and incentive pay based on selling or service requirements. An emphasis on customer relations may suggest more base pay and less incentive pay (even no incentive at all and a competitive base salary), while an emphasis on hard selling may suggest less base pay and more incentive.

5   Ensure that incentives and goals are consistent with the business plan. For example, the focus in the plan, and therefore the criteria for sales commission, could be more about getting new customers and retaining existing ones than just sales volume goals.

6   Segment the reward package as necessary to reflect the different demands made on members of the sales or customer service teams.

References

Gundy, P (2002) Sales compensation programmes: built to last, *Compensation & Benefits Review*, September/October, pp 21–28

Mercer Human Resource Consulting (2004) *Sales Effectiveness Report*, Mercer, London

West, M, Fisher, G, Carter, M, Gould, V and Scully, J (2005) *Rewarding Customer Service? Using reward and recognition to deliver your customer service strategy*, CIPD, London

24
Rewarding knowledge workers

LEARNING OUTCOMES

On completing this chapter you should be able to define these key concepts. You should also know about:

- What motivates knowledge workers
- Approaches to rewarding knowledge workers

Introduction

Knowledge workers are people whose work requires a marked degree of expertise. Their work is defined by the knowledge they need to do it. The term therefore embraces such diverse groups as scientists, accountants, HR professionals, IT specialists, lawyers, media workers and researchers.

Knowledge workers play a steadily increasing part in organizations. According to the government's *Occupational Employment Trends and Projections, UK 1982–2012*, by 2012 knowledge workers will have increased from roughly a quarter of all jobs 20 years ago to almost a half.

The importance of the contribution made by knowledge workers means that attention has to be given to how reward policies and practices can be developed to attract, retain and motivate them having taken account of their particular needs. This is an area of reward management where segmentation may be appropriate. For example, the fluid grading system used in the scientific civil service allows for much more flexibility in rewarding scientists in line with their levels of competence rather than by the levels of responsibility that characterize traditional multi-graded structures. The requirement to consider how knowledge workers should be rewarded is studied in this chapter, which starts with an analysis of what motivates them and then examines the approaches that can be adopted to their rewards.

What motivates knowledge workers?

In the words of Reeves and Knell (2001), it can be said of all knowledge workers that: 'The brightest and the best want an intellectual challenge and the chance to keep learning.' And Coyle (2001) explained that: 'Skilled programmers don't seem to fret about getting enough money. The more highly valued reward, because it is so much harder to come by, is the esteem in which they are held by their peer group.'

A study by Tampoe (1993) identified four key motivators for knowledge workers:

Personal growth: the opportunity for individuals to fully realize their potential.

Occupational autonomy: a work environment in which knowledge workers can achieve the task assigned to them.

Task achievement: a sense of accomplishment from producing work that is of high quality and relevance to the organization.

Money rewards: an income that is a just reward for their contribution to corporate success and that symbolizes their contribution to that success.

To which could be added, especially for scientific or research and development workers, the facilities required to carry out their work and the opportunity to gain recognition and prestige from their achievements. These may be more significant than financial rewards relating pay to performance.

Approaches to rewarding knowledge workers

Approaches to rewarding knowledge workers are described below under the headings of total reward, pay flexibility, pay related to competency, and career- and job-family structures.

Total rewards policies

Taking into account the factors that motivate knowledge workers mentioned above, there is an overwhelming case for adopting a total rewards policy. As explained in

Chapter 10, this would mean focusing on non-financial rewards such as recognition, opportunity to grow and achieve, and learning and development opportunities as well as financial rewards.

The following are examples of the approach used by two firms employing large numbers of knowledge workers.

Bristol-Myers Squibb

The pharmaceutical company states that 'reward is much wider than just paying its staff a competitive salary'. It has designed its total reward package knowing that everyone works for the company for different reasons and that everyone places a different emphasis on the importance of each of the elements of total reward – there is no one-size-fits-all. It has also set out to use total reward to 'elevate and differentiate' Bristol-Myers Squibb from other companies, both in the same industry and beyond.

The three elements of total reward are:

1 Compensation: salary, performance-based bonus and stock options.

2 Benefits: non-contributory pension, life cover, private health care, perks and cars.

3 Work experience: defined as: 'all the elements which contribute to providing you with an environment that enables you to optimize your contribution to the company and achieve your full potential, whilst maintaining a balance between your personal and professional life'. These include:

  – acknowledgement, appreciation and recognition;
  – balance of work and life;
  – culture of Bristol-Myers Squibb;
  – employee development;
  – the working environment.

The total rewards approach at Bristol-Myers Squibb embraces what they call the work experience, described above. This, says the company to its staff, 'recognizes that you are an individual with unique needs and offers something for everyone'. Work experience comprises acknowledgement, appreciation and recognition, balance of work and life, organizational culture, employee development and the working environment.

Elan Computers

The company's approach to total reward stresses investment in people, recognition, the quality of life and fair and competitive reward. It is part of Elan's people strategy, the stated aims of which are to:

> Support the group vision, to invest in talented people, and to maintain a people-focused environment that is fun, challenging and rewarding. Starting with our comprehensive induction programme, we aim to secure long-term commitment and inspire enthusiasm from day one. And we never stop listening to people. People are given the opportunity every year to take part in a survey to give feedback on every aspect of their life at Elan, and there are open question and answer sessions with board members. And to ensure that

we are doing what we can to keep the best people, we study the reasons why people leave, and what retains our most talented people. This strategy allows us to continually improve our position as an employer and as a market force.

The complete package, the concept of which is based on employees understanding the total value of all the rewards they receive, not just the individual elements, is designed to attract, retain, motivate and develop the best talent. The proposition for employees is that 'Total Reward' gives them the opportunity to share in the company's success, makes it easier to balance home and working life, and helps them to take care of themselves and their families.

Pay flexibility

The overall approach to rewarding knowledge workers should be flexibility within a framework. This means that a common framework of reward policies exists across the organization but within that framework some segmentation can take place. This would involve tailoring arrangements to suit the specific needs of particular groups of knowledge and professional workers and the individuals within those groups. Pay flexibility could include market rate supplements to attract and retain specific categories of staff and the use of selected market groups (separate pay structures for certain types of staff). This is in accord with the view expressed by Lawler (2002) that there should be a move away from job-based pay to person-based pay related to the market value of a person's skills and knowledge. On a wider scale, career or job families can be installed as described in Chapter 15.

Pay related to competency

If knowledge workers exist to apply their expertise then it seems reasonable to reward them according to the level of expertise (competency) they possess and apply. There are three ways of doing this, as described below: (1) by competency-related pay, (2) through structures in which grades or bands are defined in competency terms, and (3) the incorporation of skills and competencies into job evaluation factor plans.

Competency-related pay

In a competency-related pay scheme, people receive financial rewards in the shape of increases to their base pay by reference to the level of competence they demonstrate in carrying out their roles. It is a method of paying people for the ability to perform now and in the future. This seems to be a highly relevant approach for knowledge workers but there are measurement problems that have restricted its use.

Competency-defined grade and pay structures

Job or career family structures typically define levels in terms of competencies.

Use of competencies in job evaluation

Traditional job evaluation schemes have always incorporated competencies in their factor plans, although they called them knowledge, skill or know-how. Factor plans have recently been developed that deliberately include competencies. This has applied in sectors or organizations such as higher education (the HERA scheme), the senior civil service (the JESP system) and the NHS, where there are 16 measurement factors but the knowledge, skills and experience factor accounts for almost a quarter of the total points weighting. This scheme acknowledges the explicit bias towards knowledge in an organization with huge numbers of professional workers.

Job families

Job-family structures as described in Chapter 15 consist of separate families of jobs with similar characteristics. Within each family the successive levels of competency required to carry out typical activities are defined, thus indicating career paths. In a job-family structure such as that at Canon UK, each job family has its own pay structure, which takes account of different levels of market rates between families (this is sometimes called 'market grouping'). In Southampton University, the ranges of pay for each family are the same and the emphasis is on defining career progression rather than market pricing, although market supplements may be paid.

Job families are particularly appropriate for knowledge workers because they spell out the career ladders that apply specifically to the different categories employed in an organization.

Rewarding knowledge workers: six tips

1 Adopt total reward policies emphasizing scope for achievement, recognition and growth.

2 Consider segmenting the reward package for specified groups of knowledge workers.

3 Introduce competency-based pay.

4 Create a job-family structure with levels defined in competency terms.

5 Define career ladders and the rewards associated with career progression.

6 Develop a work environment that ensures that knowledge workers have the resources they need, the scope to use and develop their knowledge and skills and the recognition they deserve.

References

Coyle, D (2001) Power to the People, in *The Future of Reward*, ed N Page, CIPD, London

Lawler, E E (2002) Pay Strategies for the Next Economy: Lessons from the dot-com era, *World at Work Journal*, **11** (1), pp 6–10

Occupational Employment Trends and Projections, UK 1982–2012, Office for National Statistics, London

Reeves, R and Knell, J (2001) All of these futures are yours, in (ed) N Page, *The Future of Reward*, CIPD, London

Tampoe, M (1993) Motivating Knowledge Workers: The challenge for the 1990s, *Long-range Planning*, **26** (2), pp 37–44

25
Rewarding manual workers

KEY CONCEPTS AND TERMS

- Base rate
- Effort bargain
- Effort rating
- Harmonization
- High day rate
- Incentive scheme
- Individual job grades
- Measured day work
- Payment-by-results

- Pay/work bargain
- Performance-related pay
- Piece work
- Single status
- Skill-based pay
- Spot rate
- Taylorism
- Time rate
- Wage drift

LEARNING OUTCOMES

On completing this chapter you should be able to define these key concepts. You should also know about:

- The factors affecting the pay of manual workers
- The use of time rates
- The use of pay structures
- Types of shopfloor incentive schemes
- Considerations affecting the use of incentive schemes
- The meaning of single status and harmonization

Introduction

Manual worker pay systems that have not been harmonized – that is, brought into line with the reward system for staff – frequently differ from the systems described elsewhere in this book in three ways. First, the use of a time-rate basis of payment, second, the use of spot rates rather than grades, and third, the use of individual payment-by-results and skill-based pay schemes as described in this chapter. But first it is necessary to consider the factors affecting the pay of manual workers, which will affect both the level of pay and the methods used.

Factors affecting the pay of manual workers

The three main factors affecting the pay of manual workers are: first the local labour market, second, bargaining arrangements and third, trends in the use of technology on the shopfloor.

The local labour market

Manual workers are usually recruited from the local labour market, where the laws of supply and demand will affect the rates of pay for particular occupations if there is a skills shortage or surplus, or reluctance on the part of workers to carry out certain jobs. In the absence of trade unions (union density was only 16.8 per cent in the private sector in 2010) this is the major factor. The local labour market is a fairly perfect market in one of the senses used by economists, namely that there is widespread and easily available knowledge of rates of pay (the price of labour) and there may also exist, although not for every occupation, a fair degree of choice by buyers (employers) of where they obtain labour. There may be much less choice on the part of employees in areas of high unemployment.

Bargaining arrangements

The pay of manual workers can be influenced by local and, to a lesser extent, national agreements with trade unions, which determine rates for jobs or skill levels. This is more likely to be the case in the public sector where in 2010 the union density was 64.5 per cent.

Bargaining arrangements constitute an aspect of the effort bargain. The objective of workers and, where relevant, their trade union officials and representatives is to strike a bargain with management about what they consider the amount of pay that should be provided by their employer for their work. It is an agreement between workers and management – the pay/work bargain – that lays down the amount of work to be done for an agreed wage, not just the hours to be worked. Explicitly or implicitly, all employers are in a bargaining situation with regard to payment systems. This applies whether or not workers are unionized. Negotiated wage settlements can also affect non-unionized companies.

Non-unionized employees may be in a bargaining relationship with their employers if they are able to negotiate rates of pay when they join a company or during employment. But it is probably only those with much-wanted or scarce skills that are able to do this.

Technology

The increased use of technology on the shopfloor, for example, in the form of computer-aided manufacture, has meant that the demand for a number of the traditional skills has diminished while the demand for new ones has increased. Computer-controlled machines are more likely to be operated by technicians than by members of the old skilled trades. This is one of the factors that has led to pressures to harmonize shopfloor and office or laboratory payment systems. Shopfloor technicians are more likely to be on a spot rate or an individual job pay range with scope for merit pay than other skilled, semi-skilled or unskilled workers.

Time rates

Time rates, also known as day rates, day work, flat rates or hourly rates, provide workers with a predetermined rate for the actual hours they work. The rate is fixed by formal or informal negotiations, on the basis of local rates or, less often, by reference to a hierarchy produced by job evaluation. The rate only varies with time, never with performance or output. However, additional payments are made on top of base rates for overtime, shift working, night work, call outs, adverse working conditions and, sometimes, location.

The situation where time rates are most commonly used is where it is thought impossible or undesirable to use a payment-by-results scheme, for example in maintenance work. From the viewpoint of employees, the advantage of time rates is that their earnings are predictable and steady and they do not have to engage in endless arguments with rate fixers and supervisors about piece rate or time allowances. The argument against them is that they do not provide a direct incentive relating the reward to the effort or the results. Two ways of modifying the basic time-rate approach are to adopt high day rates or measured day work as described later.

Time rates may take the form of what are often called high day rates. These are higher than the minimum time rate and may contain a consolidated bonus rate element. The underlying assumption is that higher base rates will encourage greater effort without the problems created when operating an incentive scheme. This is in line with the theory of the economy of high wages mentioned in Chapter 13. High day rates are usually above the local market rates to attract and retain high-quality workers.

Pay structures

Pay systems for manual workers are seldom graded in the ways described in Chapter 15 unless their conditions have been harmonized. Time rates are usually paid in the form of spot rates: that is, a fixed rate for a job or an individual. However, spot rates may be designated for different levels of skill. Traditionally, a person-based pay system was adopted with three basic rates of pay attached to people – unskilled, semi-skilled and skilled – above which there might be special rates for highly skilled occupations such as toolmakers. Earnings from payment-by-results schemes were added to these rates. Other arrangements include the use of a more discerning hierarchy of rates linked to skill levels (a type of skills-based pay), a job-based pay system with different rates for different jobs, or individual job grades which are, in effect, spot rates to which a defined pay range of, say, 20 per cent on either side of the rate has been attached to provide scope for pay progression based on performance.

Incentive schemes for manual workers

Incentive schemes for manual workers consist of:

- Payment-by-results (PBR) schemes, which pay for output and include piecework, work-measured schemes and measured day work. Payments are added to base rate although, rarely, payment is entirely related to output.
- Merit or skill-based pay schemes, which relate pay to performance or skill. Increases may be consolidated or paid as lump sum bonuses.
- Collective schemes, which pay bonuses related to either team or plant performance.

Each of these methods is described below. First, however, it is necessary to deal with the considerations affecting the use of incentive schemes.

Considerations affecting the use of incentive schemes

The considerations to be taken into account in developing and maintaining incentive schemes are the criteria of effectiveness and their advantages and disadvantages.

Criteria of effectiveness

Incentive schemes aim to motivate employees to exert greater effort. They will do so effectively only if:

- the link between effort and reward is obvious and easily understood, ie there is a clear line of sight;
- the value of the reward is worthwhile in relation to the effort;
- individuals are able to influence their level of effort or behaviour in order to earn a reward;
- rewards closely follow the effort;
- the integrity of the scheme is preserved – it is not allowed to degenerate and cannot be manipulated so that individuals are over-rewarded.

The rationale for incentive schemes

The basic rationale of incentive schemes is the simple proposition that people are motivated by money. It is believed that they will work harder if rewards are tied directly to the results they achieve. This is essentially 'Taylorism' – FW Taylor's concept of scientific management, meaning the use of systematic observation and measurement, task specialism and, in effect, the reduction of workers to the level of efficiently functioning machines who will only work harder if they are paid more.

Certainly, the experience of most people who have installed a PBR scheme in a workplace where it did not previously exist is that productivity increases substantially when the scheme is new, although the level of increase is not always maintained. Studies in the United States by Binder (1990), Guzzo, Jette and Katsell (1985), Lawler (1971) and Nalbantian (1987) have shown productivity increases of between 15 per cent and 35 per cent when incentive schemes have been put into place.

Incentive schemes are used in the belief that they yield increased output, lower the cost of production and provide higher earnings for the workers concerned. It is also commonly believed that less supervision is needed to keep output up. Indeed, when direct supervision is difficult, PBR is often advocated as the only practicable form of payment.

The argument that people work harder only when they are paid more is regarded by some people as overwhelming. They do not accept the proposition that intrinsic and non-financial motivators can also be important.

Disadvantages of incentive schemes

The disadvantages of shopfloor incentive schemes are that they can:

- be unfair: earnings may fluctuate through no fault of the individual because of lack of work, shortage of materials, design modifications or the need to learn new skills. It may also be felt that the method of altering rates is unfair.
- be ineffective: workers may have their own ideas about how much they want to earn or how hard they want to work, and regulate their output accordingly.
- penalize skill: the more skilled workers may be given the more difficult and often less remunerative jobs.
- cause wage drift: the difficulty of conforming to criteria such as clearly relating pay to effort and the lax approach of some organizations to the management of incentive schemes contribute to increases in earnings at a higher rate than productivity. Degeneration and wage drift are a particular problem with work-measured schemes as discussed later in this chapter.
- lead to management escaping its responsibilities: team leaders and supervisors may rely on the incentive scheme to control output. Instead of taking poor performers to one side and informing them that their work is not up to standard, they are tempted to take the soft option and simply point to the figures.

- be costly to maintain: extra work-study engineers, rate fixers and inspectors are often needed to maintain the scheme and exercise quality control.

- produce strife in the workplace: arguments about rates and accusations of unjustified rate-cutting are common in workshops where incentive schemes are used.

- create reluctance to exert the expected level of effort: workers may believe that management will progressively increase the performance targets required to trigger the same bonus payment. They may therefore be reluctant to carry on at the incentivized level of performance they have achieved, on the grounds that this will only result in higher targets that will make the bonus more difficult to obtain.

- result in poor-quality work: concentration on output can lead to neglect of quality.

- lead to poor teamwork: individual incentive schemes by definition encourage individual rather than team effort.

- result in accidents and health hazards: workers may be tempted to cut corners and ignore safety precautions to achieve output targets; repetitive strain injury (RSI) may result if they work too hard on tasks requiring repeated small movements.

These are powerful arguments but shopfloor incentive schemes persist. The number of workers paid on this basis may have diminished, but this is because of structural (the reduction in manufacturing) and technological reasons rather than because managements have turned against it.

Payment-by-results schemes

Piecework

Piecework is the oldest and simplest form of incentive scheme for manual workers. Operators are paid at a specific rate according to their output or the number of 'pieces' they produce. Pay is directly proportional to output, although most piecework schemes provide a fallback rate at minimum earnings level. The proportion of the minimum rate to average earnings varies. It is typically set at 70 or 80 per cent, although it can be as low as 30 per cent.

Work-measured schemes

Work-measured schemes are the most popular form of incentive plan for shopfloor workers. They use work-measurement techniques to determine standard output levels over a period or standard times for tasks. The incentive pay is then linked with the output achieved relative to the standard, or to the time saved in performing each task.

The form of work measurement used is time study. Jobs are broken down into their constituent parts or tasks and the time taken by workers to complete each part is measured with a stopwatch by a work-study or industrial engineer. A number of measurements will be made of the time taken by different workers on the same task or the same worker carrying out the task at different times of the day and night. Time study is based on objective measurements, but account has to be taken of the fact that there will probably be significant differences between the rates at which operators work – the effort they put into the job. Work-study engineers have therefore to assess what that rate is, a process known as effort rating.

Individual effort is rated in terms of 'standard performance'. This is the performance that a qualified and motivated worker should be able to achieve without overexertion. The effort needed to achieve standard performance is sometimes represented as equivalent to walking at four miles an hour (ie quite briskly). All the operators studied are given an effort rating relative to this standard. The raw times observed in the work study are then adjusted by the work-study engineer to produce a basic time that represents a rating of 100 to indicate the performance of an average operator working conscientiously without financial motivation. This involves a large element of subjectivity, although experienced and well-trained engineers should be capable of making reasonably accurate and consistent assessments.

The basic time will be further adjusted to incorporate allowances for relaxation, personal needs, fatigue and any time regularly taken up by other aspects of the work such as cleaning or resetting machines. The result is the standard time for the task, usually expressed as 'standard minutes'.

Work-measured schemes can use performance ratings that are calculated by a formula as in the following example:

$$\frac{\text{Number of units produced per day (132)} \times \text{standard minutes per unit (4)}}{\text{Actual time taken in minutes per day (480)}} = \frac{528}{480} \times 100 = 110\%$$

In the most common proportionate system of payment, the performance rating is applied directly to the base rate, so that in the above example the incentive payment would be an additional 10 per cent.

The problem with time study is that, although it is based on objective measurements, the standard time that is ultimately obtained is the product of a number of additional subjective judgements. Employees who are being timed may deliberately restrict their performance in order to achieve low standard times and therefore higher bonuses with less effort. It is up to the work-study engineer's skill and judgement to detect such restrictions, and this can lead to arguments and even strife. In organizations with trade unions it is common practice to train some representatives in work-measurement techniques to promote the achievement of acceptable judgements on standard times.

Alternatively, PBR payments can be based on the time-saved principle. The amount of the bonus depends on the difference between the actual time taken to perform the task and the standard time allowed. If a task is done in less than the standard time, then the percentage of time saved is applied to the base rate to calculate the bonus. The standard times may be determined by work measurement, although traditionally 'rate fixers' were employed to make more subjective and therefore often more controversial judgements.

Measured day work

Measured day work schemes were originally developed for large batch or mass-production factories in the 1950s and 1960s, when it became evident that, despite all efforts, it was impossible to control wage drift. They are, however, much less common now. Manufacturing firms often prefer to pay a high day rate.

When they exist, measured day work schemes provide for the pay of employees to be fixed on the understanding that they will maintain a specified level of performance, but in the short term pay does not fluctuate with their performance. The arrangement depends on work measurement to define the required level of performance and to monitor the actual level. The fundamental principles of measured day work are that there is an incentive level of performance and that the incentive payment is guaranteed in advance, putting employees under the obligation to perform at the effort level required. In contrast, a conventional work-measured incentive scheme allows employees discretion as to their effort level but relates their pay directly to the results they achieve. Between these two extremes there are a variety of alternatives, including banded incentives, stepped schemes and various forms of high day rate.

Performance-related pay

Performance-related pay systems such as those described in Chapter 18 can be used for manual workers. Employees receive a high base rate and an additional performance-related payment, which is either a lump sum bonus or consolidated into basic pay. The award is governed by assessments of skill and performance ratings under headings such as quality, flexibility, contribution to teamworking and ability to hit targets. The percentage award is usually small – up to 5 per cent. Where payments are consolidated the scope for progression may be defined in individual job grades.

Performance-related pay is sometimes introduced for manual workers as part of a programme for harmonizing their conditions of employment with those of salaried staff. It can be appropriate in circumstances where work measurement is difficult or impossible to use, in high-technology manufacturing where operations are computer-controlled or automated and teamwork and multiskilling are important, in organizations where the emphasis is on quality, and in those where just-in-time systems are used. But it is difficult to operate and trade unions tend to be hostile and it is therefore uncommon.

Skill-based pay

Skill-based pay provides employees with a direct link between their pay progression and the skills they have acquired and can use effectively. It focuses on what skills the business wants to pay for and what employees must do to demonstrate them. It is therefore a people-based rather than a job-based approach to pay. Rewards are related to the employee's ability to apply a wider range or a higher level of skills to different jobs or tasks. It is not linked simply with the scope of a defined job or a prescribed set of tasks.

A skill may be defined broadly as a learned ability that improves with practice in time. For skill-based pay purposes the skills must be relevant to the work. Skill-based pay is also known as knowledge-based pay, but the terms are used interchangeably, knowledge being regarded loosely as the understanding of how to do a job or certain tasks.

Skill-based pay in the UK has been mainly applied to manual workers. The broad equivalent of skill-based pay for managerial, professional and administrative staff and knowledge workers is competency-related pay, which refers to expected behaviour as well as often to knowledge and skill requirements. There is clearly a strong family resemblance between skill- and competency-related pay – they are both person-based pay schemes. But they can be distinguished both by the way in which they are applied, as described below, and by the criteria used.

Skill-based pay works as follows:

- Skill blocks or modules are defined. These incorporate individual skills or clusters of skills that workers need to use and that will be rewarded by extra pay when they have been acquired and the employee has demonstrated the ability to use them effectively.
- The skill blocks are arranged in a hierarchy, with natural break points between clearly definable different levels of skills.
- The successful completion of a skill module or skill block will result in an increment in pay. This will define how the pay of individuals can progress as they gain extra skills.
- Methods of verifying that employees have acquired and can use the skills at defined levels are established.
- Arrangements for 'cross-training' are made. These will include learning modules and training programmes for each skill block.

Skill-based pay systems are expensive to introduce and maintain. They require a considerable investment in skill analysis, training and testing. Although in theory a skill-based scheme will pay only for necessary skills, in practice individuals will not be using them all at the same time and some may be used infrequently, if at all. Inevitably, therefore, payroll costs will rise. If this increase is added to the cost of training and certification, the additional costs may be considerable. The advocates of skill-based pay claim that their schemes are self-financing because of the resulting increases in productivity and operational efficiency, but there is little evidence that such is the case. For this reason, skill-base schemes have never been popular in the UK.

Collective schemes

Group or team incentive schemes

Group or team incentive schemes provide for the payment of a bonus to members of a group or team related to the output achieved by the group in relation to defined targets or to work-measured standards.

Factory or plant-wide schemes

Factory or plant-wide schemes pay a bonus to individuals that is related to the performance of the factory as a whole, which may be measured in terms of added value as in a gain-sharing scheme (see Chapter 20) or some other index of productivity (eg units produced, cost per unit of output). The bonus may be added to individual incentive payments.

Summary of schemes

Shopfloor incentive schemes are summarized in Table 25.1. This contains an assessment of the advantages and disadvantages of each type of scheme from the viewpoint of employers and employees and a review of the circumstances when the scheme is more likely to be appropriate.

Single status and harmonization

Single status means that manual or shopfloor workers are no longer on wages and are instead placed on salaried terms and conditions and are entitled to the same conditions of employment as other members of staff, such as sick pay. Harmonization means the reduction of differences in the pay structure and other employment conditions between categories of employee, usually manual and staff employees. It involves the adoption of a common approach and criteria to pay and benefits for all employees.

The pressure for harmonization has occurred because of the belief that status differentials between people in the same employment cannot be justified. Harmonization facilitates the more flexible use of labour, and the impact of technology has enhanced the skills of shopfloor workers and made differential treatment harder to defend. Equal pay legislation has been a major challenge to differentiation between staff and manual workers.

Before pursuing a programme of harmonization the following questions should be answered:

- What differences in the treatment of groups of employees are a rational result of differences in the work or the job requirements?
- Is it possible to estimate the direct costs of removing these differences?
- What differences in status are explicitly recognized as part of the reward package for different groups in the labour force?
- What would be the possible repercussive effects of harmonization?
- How do the existing differences affect industrial relations in the organization?

TABLE 25.1 Comparison of shopfloor incentive schemes

Scheme	Main features	For employers		For employees		When appropriate
		Advantages	Disadvantages	Advantages	Disadvantages	
Piecework	Bonus directly related to output.	Direct motivation; simple, easy to operate.	Lose control over output; quality problems.	Predict and control earnings in the short term; regulate pace of work themselves.	More difficult to predict and control earnings in the longer term; work may be stressful and produce RSI.	Fairly limited application to work involving unit production controlled by the person, eg agriculture, garment manufacture.
Work-measured schemes	Work measurement used to determine standard output levels over a period or standard times for job/tasks; bonus based by reference to performance ratings compared with actual performance or time saved.	Provides what appears to be a 'scientific' method of relating reward to performance; can produce significant increases in productivity, at least in the short term.	Schemes are expensive, time-consuming and difficult to run, and can too easily degenerate and cause wage drift because of loose rates.	Appear to provide a more objective method of relating pay to performance; employees can be involved in the rating process to ensure fairness.	Ratings are still prone to subjective judgement and earnings can fluctuate because of changes in work requirements outside the control of employees.	For short-cycle repetitive work where changes in the work mix or design changes are infrequent, down time is restricted, and management and supervision are capable of managing and maintaining the scheme.
Measured day work	Pay fixed at a high rate on the understanding that a high level of performance against work-measured standards will be maintained.	Employees are under an obligation to work at the specified level of performance.	Performance targets can become easily attained norms and may be difficult to change.	High predictable earnings are provided.	No opportunities for individuals to be rewarded in line with their own efforts.	Everyone must be totally committed to making it work; high standards of work measurement are essential, with good control systems to identify shortfalls on targets.

TABLE 25.1 continued

Scheme	Main features	For employers		For employees		When appropriate
		Advantages	Disadvantages	Advantages	Disadvantages	
Performance-related pay	Payments on top of base rate are made related to individual assessments of performance.	Reward individual contribution without resource to work measurement; relevant in high-technology manufacturing.	Measuring performance can be difficult; no direct incentive provided.	Opportunity to be rewarded for own efforts without having to submit to a pressured PBR system.	Assessment informing performance pay decisions may be biased, inconsistent or unsupported by evidence.	As part of a reward harmonization (shopfloor and staff) programme; as an alternative to work-measured schemes or an enhancement of a high day rate system.
Skill-based pay	Payments for acquiring and using new skills.	Encourage skills acquisition.	May pay for skills not used.	Scope to develop.	Proper training may not be available.	Where skills requirements are exacting.
Group or team basis	Groups or teams are paid bonuses on the basis of their performance as indicated by work measurement ratings or the achievement of targets.	Encourage team cooperation and effort; not too individualized.	Direct incentive may be limited; depends on good work measurement or the availability of clear group output or productivity targets.	Bonuses can be related clearly to the joint efforts of the group; fluctuations in earnings minimized.	Depend on effective work measurement, which is not always available; individual effort and contribution not recognized.	When teamworking is important and team efforts can be accurately measured and assessed; as an alternative to individual PBR if this is not effective.
Factory-wide bonuses	Bonuses related to plant performance – added value or productivity.	Increase commitment by sharing success.	No direct motivation.	Earnings increased without individual pressure.	Bonuses often small and unpredictable.	As an addition to other forms of incentive when increasing commitment is important.

Rewarding manual workers: six tips

1 Consider scope for single status or harmonization.

2 Ensure that rates of pay for jobs and people are linked to the level of skill or the degree of multiskilling required.

3 If planning to introduce new payment-by-results schemes or amend existing ones, involve employees and their representatives in discussions on what needs to be done and reach agreement on how the changes should be introduced.

4 Consider introducing team pay or gain-sharing.

5 Ensure that payment-by-results schemes are based on work measurement and provide a clear line of sight between effort and reward.

6 Review all existing payment-by-results schemes to ensure that they are functioning properly and are not encouraging wage drift.

References

Binder, A S (1990) *Paying for Productivity*, Brookings Institution, Washington, DC

Guzzo, R A, Jette, R D and Katsell, R A (1985) The Effect of Psychological-Based Intervention Programmes on Worker Productivity: A meta analysis, *Personnel Psychology*, 38, pp 275–91

Lawler, E E (1971) *Pay and Organizational Effectiveness*, McGraw-Hill, New York

Nalbantian, H (1987) *Incentives, Cooperation and Risk Sharing*, Rowman & Littlefield, Totowa, NJ

26
International reward

LEARNING OUTCOMES

On completing this chapter you should be able to define these key concepts. You should also know about:

- The international scene
- International reward strategy
- Convergent or divergent reward policies and practices
- Guiding principles for international reward
- Expatriate pay and allowances

Introduction

International reward management is concerned with two special groups of employees: (1) all those working in foreign or overseas subsidiaries or associated companies and (2) expatriates, nationals of the parent company or another company in the group (third country nationals) who work abroad in another subsidiary. This chapter starts with a review of the international scene, including definitions of what is meant by international and multinational firms and globalization. It then examines reward management policy and practice for the two groups referred to above in turn.

The international scene

The international scene is composed of international and multinational firms working in the context of globalization.

International firms are those in which operations take place in subsidiaries overseas that rely on the business expertise or manufacturing capacity of the parent company. They offer products or services that are rationalized and standardized to enable production or provision to be carried out locally in a cost-efficient way. Perkins and Hendry (1999) stated that international firms seem to be polarizing around two organizational approaches: a) regionalization, where local customer service is important, or b) global business streams that involve setting up centrally controlled business segments that deal with a related range of products worldwide.

Multinational firms are those in which a number of businesses in different countries are managed as a whole from the centre. The degree of autonomy they have will vary and the subsidiaries are not subject to rigid control except over the quality and presentation of the product or service. They rely on the technical know-how of the parent company but usually carry out their own manufacturing, service delivery or distribution activities.

The international scene is linked to the notion of globalization, that is, international economic integration in worldwide markets. This is defined by the International Monetary Fund (1997) as 'the growing economic interdependence of countries worldwide through increasing volume and variety of cross-border transactions in goods and services, freer international capital flows, and more rapid and widespread diffusion of technology'. Globalization is associated with easily transferable technology and reductions in international trade barriers. As Ulrich (1997) pointed out, it requires organizations to move people, ideas, products and information around the world to meet local needs. New and important ingredients must be added to the mix when making business strategy: volatile political situations, contentious global trade issues, fluctuating exchange rates and unfamiliar cultures.

Firms are being forced to react to these issues in their international resourcing and reward approaches by moving more staff between locations to meet their increasingly global businesses' needs and to transfer relevant knowledge and skills. But there are problems in doing this including the growth of dual-career couples and political instability contributing to an apparent greater reluctance to move overseas.

Stephen Perkins (2006) explained that achieving an appropriate balance between global and local requirements in international staffing and rewards has therefore become a much more strategic and challenging issue for HR and reward managers. Major organizations such as BP and The World Bank have overhauled their policies in recent years to achieve their key strategic reward goals of mobility and affordability in this more demanding global context.

Reward management for employees working in international subsidiaries

The following main concerns in global reward management were listed by Baeten and Leuven (2010):

- the extent of centralization or decentralization of reward policies and practices;
- balancing corporate and national cultures;
- the sustainability and span of global reward policies;
- the choice of reward instruments to be included in global reward policies;
- global benchmarking;
- measuring the efficiency of a global reward approach.

Design of international reward systems

The factors that are likely to impact on the design of reward systems, as suggested by Bradley *et al* (1999), are the corporate culture of the multinational enterprise, expatriate and local labour markets, local cultural sensitivities and legal and institutional factors. They refer to the choice that has to be made between on the one hand seeking internal consistency by developing common reward policies in order to facilitate the movement of employees across borders and preserve internal equity, and on the other hand, responding to pressures to conform to local practices. But they point out that studies of cultural differences suggest that reward system design and management needs to be tailored to local values to enhance the performance of overseas operations. Although Sparrow (1999) indicated that differences in international reward are not just a consequence of cultural differences, but also of differences in international influences, national business systems and the role and competence of managers in the sphere of HRM.

International reward strategy

International reward strategy is concerned with the development of an integrated approach to building reward policies and practices across international boundaries. It should be integrated in the sense that it takes into account the business goals and drivers of the parent company while at the same time fitting the strategy to the different contexts and cultures across the globe. The issue of the extent to which the reward strategy should be centralized or decentralized (convergence or divergence) needs to be addressed.

As White (2005) stated: 'Best practice tells us that global rewards must not be considered piecemeal.' He explained that:

> The development of any reward programme calls for an integrated approach whereby each individual element of reward supports the others to reinforce organizational objectives. A global rewards philosophy and total rewards approach can facilitate alignment of an organization's rewards with business strategy, focus employees on the business goals, and reinforce consistent pay practices.

But he also commented that 'different local market practices, regulations and culture are indicators that a one-size-fits-all system will not be truly effective'.

International reward management objectives

Briscoe *et al* (2012) gave the following objectives for a typical multinational enterprise (MNE) global reward programme:

- attraction and retention of the best-qualified talent to staff the MNE in all its locations;
- attraction and retention of employees who are qualified for international assignments;
- facilitation of transfers between different locations within the MNE;
- establishment and maintenance of consistent and reasonable relationships between the pay and benefit of employees at home and abroad;
- maintenance of rewards which are reasonable in relation to the practices of competitors yet minimize costs to the extent possible.

They noted that national and organizational cultures influence how people perceive the value of the various reward available and commented that: 'The culture may be performance driven (and pay for performance is an established norm) or it may be entitlement orientated (with longevity of service rewarded. In some cultures people are more willing to accept risk in their compensation while in others people are quite risk-averse.).'

The convergence or divergence of international reward management policy and practice

White (2005) argued that: 'Global consistency in management's messages to employees, as well as in the reward programs that reinforce these messages is critical in building a cohesive entity that will create shareholder value.'

A consistent approach to international reward management will be developed if a global business strategy exists which encourages similarities in reward management policies and practices amongst MNE subsidiaries. But this might violate local cultural norms or business conditions. International reward management practices are affected by differences in three areas: (1) the labour market where in each country there will be unique labour demand and supply pattern; (2) institutions such as government regulations, tax systems and trade unions and (3) national cultures where, for example, there may be difference in the extent to which financial incentives will affect motivation.

As Yanadori (2011) stated:

> Managing employee compensation in multinational corporations (MNCs) involves carefully balancing two pressures: localization and strategic alignment. On the one hand, the compensation systems in foreign subsidiaries need to be customized to address unique local contexts... On the other hand, MNCs are increasingly interested in establishing, across different subsidiaries, consistent compensation systems that are aligned with their global business strategies.

His research in a multinational finance firm established that different pay rates were adopted to reflect differences in the local labour market.

Research by Baeten and Leuven (2010) in 31 international companies aimed at providing answers to the issue of centralization versus decentralization of compensation policies and systems. It was established that the degree of centralization was very high for senior management (94 per cent), moderate for middle management (54 per cent) and low for operational employees (12 per cent). Decision making on base pay and incentives was centralized for senior managers. In the case of middle managers, it was centralized for some issues such as grading and criteria for pay reviews, but decentralized for others such as pay ranges and actual base pay increases. It was mainly decentralized for operational employees.

There are four levels of convergence as set out in Table 26.1.

TABLE 26.1   Levels of convergence in reward management policy and practice

Level 1: Total convergence	Central reward policies and practices have to be followed by each operating unit in accordance with a set of guiding principles. These may include a standard job evaluation scheme, uniform grade and pay structure (with scope for local market differentiation), a common approach to incentives and a common set of benefits.
Level 2: Partial convergence	Central reward policies are applied in some but not all aspects of reward management. Centralization may be limited to senior management or international staff (expatriates or nationals from countries other than the parent company working in the local country – third country nationals). Reward policies and practices for local nationals are decentralized.
Level 3: Partial divergence	Corporate job evaluation schemes and grade structures are recommended but modification is permitted to fit local conditions. However, all locations are expected to comply with the international guiding principles for reward. There may still be centralized policies for senior managers, expatriates, and third country nationals, and some benefits may be standardized. But pay levels and pay progression and incentive arrangements are determined locally.
Level 4: Total divergence	Local companies have complete freedom to develop and apply their own reward policies and practices, although they may be made aware of the international guiding principles.

Briscoe *et al* (2012) listed the following options for establishing a worldwide reward system:

- Create worldwide salary levels at HQ with differentials for each subsidiary according to their differing costs of living.

- Base pay on local levels (usually excluding executives and globally mobile employees).
- Establish a global base per position where there is a global market for particular occupations or for senior managers and global employees.
- Set up two classifications – local and national – for pay. All local nationals above a certain level are placed on the headquarters scale. The others are paid on a local scale.

International reward management in action

Case study 1 – US-owned MNC

A case study by Almond *et al* (2005) of the pay policies of a large US-owned MNC operating in Europe found that over the years the degree of centralization or decentralization changed frequently. Until the 1980s, corporate HQ had issued a number of global policies which national managers were expected to implement. Some room was given for the policies to be adapted to fit local circumstances but management in subsidiaries had to justify these changes to headquarters.

During the late 1980s, the firm moved away from this highly centralized approach, allowing more scope for subsidiaries to develop policies that suited their own situation. For example, job evaluation systems could be developed independently of the US system. The decentralizing tendency was reversed in the early 1990s, and there has followed a period during which strong coordination of HR policies between countries and central control has been re-established.

Case study 2 – General Motors (GM)

As reported by Mercer Human Resource Consulting (2009) GM moves people round the globe frequently because its products are designed and built on global platforms. The international philosophy of GM was expressed in the mantras 'One GM, one global team' and 'Global perspective: local engagement'.

But different locations were using different level pay structures and job evaluation schemes. A 'leading change' programme involved compensation chiefs around the world. Under the banner of the phrase 'Global compensation takes the approach that what can be should be', the global team:

- analysed the various strategies, structures and practices in place around the world;
- used corporate governance to decide what needed to be global, regional or local;
- identified 'best practices' in compensation to establish a common philosophy, tools and structure for the salaried workforce;
- engaged key stakeholders in the process;
- provided tools, support and education;
- created with the help of Mercer Consultants more than 200 benchmarks in 30 job functions and then slotted them into global salary grades.

Research by Scullion and Starkey (2000)

This research established that in the global companies they analysed, centralized control was reinforced through corporate HR control over the design and management of the rewards system for the top 250 to 400 managers worldwide. Reflecting the more general trend to align HRM with the strategic goals of the organization, senior managerial rewards were aligned not only with short-term divisional or business unit objectives but increasingly with longer-term corporate objectives. A major advantage of a global reward system for top executives over a multi-focal strategy, which reflected a significant reform to international rewards for many organizations, was the aligning of reward strategy with global business strategy.

Rewards for expatriates

As businesses expand globally, they tend to send an increasing number of staff abroad as expatriates. The assignment may be a short-term attachment to provide guidance and expertise, or it may be a secondment to an overseas location that lasts two or three years or is even a permanent appointment. Managing expatriates presents a number of problems: for example, persuading people to work in possibly unpleasant or even dangerous countries, convincing them that an overseas assignment is a good career move, dealing with the issues raised by the partners of employees who do not want their career or life at home disrupted, and coping with the fact that on returning to their home country, expatriates often find that their real earnings have fallen. A particularly difficult problem is that of remuneration (pay, benefits and allowances) and the approaches available to solving it are considered below.

Expatriate remuneration policies

Expatriate remuneration policies may be based on the following propositions:

- Expatriates should not be worse off as a result of working abroad; neither should they be significantly better off for doing essentially the same job, although they may be compensated for the extra demands made overseas or for the living and working conditions there.
- Home-country living standards should be maintained as far as possible.
- Higher responsibility should be reflected in the salary paid (this may be a notional home salary).
- The remuneration package should be competitive.
- In developing the remuneration package, particular care has to be taken to giving proper consideration to the conditions under which the employee will be working abroad.
- Account should be taken of the need to maintain equity as far as possible in remuneration between expatriates, some of whom will be from different countries.

- Account also has to be taken of the problems that may arise when expatriates are paid more than nationals in the country in which they are working who are in similar jobs.
- The package should be cost-effective; in other words, the contribution made by expatriates should justify the total cost of maintaining them abroad – assignment costs can total three or four times the equivalent package in the home country.

Expatriate pay

There are four approaches to calculating expatriate pay: home country, host country, selected country and hybrid.

Home-country basis

The home-based method (sometimes called the balance sheet approach) 'builds up' the salary to be paid to the expatriate in the following steps:

1 Determine the salary that would be paid for the expatriate's job in the home country, net of income tax and National Insurance contributions.

2 Calculate the 'home-country spendable' or 'net disposable' income. This is the portion of income used for day-to-day expenditure at home.

3 Apply a cost of living index to the 'host-country expendable income' to give the equivalent buying power in the host country. This is used as a measure of expenditure levels in the host country and is an important yardstick that is used to ensure that the expatriate will be no worse off abroad than at home.

4 Add extra allowances for working abroad (see below).

This is the most popular approach.

Host-country basis

This involves paying the market rate for the job in the host country. Allowances may be paid for the expenditure incurred by expatriates because they are living abroad, such as second-home costs and children's education.

Selected-country basis

The salary structure in a selected country (often where the company's headquarters are sited) provides the base and this is built up as in the home-country method.

Hybrid basis

This approach divides the expatriate's salary into two components. One – the local component – is the same for all expatriates working in jobs at the same level irrespective of their country of origin. The other local component is based on a calculation of the spendable income in the host country required to maintain a home-country standard of living.

TABLE 26.2 Advantages and disadvantages of the home- and host-based methods of paying expatriates

Method	Advantages	Disadvantages
Home-based	• Ensures that expatriates do not lose out by working abroad. • Easy to communicate to expatriates. • Easier to slot back into home country salary on return. • Particularly appropriate for shorter assignments after which the employee will return home.	• Expatriates may be paid significantly more than local nationals doing the same jobs, thereby causing dissatisfaction and possible friction. • In effect there will be two reward systems in the same country, which can cause confusion.
Host-based	• Avoids the possible dissatisfaction and friction which can arise when expatriates are paid significantly more than local nationals doing the same jobs. • Enables one coherent pay system to be maintained.	• Expatriates might lose out, making it more difficult to persuade people to work abroad. • May be harder to assimilate expatriates back into their own country's pay systems.

Choice of approach

The choice is often between the two most popular approaches – the home- and host-based methods. Their advantages and disadvantages are set out in Table 26.2.

The choice will depend upon the organization's convergence or divergence strategy. To a large extent it also depends on how important it is to encourage people to work overseas for limited-duration assignments, and how much importance is attached to ensuring the motivation and commitment of the host-country staff.

Allowances

Companies add a number of allowances, as described below, to the expatriate's salary to calculate the total expatriate remuneration package. They are designed to compensate for disruption and to make the assignment attractive to the employee. Most are applied to the notional home salary but one of them, the cost of living allowance, is based on spendable income.

- Cost of living allowance: the cost of living allowance is reached by applying an index to the home-country spendable income. The index measures the relative cost, in the host country, of purchasing conventional 'shopping basket' items such as food and clothing.

- Incentive premium: this offers the expatriate a financial inducement to accept the assignment. It may be intended to compensate for disruption to family life. But companies are tending to reduce this premium or do away with it altogether, particularly for intra-European assignments. They are questioning why an employee should receive 10–15 per cent of gross salary for simply moving from one country to a culturally similar one when no such allowance would be payable in the case of a relocation within the UK.
- Hardship allowance: this compensates for discomfort and difficulty in the host country such as an unpleasant climate, health hazards, poor communications, isolation, language difficulties, risk and poor amenities.
- Separation allowance: this may be paid if expatriates cannot take their family abroad.
- Clothing allowance: a payment for special clothing and accessories that expatriates need to buy.
- Relocation allowance: this covers the cost of expenses arising when moving from one country to another.
- Housing/utilities: any additional costs of accommodation or utilities.

Benefits

The benefits provided to expatriates include cars, the costs of educating children, home leave, rest and recuperation leave if the expatriate is working in a high-hardship territory.

International reward: six tips

1 Decide on the extent to which you want international reward policies to be uniformly based on those in headquarters or varied in different countries (a convergence or divergence policy).

2 If the policy is inclined to convergence, decide what elements of corporate reward policy and practice you want to be applied internationally.

3 If the policy is inclined to divergence, decide what guiding principles, if any, you wish to be adopted in overseas territories.

4 Take steps to ensure that managements in overseas territories are capable of applying the central policies or following the guidelines, and monitor how these policies and guidelines are implemented.

5 Evaluate the advantages and disadvantages of each method of rewarding expatriates in different countries and decide on the most appropriate method.

6 Remember that important aspects of the total reward package for expatriates will be their working environment, the existence of family-friendly policies, career opportunities abroad and when they return and the existence of satisfactory re-entry policies (job placement and career choice).

References

Almond, P, Edwards, T, Colling, T, Ferner, A, Gunnigle, P, Müller-Camen, M, Quintanilla, J and Wächter, H (2005) Unravelling Home and Host Country Effects: An investigation of the HR policies of an American multinational in four European countries, *Industrial Relations*, **44** (2), pp 276–306

Baeten, X and Leuven, V (2010) Global Compensation and Benefits Management: The need for communication and coordination, *Compensation & Benefits Review*, **42** (3), pp 392–402

Bradley, P, Hendry, C and Perkins, P (1999) Global or Multi-Local? The significance of international values in reward strategy, in *International HRM: Contemporary issues in Europe*, eds C Brewster and H Harris, Routledge, London

Briscoe, D, Schuler, R and Tarique, I (2012) *International Human Resource Management*, 4th edn, Routledge, New York

International Monetary Fund (1997) *World Economic Outlook*, IMF, Washington, DC

Mercer Human Resource Consulting (2009) *A Whole New World*, Mercer, New York

Perkins, S (2006) *Guide to International Reward and Recognition*, CIPD, London

Perkins, S and Hendry, C (1999) *The IPD Guide on International Reward and Recognition*, IPD, London

Scullion, H and Starkey, K (2000) In Search of the Changing Role of the Corporate Human Resource Function in the International Firm, *The International Journal of Human Resource Management*, 11 (6), pp 1061–81

Sparrow, P R (1999) *The IPD Guide on International Recruitment, Selection and Assessment*, IPD, London

Ulrich, D (1997) *Human Resource Champions*, Harvard Business School Press, Boston, MA

White, R (2005) A Strategic Approach to Building a Consistent Global Rewards Program, *Compensation & Benefits Review*, July/August, pp 23–40

Yanadori, Y (2011) Paying Both Globally and Locally: An examination of the compensation management of a US multinational finance firm in the Asia pacific region, *The International Journal of Human Resource Management*, **22** (18), pp 3867–87

PART FIVE
Employee benefits

27
Provision of employee benefits

LEARNING OUTCOMES

On completing this chapter you should be able to define these key concepts. You should also know about:

- The meaning of employee benefits
- The rationale for employee benefits
- Employee benefits strategies and policies
- Types of employee benefits
- Choice of benefits
- Administering benefits
- Total reward statements

Introduction

Employee benefits consist of arrangements made by employers for their employees that enhance the latter's well-being. They are provided in addition to pay and form important parts of the total reward package. As part of total remuneration, they may be deferred or contingent, like a pension scheme, insurance cover or sick pay, or they may be immediate, like a company car or a loan. Employee benefits also include holidays and leave arrangements, which are not strictly remuneration. Benefits are sometimes referred to dismissively as 'perks' (perquisites) or 'fringe benefits', but when they cater for personal security or personal needs they could hardly be described as unimportant.

Employee benefits are a costly part of the remuneration package. They can amount to a third or more of basic pay costs and therefore have to be planned and managed with care.

Note that many benefits such as company cars, interest-free loans, private medical insurance, and prizes, gifts and vouchers can be taxed quite heavily. It is worth seeking advice from a tax specialist if in any doubt.

Rationale for employee benefits

Employee benefits provide for the personal needs of employees and they are a means of increasing their commitment to the organization and demonstrating that their employers care for their well-being. Not all employers care but, like the ones that do, they still provide benefits to ensure that the total remuneration package is competitive. And some benefits, such as maternity leave, have to be provided by law in the UK.

Employee benefit strategies and policies

Employee benefit strategies will be concerned in general terms with what the organization wants to do about the range and scale of benefits it provides and the costs it is prepared to incur. The strategy forms the foundation for the formulation of employee benefit policies.

Employee benefit policies deal with:

- the types of benefits to be provided, taking into account their value to employees, their cost and the need to make the benefit package competitive;
- the size of the benefits;
- pensions arrangements;
- the need to harmonize benefits;
- the total costs of benefits provision in relation to the costs of basic pay;
- the use of flexible benefits, as described in Chapter 28.

Types of benefit

The main benefits are pensions, personal security, financial assistance, personal needs, holidays, company cars, other benefits, voluntary benefits and concierge services as described below.

Pensions

Pensions offer an income to employees when they retire and to their surviving dependants on the death of the employee, and deferred benefits to employees who leave. Occupational schemes offered by organizations, as distinct from state pensions, are funded by contributions from the organization and usually, but not always, the employee. Occupational pensions are the most significant employee benefit and are a valuable part of the total reward package. But they are perhaps the most complex part. Pensions are provided because they demonstrate that the organization is a good employer concerned about the long-term interests of its employees who want the security provided by a reasonable pension when they retire. Good pension schemes help to attract and retain high-quality people by maintaining competitive levels of total remuneration. The two main types of occupational pension schemes are described below.

Defined contribution schemes

The main features of a defined contribution scheme (formerly known as a money purchase scheme) are:

- Pension entitlement. The employee receives a pension on retirement that is related to the size of the fund accumulated by the combined contributions of the employee and employer. The amount of the pension depends on the size of contributions, the rate of return on the investment of the accumulated fund and the rate of return on an annuity purchased by the employer. It is not related to the employee's final salary.
- Contributions. The employer contributes a defined percentage of earnings, which may be fixed, age related or linked to what the employee pays. The employee also contributes a fixed percentage of salary.
- Dependants. Receive death in service and death in retirement pensions.
- Lump sum. One-quarter of the pension can be taken as a tax-free lump sum on retirement.

Defined benefit schemes

The main features of a defined benefit scheme are:

- Pension entitlement. On retiring the employee is entitled to a pension that is calculated as a fraction of their final salary (on retirement or an average of the last two or three years) or their average earnings multiplied by the length of pensionable service. The maximum proportion of salary allowed by Inland Revenue and Customs is two-thirds of final salary after 40 years' service. In a final salary scheme (the most typical) the accrual rate refers to the fraction of final salary that can be earned per year of service. When a pension is described as 1/60th it means that 40 years' service would produce a two-thirds of final salary pension.
- Employer and employee contributions. Employer contributions can be a fixed percentage of salary. Alternatively the percentage increases with service or is a multiple of the employee's contribution (eg the employer contributes 15 per cent if the employee contributes 5 per cent).

- Dependants. Entitled to a percentage of the employee's pension entitlement if he or she dies during retirement or in service with the company.
- Lump sum. Part of the pension may be exchanged for a tax-free lump sum.

Comparison of defined contribution and defined benefits schemes

The main differences are that a defined contribution scheme provides an uncertain pension and the cost to the employer is predictable while a defined benefits scheme provides a guaranteed pension to the employee but the employer is unable to predict the costs.

Changes in occupational pensions provision

Because of the cost implications employers in the private sector have rapidly replaced defined benefit schemes with defined contribution ones. The CIPD 2013 reward survey established that 55 per cent of pension schemes were defined contribution (a decline from the figure of 63 per cent in 2012) and 28 per cent defined benefit but that in manufacturing and production and private sector services the proportions of defined contribution schemes were only 10 and 4 per cent respectively. The proportion of defined benefits schemes in the public sector was 74 per cent although the government is taking steps to reduce the costs involved.

State pension arrangements

State pension arrangements are subject to change, and this section is based on the current (2015) arrangements. The State Pension Scheme has two parts:

The Basic State Pension. This is paid at a standard rate, which may be increased each year.

The State Second Pension. The State Second Pension (also known as the State Additional Pension) pays a pension on earnings for which Class 1 National Insurance contributions have been paid over the years that fall between the lower and the upper earnings limit. The lower earnings limit corresponds roughly with the flat-rate pension for a single person while the upper limit is currently about eight times the lower earning limit. Both limits are adjusted from time to time.

Employers and individuals with a personal pension plan can contract out of the State Second Pension. Occupational pension schemes can contract out if they meet an overall quality test. When a scheme is contracted out, both the employer and the employee pay National Insurance contributions at a lower rate.

Auto-enrolment

The Workplace Pension Reform Regulations of 2010 provided for auto-enrolment into workplace pension schemes, from which an individual would need to actively opt out, to build private saving. This was combined with a minimum employer contribution, and the creation of a pension scheme – now known as the National Employment Savings Trust (NEST) – that could be used by any employer.

Stakeholder pension

A stakeholder pension is a government-sponsored scheme, primarily designed for lower-paid employees. It is a low-cost personal pension scheme regulated by the government and provided through pension companies. Employers who employ five or more staff and do not provide a suitable occupational pension scheme for their employees are required by law to offer access to a stakeholder scheme and deduct and pass on employee contributions to the scheme. But employers do not have to make contributions themselves.

Advising employees on pensions

The Financial Services Act 1986 and the Pensions Act 1995 place restrictions on the provision of financial advice to employees. Only those who are directly authorized by one of the regulatory organizations or professional bodies are permitted to give detailed financial advice on investments. Specific advice on the merits or otherwise of a particular personal pension plan – personal pensions are classed as investments by the Financial Services Act – can, however, be given to employees:

- On the company's occupational pension scheme, since it is not classed as an investment.
- About the general principles to be borne in mind when comparing an occupational pension scheme with a personal pension; these could include spelling out the benefits of the company's scheme, thus leaving employees in a better position to compare the benefits with whatever an authorized adviser may indicate are the benefits from a personal plan. What should not be done is to tell people categorically that they will be better off with the company's scheme or to advise them to look elsewhere.
- On their rights, for staff who are leaving, to preserve their pension and the advisability of finding out from their prospective employer whether existing rights can be transferred to their scheme and, if so, what the outcome will be in terms of pension rights at the new company.
- On the general advantages of making additional voluntary contributions.
- HR specialists should restrict themselves to giving factual information. They should never suggest what people should do. If in any doubt as to how to respond to a request for information or advice, it is best to refer the matter to the company's own pension specialist or adviser or, if none is available, suggest that the employee should talk to an authorized adviser, for example the individual's own insurance company or bank.

Personal security

Personal security benefits include:

- Health care: the provision through medical insurance of private health care to cover the cost of private hospital treatment (permanent health insurance), making periodic health screening available and, sometimes, dental insurance.

- Insurance cover: for death in service (if not already provided in a pension scheme), personal accident and business travel.
- Sick pay: providing full pay for a given period of sickness and a proportion of pay (typically half pay for a further period). Sick pay entitlement is usually service related. Sick pay can be costly unless attendance management and control practices are introduced.
- Redundancy pay: additions can be made to the statutory redundancy pay, including extra notice compensation, extra service-related payments (eg one month per year of service) and ex gratia payments to directors and executives in compensation for loss of office (sometimes called golden handshakes).
- Career counselling (outplacement advice) can be provided by specialist consultants to employees who have been made redundant.

Financial assistance

Financial assistance can take the following forms:

- Company loans: interest-free modest loans, or low interest on more substantial loans, which are usually earmarked for specific purposes such as home improvements.
- Season ticket loans: interest-free loans for annual season tickets.
- Mortgage assistance: subsidized interest payments on mortgages up to a given price threshold. This benefit is most likely to be provided by financial services companies.
- Relocation packages: for staff who are being relocated by the organization or recruited from elsewhere, the costs of removal and legal/estate agents' fees may be refunded.
- Fees to professional bodies: eg the CIPD.

Personal needs

Employee benefits satisfying personal needs include:

- maternity and paternity leave and pay above the statutory minimum;
- leave for personal reasons;
- childcare through workplace nurseries or vouchers;
- pre-retirement counselling;
- personal counselling through employee assistance programmes;
- sports and social facilities;
- company discounts, whereby employees can buy the products or services offered by the company at a reduced price;
- retail vouchers to buy goods at chain stores.

Holidays

Before the European Working Time Directive in 1998, there was no statutory obligation to offer any paid holiday except for the standard 'bank' holidays. Employers are now obliged to offer a minimum of 20 days' paid holiday per year, including bank holidays.

In practice, many organizations in the UK give four or five weeks' holiday. UK organizations are obliged by statute to provide paid maternal and paternal leave and unpaid family leave.

Company cars

Although the tax liability for individuals with company status cars has been increasing steadily, they still remain one of the most valued perks, perhaps because people do not have to make a capital outlay, do not lose money through depreciation and are spared the worry and expense of maintenance.

Other benefits

Other benefits include free car parking, Christmas parties and tea/coffee/cold drinks.

Voluntary (affinity) benefits

Voluntary benefit schemes provide opportunities for employees to buy goods or services at discounted prices. The employer negotiates deals with the providers but the scheme does not cost them anything.

Popular voluntary benefits include:

- Health: private medical insurance, dental insurance, health screening.
- Protection: critical illness insurance, life insurance, income protection insurance, personal accident insurance.
- Leisure: holidays, days out, travel insurance, computer leasing, bicycle leasing, pet insurance, gym membership.
- Home: household goods, online shopping.

Concierge services

Concierge services can include dealing with home and car repair and maintenance, financial services, buying presents, restaurant reservations, theatre tickets and travel arrangements. They originated in the United States in response to the long-hours culture that limited personal time away from the workplace. Businesses benefit from providing these services because they enable staff to concentrate on their jobs by freeing them from mundane personal tasks such as waiting at home for deliveries or getting their cars serviced.

Incidence of benefits

The proportion of respondents to the 2012 CIPD reward management survey providing the following benefits were:

- 25 days' paid leave: 65 per cent;
- childcare vouchers: 62 per cent;
- life insurance: 48 per cent;
- an employee assistance programme: 42 per cent;
- enhanced maternity/paternity leave: 43 per cent;
- cycle to work loan scheme: 38 per cent.

Choice of benefits

Some benefits, such as holidays, maternity leave and redundancy pay, have to be provided by statute – there is no choice except on the extent to which statutory provisions may be enhanced. Neither, for a responsible employer, is there any real choice over the provision of pensions, life insurance or sick pay. Company cars for executives are still popular in spite of the tax penalties because of the felt need to be competitive.

Some optional benefits such as health insurance, childcare and low-interest loans may be selected because they will be appreciated and because they help to make the reward package competitive.

The factors affecting the choice of provision or scale will be:

- what employees want, as established by opinion surveys;
- what other employers are providing, as established by market surveys;
- what the organization can afford.

Flexible benefit schemes give employees a choice within limits of the type or scale of benefits offered to them by their employers.

Administering employee benefits

Employee benefits can be expensive and it is necessary to monitor the costs of providing them and the extent to which a cost–benefit comparison justifies continuing with them on the present scale or at all. There should be a budget for employee benefit costs and expenditure should be monitored against it. Regular surveys should be undertaken of the attitude of employees to the benefits package. They may suggest where benefit expenditure could be redirected to areas where it would be more appreciated. They may also suggest that there is a need to adopt a flexible benefit policy, as described in the next chapter.

Total reward statements

Total reward statements communicate to employees the value of the employee benefits such as pensions, holidays, company cars, free car parking and subsidized meals they receive in addition to their pay. They also describe any other rewards they get, such as learning and development opportunities. The aim is to ensure that they appreciate the total value of their reward package. Too often, people are unaware of what they obtain in addition to their pay. Table 27.1 shows how a total reward statement can be set out.

TABLE 27.1 Example of total reward statement

Total reward statement		
Pay	Basic annual salary	£30,000
	Bonus	£3,000
	Total	£33,000
Employee benefits	Retirement, life insurance and ill-health	£5,000
	Holidays	£1,000
	Other fringe benefits (subsidized meals, employee assistance programme, concierge service, voluntary benefits, staff discount, free car parking)	£2,000
	Total	£8,000
Total remuneration		£41,000
Other rewards/benefits	Learning and development programmes Further education assistance Flexible hours Additional maternity/paternity leave	

> ### Employee benefits: six tips
>
> 1 Review the benefit package regularly to establish that the benefits provided are desirable and cost-effective, that they are appreciated and that they are administered efficiently.
>
> 2 Survey employees to find out what they think of the benefits package and what they think it should look like.
>
> 3 Ensure that the benefits package reflects good practice as established by benchmarking.
>
> 4 Ensure that the benefits package is competitive and enhances the reputation of the business as a good employer.
>
> 5 Ensure that employees appreciate the value of the benefits they receive by issuing total reward statements.
>
> 6 Consider giving employees the opportunity to choose their benefits through a flexible benefits scheme.

References

CIPD (2012) *Survey of Reward Management*, CIPD, London
CIPD (2013) *Survey of Reward Management*, CIPD, London

28
Flexible benefits

LEARNING OUTCOMES

On completing this chapter you should know about:

- The meaning of flexible benefits
- Reasons for introducing flexible benefits
- Types of flexible benefit schemes
- Salary sacrifice
- How to introduce flexible benefits

Introduction

Flexible benefit schemes give employees a choice within limits of the type or scale of benefits offered to them by their employers. As described in this chapter, there are a number of varieties of flexible benefit schemes as well as the increasingly popular salary sacrifice system.

Interest in such schemes has been generated because employee benefits are not all equally wanted or appreciated by the staff that receive them and, from the employer's point of view, some benefits will not therefore provide value for money. The number of employers who have introduced formal flexible schemes is growing – it was only 13 per cent of the respondents to the CIPD 2008 Reward Management Survey but by 2013 the proportion had increased to 34 per cent. In this chapter the reasons for introducing flexible benefits are set out, the different types of flexible benefit schemes are defined and the steps required to introduce a scheme are explained.

Reasons for introducing flexible benefits

Flexible benefit schemes may be introduced in order to:

- meet the diverse needs of employees and increase the perceived value of the package to them – enabling them, to a degree, to decide for themselves what benefits they want and the size of particular benefits to suit their own lifestyle rather than being forced to accept what their employers think is good for them;
- enable employers to get better value for money from their benefits expenditure because it meets the needs and wants of employees;
- control costs by providing employees with a fund to spend rather than promising a particular level of benefits;
- aid recruitment and retention – as flexible benefits are generally preferred by employees to fixed benefits of equivalent value;
- help to harmonize terms and conditions in a merger.

Types of flexible benefits schemes

The main types of schemes are described below.

Flex individual benefits

Employees are given the opportunity to vary the size of individual benefits, paying extra if they want more or receiving cash if they want less. A typical example is a flexible car scheme that enables people to pay more for a better model or, if they decide to downsize, receive the reduction in cost to the company in cash. Choices are made on recruitment or when the car is replaced.

Another common arrangement is to provide scope, within limits, to buy or sell holiday time over the holiday year; for example, so many extra days could be bought at the daily rate of the employee or so many could be sold and the amount at the daily rate added to pay.

This is a simple approach that is easy to introduce and administer and is therefore the most common method of flexing benefits. The disadvantage is that the impact may be limited.

Flex existing entitlement

Employees may choose to increase, decrease or end their current benefits and select new benefits from the menu provided. The value of the benefits bought and sold is then aggregated and the net amount added to or deducted from pay. An example of how this might look for an employee whose annual salary is £30,000 is shown in Table 28.1.

TABLE 28.1   Example of variation around existing entitlement

Benefit	Standard entitlement	Selected entitlement	Monthly cost saving (or extra cost)
Holidays	25 days	22 days	£35
Car	Lease cost £300 per month	£240 per month	£60
Company pension contribution	10% of salary	10% of salary	Nil
Private medical insurance	Cover for self	Cover for self, partner and child	(£45)
Dental insurance	Nil	Nil	Nil
Childcare vouchers	Nil	£200 per month	(£200)
Total monthly adjustment			(£150)

This arrangement can be simplified by making only two or three benefits flexible. The rules often stipulate that such essential core benefits as pensions and life insurance cannot be reduced, and limits may be placed on the scope for flexing other benefits, for example holidays.

Flex fund

Employees are allocated a fund of money to spend on benefits from a menu. This is therefore sometimes described as the cafeteria approach. Certain core compulsory benefits such as pensions and life insurance have to be maintained. The value of the flex fund is big enough to enable individual employees to buy their existing benefits and thus retain them without additional cost.

A simplified example of a flex fund benefits-choice menu for someone with a salary of £30,000 with a flex fund of £12,000 is shown in Table 28.2. The impact of the choices made is shown in Table 28.3.

TABLE 28.2   Example of flex fund benefits-choice menu

Benefit	Minimum choice	Maximum choice	Price
Holidays	20 days	30 days	0.4% of salary per day
Lease car	£300 per month (£3,600 per annum)	£500 per month (£6,000 per annum)	Annual lease times 1.25 (to allow for insurance and maintenance)
Company pension contribution	5% of salary	15% of salary	Face value less 10%*
Private medical insurance	Cover for self only	Cover for self, partner and children	£500 each per adult. £200 for one or more children
Dental insurance	n/a	Level 3 cover for self, partner and children	£40, £100, £180 per individual for Level 1, 2 or 3 cover, respectively
Childcare vouchers	n/a	20% of salary	Face value less 5%*

* The adjustment reflects the fact that Employer NICs are not payable on these benefits. The adjustment for childcare vouchers is lower to allow for the charge payable to the provider.

Any overspend would be funded by salary sacrifice. In this example, where less than £12,000 has been spent, the unspent flex fund would be paid as a monthly, non-consolidated cash sum.

Most schemes show each of the benefits with a cash value and the employee uses this as the basis for calculating the effect of their choices. Other schemes use a points plan, where each benefit has a points rating and the employee has an allowance of a certain number of points.

The advantage of showing a cash value is that it gives employees an idea of what the benefit is truly worth and the cost that the employer is bearing. The danger of a cash system is that it may encourage employees to feel that they are being forced to buy benefits out of their own salary.

Whether or not a points or a cash value scheme is used, schemes make a clear distinction between notional or reference salary and the final value of salary that is actually paid in the year including benefit allowances (regardless of whether this is higher or lower than the notional salary). The notional salary continues to be used as the basis for items such as pension calculations and salary reviews.

TABLE 28.3 Example of impact of flex fund choices made (shown in Table 28.2)

Benefit	Choice	Cost
Holidays	25 days	£3,000
Lease car	£350 per month	£5,250
Company pension contribution	10% of salary	£3,000
Private medical insurance	Cover for self and partner	£1,000
Dental insurance	Level 2 cover for self and partner	£200
Childcare vouchers	Nil	Nil
Total		£11,400
Flex fund		£12,000
Under (over) spend		£600

Salary sacrifice

Salary sacrifice provides employees with benefits such as childcare vouchers and additional annual leave in return for employees agreeing to a reduction of their contractual salary. It is advantageous for both employees and employers as it saves each of them National Insurance contributions. It can also reduce employees' income tax liabilities. It has become a popular alternative to a fully-fledged flexible benefit scheme such as one of those described earlier.

Introducing flexible benefits

The steps required to introduce flexible benefits are:

1 *Define business need*: the benefits in terms of meeting the diverse needs of employees, helping recruitment and retention and getting better value for money from expenditure on employee benefits.

2 *Seek views*: conduct an opinion survey of employees on what they think of present benefit arrangements, what they think about flexible benefits and what benefits they would like to be eligible for flex (this could be accompanied by information about how flexible benefits might work, and would therefore be the first shot in a communications campaign – communicating about flexible benefits is important).

3 *Decide objectives and essential elements*: the objectives of the scheme should be determined and its essential elements defined. This will include broadly the extent to which it is believed that the approach should be to go for a full scheme based either on flexing existing benefits or a flex fund, or whether the approach should be to flex individual benefits. There may be something to be said for starting with the latter, simpler approach (which will be cheaper to install) with the possibility of extending it at a later stage when experience has shown that it is working well. The strategy should also explore the need for outside advice and, on the basis of initial discussions with potential advisers, how much would need to be spent on developing and maintaining the scheme. One of the common objections to flexible benefits is the cost of administration, especially when the proposed scheme is a fairly complex one and outside professional advice and support are required. Preliminary decisions need to be made at this stage on the likelihood that such advice will be required so that the costs involved can be estimated. It is also necessary to decide on the need for a project team with employee involvement.

4 *Set up project team*: this could be a joint management/employee team (involvement is very desirable) with the responsibility of planning and overseeing the development programme.

5 *Decide who is going to carry out the development work*: someone from within the organization should be in charge of the project, with help as required and available from flexible benefit, finance, tax and pensions specialists. The development of a scheme requires considerable expertise in these areas in developing and costing schemes, exploring tax considerations and setting up the administration.

6 *Design scheme*: this involves deciding on core benefits, which will have to be maintained, identifying benefits that can be flexed and any limits on the extent to which these benefits can be flexed, costing the benefits as necessary to enable menus to be produced and flex funds set up, if appropriate, and considering how the scheme should be administered. Simple schemes can be administered on paper but there is software available to administer more elaborate ones. An intranet can be used to help with administration – employees can make their choice of benefits from the screen and calculate the financial implications.

7 *Communicate details of the scheme*: employees need to be given detailed but easily understood information about the proposed scheme – how it will work, how it will affect them, its advantages, and how and when it will be introduced.

8 *Pilot test*: there is much to be said for piloting the scheme in a part of the organization to test reactions and administrative arrangements.

9 *Introduce scheme*: the earlier communications need to be reinforced generally at this stage and arrangements must be made to provide individual employees with advice through personal contact, a helpline or a help screen on the intranet.

10 *Evaluate scheme*: monitor and measure impact.

Flexible benefits: six tips

1   Define business need for flexible benefits.

2   Obtain views of employees about their benefits and the degree to which they would like them to be flexed.

3   Decide on essential elements of the scheme: core benefits which have to be maintained, benefits that can be flexed and limits on the extent to which these benefits can be flexed, and costing the benefits as necessary to enable menus to be produced and flex funds set up, if appropriate.

4   Decide how the scheme should be administered and develop administrative systems.

5   Communicate to staff how the flexible benefits scheme works and its advantages for them.

6   Provide for advice to employees as required.

References

CIPD (2008) *Reward Management Survey*, CIPD, London
CIPD (2013) *Reward Management Survey*, CIPD, London

PART SIX
The practice of reward management

29
Evidence-based reward management

LEARNING OUTCOMES

On completing this chapter you should be able to define these key concepts. You should also know about:

- Evidence-based management
- Evidence-based reward management
- Reviewing reward
- Measuring reward
- Evaluating reward
- Developing and implementing reward systems

Introduction

Evidence-based reward is an approach to reward management based on facts and measurements rather than supposition. It follows the principles of evidence-based management as explained in the first part of this chapter. The chapter continues with a description of the concept of evidence-based reward management and the processes involved, namely: reviewing, measuring and evaluating. The approaches described in this chapter inform the process of developing reward systems as covered in Chapter 2.

Evidence-based management

Evidence-based management uses information derived from the analysis of the messages delivered by relevant research, systematic benchmarking and surveys of current practice and the evaluation of the impact of HR and reward practices. This informs decisions on innovations and improvements to HR and reward policy and practice.

Briner *et al* (2009) defined evidence-based management as follows:

> Evidence-based management is about making decisions through the conscientious, explicit and judicious use of four sources of information: practitioner expertise and judgment, evidence from the local context, a critical evaluation of the best research evidence and the perspectives of those people who might be affected by the decision.

They listed four points, which summed up the essence of evidence-based management:

1 Evidence-based management is something practitioners do (or do not do).
2 Evidence-based management represents a family of approaches.
3 Academics are needed to provide input.
4 Managers need to fully understand how to conduct and use systematic reviews.

Evidence-based reward management

Evidence-based reward management uses the information obtained from internal and external surveys and the measurement and evaluation of reward practices for two purposes: (1) to review, measure and evaluate the operation of the reward system as described in the next three sections of this chapter, and (2) to provide guidance on the development and implementation of new or improved reward practices in accordance with defined reward goals and success criteria as described in the last section of the chapter.

Internally, it gathers data on the impact of reward strategies and the effectiveness of the innovations resulting from them. The aim is to improve the reward strategy formulation and implementation process in order to ensure that rewards more effectively support the achievement of organization goals and meet employee needs. It deals with issues relating to organizational performance and processes such as valuing and pricing jobs, contingent pay, base pay management (the design and management of grade and pay structures), the provision of employee benefits and the administration of rewards. It is concerned with the non-financial elements of reward, which comprise the total reward package. Importantly, it involves seeking the views of stakeholders.

Externally, it carries out systematic benchmarking of good reward practices and analyses and makes use of the practical outcomes of reward research projects. Evidence-based reward management provides the information and impetus which make an integrated approach to reward management effective.

Evidence-based reward management is the management of reward systems based on fact rather than opinion, on understanding rather than assumptions, on grounded

FIGURE 29.1 A model of evidence-based reward management

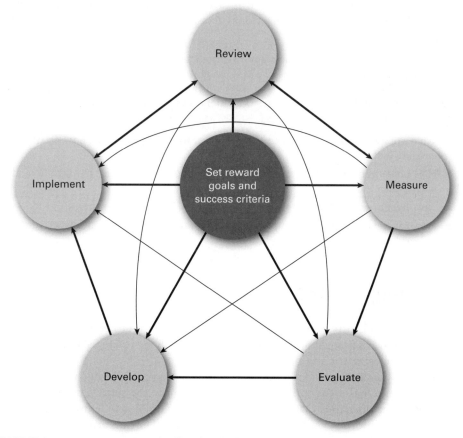

SOURCE: Armstrong, M, Brown, D and Reilly, P (2010) *Evidence-Based Reward Management*, London, Kogan Page

theory rather than dogma. It makes use of the process of surveys, measurement and evaluation, which lead to the development and implementation of reward systems as modelled in Figure 29.1 and described in the rest of this chapter.

As pointed out by Armstrong *et al* (2010), this model appears to describe a sequential progress in the form of a continuous cycle from goal setting, through review, measurement, evaluation, and development activities to implementation and further review. This can happen in some circumstances but the components are not necessarily specified, or defined and managed in an orderly sequence. They are closely interlinked and they may overlap. Goal setting affects all the other components. Similarly, those concerned with review, measurement and evaluation, ie the fundamental aspects of evidence-based reward management, can take place at any time (or all at once) and all of them directly influence the ultimate activities of development and implementation.

The model illustrates the complex and varied ways in which evidence-based reward management works. It is in accordance with the view of evidence-based management expressed by Briner *et al* (2009) that it is 'a family of practices, not a single rigid formulaic method of making organizational decisions'. But as Armstrong *et al* (2010) contended:

> Even in the messiest and most reactive of situations an approach, which makes appropriate use of these components, will be helpful. Using them appropriately means applying and linking the components in ways which fit the demands of the situation. It becomes a way of thinking that reward practitioners can apply to any situation or issue by asking themselves:

- What are we trying to do here, what's important to this organization, how do we measure that?
- How are current reward practices helping or hindering what we are trying to do and what evidence do we have of this?
- How might reward changes improve the delivery of the desired outcomes?
- How can we best implement improvements and how can we show ourselves that they are working?

Reviewing reward

Reward reviews identify and assess what is being done about reward; internally in the shape of reward policies and practices and externally by reference to evidence on reward and wider trends and developments.

Reward reviews should be conducted within a framework which sets out the internal and external areas to be covered, explains how the success criteria will be used, defines the questions that the review needs to address, and helps to categorize and analyse the information emerging from the review. They involve:

- researching and gathering both quantitative and qualitative information and evidence on existing reward policies and practices from inside the organization;
- gathering information on external reward practices, levels and trends; this can be used to assess the competitiveness and distinctiveness of rewards in the organization, as well as drawing out learning from relevant organizations externally, and from external research on specific reward practices;
- using this information to make assessments of the effectiveness of the delivery of reward goals and of the various pay and reward practices;
- thereby agreeing key reward issues to address;
- considering possible options and changes to improve the delivery of the reward goals, and their strengths and weaknesses relative to the current reward practices;
- agreeing the optimum rewards changes and improvements for the future to improve effectiveness and planning their implementation.

The information and evidence to make this reward assessment typically come from both internal and external sources. A reward checklist is set out in Table 29.1.

TABLE 29.1 Checklist: reward arrangements

Reward area	Points to be covered
Reward strategy	• Is there a recognized reward strategy linked to the organization's goals and employee needs?
Total reward	• What steps have been taken to install and maintain a total reward approach?
Job evaluation	• What job evaluation approach is in place? • Does it facilitate the design and management of an equitable pay structure? • Is it in line with the organization's values? • Is there any evidence that the scheme has decayed, eg by allowing grade drift?
Equal pay	• Has an equal pay survey been carried out? • Is the organization vulnerable to an equal pay claim?
Base pay management	• Are pay levels competitive? • What type of grade and pay structures does the organization have for different groups? • Are the structures appropriate to the business's culture and organization and the different groups? • Is the structure flexible enough to cater for different needs? • Are there too many grades or levels? • What is the distribution of pay in different grades? To what extent does this conform to policy guidelines? • What is the amount of pay dispersion? Is it justified? • Is there sufficient scope for pay progression? • Is the structure reasonably easy to manage?
Performance management	• Is there an effective system of performance management?
Pay progression	• What is the basis for pay progression within the structure, eg performance or service? • Do pay progression arrangements vary for different employee groups? If so, how? • Are the arrangements for pay progression for different groups fair, equitable, consistent and transparent?

TABLE 29.1   *continued*

Reward area	Points to be covered
Bonuses	• What bonus schemes are in place for different groups? • To what extent do the schemes fairly and appropriately reward achievement and effort?
Employee benefits and pensions	• What benefits are provided for different groups and are they appropriate? • What are the pension arrangements and what changes, if any, are required or contemplated? • Is there a flexible benefits scheme? If so, how does it work and what is the take-up? • Are employees aware of the value of their total remuneration?
Pay reviews	• How are pay reviews (general and individual) conducted and how well run are they?
Communications	• How well are reward policies and practices communicated to employees?
Reward evaluation	• Is any attempt made to evaluate reward? If so, how?
Value for money	• What evidence is there that the organization is getting value for money from its reward practices?

Measuring reward

The purpose of measuring reward is to collect, record, analyse and interpret data as a basis for evaluating the effectiveness of reward policy and practice and for informing reward development decisions. The process of measurement involves:

- setting reward goals and success criteria, linked in to the business and HR strategy and vision, deciding what improvement is wanted and where it is essential and deciding whether reward measurement needs to be part of a wider human capital management exercise;
- specifying and gathering the relevant information, or putting processes in place to gather it;
- analysing, monitoring and drawing conclusions from that information;
- taking action and making changes to improve effectiveness, which may well be improvements to the effectiveness measures as well as the reward practices themselves.

The measures of effectiveness

Research conducted by Armstrong *et al* (2011) revealed the variety of effectiveness measures being used, from organization to organization and also from year to year; there was a fair degree of consistency in some of the main ones employed. Corby *et al* (2005) classified them into the categories of cost outcomes, HR outcomes and business performance outcomes. Another common classification is in terms of strategic business and financial measures, measures of employee satisfaction and measures of external comparability.

A list of commonly used measures under different assessment headings is set out in Table 29.2.

TABLE 29.2   Commonly used reward measures

Assessment area	Measures
Productivity, performance and reward costs	• Productivity per employee • Profit, value added or sales per employee • Trends in performance appraisal ratings • Total pay and reward costs compared to competition
Financial rewards	• Return on investments in contingent pay • Surveyed contingent pay scheme satisfaction rates
Employment	• Employee turnover rates • Employee absence rates • Retention (survival rates) of high-performance/key-skill staff • Ratio of job offers/acceptances • Time taken to fill vacancies • Proportion of vacancies filled by people who fully meet the specification
Reward management general	• Actual market position compared to policy market stance • Take up and level of activity in flexible rewards • Reduction in gender pay gap following equal pay reviews
Engagement and satisfaction with rewards	• Trends in surveyed overall employee engagement levels • Trends in surveyed employee satisfaction with rewards • Employee opinions that rewards are competitive • Employee opinions that performance is rewarded and managed effectively • Manager opinions that reward arrangements meet their needs

SOURCE: Armstrong, M, Brown, D and Reilly, P (2010) *Evidence-Based Reward Management*, London, Kogan Page

Attitude surveys

Perhaps one of the most valuable measures of reward effectiveness, and also one which is most likely to reveal the need for action, is an employee attitude survey. An example is set out in Table 29.3.

TABLE 29.3   Reward attitude survey

Please state the extent to which you agree or disagree with the following statements by placing a circle around the number which most closely matches your opinion.

	Strongly agree	Agree	Disagree	Strongly disagree
My contribution is adequately rewarded	1	2	3	4
Pay increases are handled fairly	1	2	3	4
I feel that my pay does not reflect my performance	1	2	3	4
My pay compares favourably with what I could get elsewhere	1	2	3	4
I am not paid fairly in comparison with other people doing similar work in the organization	1	2	3	4
I think the organization's pay policy is overdue for a review	1	2	3	4
Grading decisions are made fairly	1	2	3	4
I am not clear how decisions about my pay are made	1	2	3	4
I understand how my job has been graded	1	2	3	4
I get good feedback on my performance	1	2	3	4
I am clear about what I am expected to achieve	1	2	3	4

TABLE 29.3 *continued*

	Strongly agree	Agree	Disagree	Strongly disagree
I like my job	1	2	3	4
The performance pay scheme encourages better performance	1	2	3	4
I am proud to work for the organization	1	2	3	4
I understand how my pay can progress	1	2	3	4
The job evaluation scheme works fairly	1	2	3	4
The benefits package compares well with those in other organizations	1	2	3	4
I would like more choice about the benefits I receive	1	2	3	4
I feel motivated after my performance review meeting	1	2	3	4
I do not understand the pay policies of the organization	1	2	3	4

Evaluating reward

To produce the evidence required to develop and improve the reward system, it is important to evaluate reward. This involves the use of reviews, measurements and other evaluating tools such as checklists to determine (1) the extent to which the reward system as a whole or parts of it are functioning effectively and (2) the impact made by reward – the ultimate measure of effectiveness.

Reward system effectiveness

The criteria for judging the effectiveness of a reward management system are the extent to which it:

- is fit for purpose – the contribution it makes to achieving organizational objectives and recognizing the needs and wants of stakeholders;
- is appropriate – it fits the culture and context of the organization;

- is designed in accord with what is generally regarded as good practice in the particular context of the organization, subject to the requirement that it must be appropriate;
- functions in line with well-defined guiding principles which include the need to achieve fairness, equity, consistency and transparency in operating the reward system;
- includes processes for valuing and grading jobs and rewarding people according to their performance or contribution which are properly conceived and function well;
- maintains competitive and equitable rates of pay;
- incorporates successfully a total rewards approach;
- manages reward processes carefully and obtains value for money;
- provides for the evaluation of reward processes and taking corrective action as necessary;
- communicates to all concerned how the reward system operates and how it affects them;
- provides for the devolution of a reasonable degree of authority to line managers to make reward decisions, taking steps to ensure that they have the skills and support required and that their decisions are in line with reward policy guidelines.

Evaluating the impact of reward

The e-reward (2010a) survey on reward effectiveness elicited a variety of reasons why those who evaluated the impact of reward did so. One respondent advised that it was essential to establish a direct link between reward spend and benefit to the organization. Another respondent wondered why a company spending thousands or millions of pounds on reward wouldn't try to understand the effect of such a large investment. Some respondents simply maintained that every organization needs to know what is going on and should 'give it a try', while others said that it at least provides a starting point to build from. Another respondent made the point that the process helps highlight the links between rewards and business performance and once this is clear, particularly for others in the organization, much progress can be made. As a respondent explained: 'By building on a reward evaluation process, a company gains more tools to improve understanding of what is going on in order to enhance its contextual as well as empirical analysis capabilities.'

The e-reward research revealed that the organizations most likely to conduct comprehensive reward evaluations were those in which a powerful tradition of human capital measurement existed, such as an international bank, or those with a highly disciplined and performance-orientated approach to measurement, such as a restaurant chain where, as the compensation and benefits manager put it: 'If it moves, we measure it.'

The criteria used by the respondents to the e-reward (2010b) survey who evaluated reward effectiveness are given in Table 29.4.

TABLE 29.4   Criteria for evaluating reward effectiveness used by survey respondents

Criteria	Proportion using
Employee attitudes	75%
Analysis of pay market positioning	72%
Employee turnover	62%
Assessment against reward strategy objectives	42%
Financial costs	41%
Business financial performance	40%
Impact on employee performance/productivity	30%
Length of service	29%
Absenteeism	29%
Other business metrics, eg sales; customer service	27%
Vacancy rates	26%
Job retention rates	12%

The following advice on reward evaluation was given by a head of reward interviewed during the e-reward research:

1 The best starting point before setting any targets or measuring anything is to decide what the organization wants to achieve.

2 Once this has been decided, you should use as much data as you can and benchmark this against the market, before deciding where the company should be positioned.

3 Take care when interpreting data such as high staff satisfaction scores and other perception-related measures – they could simply be reflecting generous, rather than effective, rewards.

4 In some cases evaluation is not necessary – it is plain to see when certain elements of the reward system are working or not.

5 It is your job to place evidence in context and try to interpret what is really happening and why.

6 Some of the reward evaluation software packages available, although clever, tend only to use quantitative measures, so they don't take account of some of the other factors that might be at work. This is where you come in – to interpret and make sense of the grey as well as black and white areas.

Conclusions

The key message of this chapter was well-expressed by Reay *et al* (2009) as 'evidence before action'. This means adopting an evidence-based reward management approach which involves:

- setting reward strategy goals and defining success criteria;
- conducting a review of current reward policies and practices against these criteria, using both general research and situation-specific evidence in the organization and identifying key issues and problems to address;
- measuring the impact of those reward policies and practices;
- evaluating the effectiveness of the reward policies and practices by reference to the measures and success criteria.

These survey, measurement and evaluation activities provide the basis for considering and agreeing reward system alternatives and changes to address issues, and designing, testing, modelling and preparing to implement new and improved reward practices as described in the next chapter.

References

Armstrong, M, Brown, D and Reilly, P (2010) *Evidence-Based Reward Management*, Kogan Page, London

Armstrong, M, Brown, D and Reilly, P (2011) Increasing the Effectiveness of Reward Management: An evidence-based approach, *Employee Relations*, **33** (1) pp 106–20

Briner, R B, Denyer, D and Rousseau, D M (2009) Evidence-Based Management: Concept clean-up time? *Academy of Management Perspectives*, September, pp 19–32

Corby, S, White, G and Stanworth, C (2005) No News is Good News? Evaluating new pay systems, *Human Resource Management Journal*, **15** (1), pp 4–24

e-reward (2010a) *Survey of Reward Effectiveness*, e-reward [online] www.e-reward.co.uk [accessed 20 July 2015]

e-reward (2010b) *Evaluating Reward Effectiveness*, e-reward [online] www.e-reward.co.uk [accessed 20 July 2015]

Reay, T, Berta, W and Kohn, M K (2009) What's the Evidence on Evidence-Based Management? *Academy of Management Perspectives*, November, pp 5–18

30
Managing reward systems

LEARNING OUTCOMES

On completing this chapter you should be able to define these key concepts. You should also know about:

- Reward forecasting
- Reward budgets
- Compa-ratio analysis
- Attrition analysis
- Assessing added value

- Conducting general pay reviews
- Conducting individual pay reviews
- Reward procedures
- Computer-assisted reward
- Communicating to employees

Introduction

Reward management involves the management of complex systems. As explained in this chapter, this is a demanding task requiring the formulation and implementation of policies, control, monitoring and evaluation, pay reviews, procedures, using computers and communicating to employees. The starting point is a clear set of policies as described in Chapter 4.

Controlling reward

Affordability is a potent word for many managements. In reward management it means getting value for money – not spending more on pay and benefits than the organization can afford and ensuring that reward practices add value rather than simply consuming scarce financial resources which could be better deployed elsewhere.

The implementation of reward policies and procedures should be monitored and controlled to ensure that value for money is obtained. Control is easier if the grade and pay structure is well defined and clear guidelines exist on how it and the benefits arrangements should be managed. It is particularly necessary to control pay reviews by reference to budgets on the proportion of the payroll, say 3 per cent, that can be allocated for increments or bonuses. It is also essential to review any proposed changes to reward practice to ensure that they will add value.

Control should be based on forecasts, budgets and costings, as described below, and by monitoring and evaluating the implementation of reward policies as discussed in the next part of this chapter.

Reward forecasts

It is necessary to forecast future payroll costs taking into account the number of people employed and the impact of pay reviews and contingent pay awards. The cost implications of developments such as a revised job evaluation scheme, a new grade and pay structure or a flexible benefits scheme also have to be forecast.

Total payroll budgets

Total payroll budgets are based on the number of people employed in different jobs and their present and forecast rates of pay. In a budgetary control system payroll budgets may be aggregated from the budgets prepared by departmental managers who will be provided with guidelines on any increases allowed. The aim is to provide a basis for controlling payroll costs by monitoring actual costs against budgeted costs.

Pay review budgets

Pay review budgets set out the increase in payroll costs that will result from either general or individual pay reviews and are used as the basis for the guidelines issued to line managers on conducting individual reviews and for controlling how much is allocated for pay increases. A pay review budget creates what is sometimes called a pot from which payments are funded. The budget may be expressed as the percentage increase allowable in departmental and total payroll costs, for example 3 per cent.

Costing reward processes

Proposed changes to the reward system need to be costed for approval by senior management. The costs would include development costs such as consultants' fees, software, literature and additional staff.

Implementation costs also have to be projected. A new grade and pay structure, for example, can easily result in an increase to the payroll of 3 to 4 per cent. New contingent pay schemes may also cost more, although the aim should be to make them self-financing.

Monitoring and evaluating reward policies and practices

The effectiveness of reward policies and practices should be monitored and evaluated against the requirements of the organization. Monitoring is carried out through compa-ratio analysis associated with mid-point management techniques, attrition analysis, assessing added value and the use of attitude surveys. Evaluation, as described in more detail in Chapter 29, should compare outcomes with the objectives set for the new practice (this is why setting objectives for reward initiatives is so important).

Compa-ratio analysis

A compa-ratio (short for comparative ratio) measures the relationship in a graded pay structure between actual and policy rates of pay as a percentage. The policy value used is the mid-point or reference point in a pay range, which represents the target rate for a fully competent individual in any job in the grade. This point is aligned with market rates in accordance with the organization's market stance (its policy on the relationship between its levels of pay and market rates).

Compa-ratios can be used to define the extent to which pay policy is achieved (the relationship between the policy and actual rates of pay). Compa-ratios are calculated as follows:

$$\frac{\text{actual rate of pay}}{\text{mid or reference point of range}} \times 100$$

A compa-ratio of 100 per cent means that actual pay and policy pay are the same. Compa-ratios that are higher or lower than 100 per cent mean that, respectively, pay is above or below the policy target rate. Compa-ratios establish differences between policy and practice. The reasons for such differences need to be established.

Compa-ratios can also be used to measure where an individual is placed in a pay range, and therefore provide information on the size of pay increases when a pay matrix is used, as described later in this chapter.

Mid-point management

Mid-point management involves the use of compa-ratios to show the extent to which the distribution of pay for people in the grades of a grade and pay structure deviate from the mid-point when this is regarded as the target rate or policy level. If compa-ratios are too high or too low compared with the policy level an indication is given that action may be necessary to slow down or accelerate increases.

For example, if the target (policy) rate in a range were £20,000 and the average pay of all the individuals in the grade were £18,000, the compa-ratio would be 90 per cent.

Analysing attrition

Attrition or slippage takes place when employees enter jobs at lower rates of pay than the previous incumbents. If this happens payroll costs will go down, given an even flow of starters and leavers and a consistent approach to the determination of rates of pay. In theory attrition can help to finance pay increases within a range. It has been claimed that fixed incremental systems can be entirely self-financing because of attrition, but the conditions under which this can happen are so exceptional that it probably never happens.

Attrition can be calculated by the formula: total percentage increase to payroll arising from general or individual pay increases minus total percentage increase in average rates of pay. If it can be proved that attrition is going to take place, the amount involved can be taken into account as a means of at least partly financing individual pay increases. Attrition in a pay system with regular progression through ranges and a fairly even flow of starters and leavers is typically between 2 per cent and 3 per cent, but this should not be regarded as a norm.

Assessing added value

Assessing the added value or value for money provided by existing practices, or by new practices when they are implemented, is a major consideration when monitoring and evaluating reward management processes. Evaluating the cost of innovations may lead to the reconsideration of proposals in order to ensure that they will provide added value. Evaluating the value for money obtained from existing reward practices leads to the identification of areas for improvement.

Affordability should be a major issue when reviewing reward management developments and existing practices. Added value is achieved when the benefits of a reward practice either exceed its cost or at least justify the cost. At the development stage it is therefore necessary to carry out cost–benefit assessments. The two fundamental questions to be answered are: (1) 'What business needs will this proposal meet?' and (2) 'How will the proposal meet the needs?' The costs and benefits of existing practices should also be assessed on the same basis.

Attitude surveys

An attitude survey is a valuable means of evaluating and monitoring reward practices by assessing the views of those at the receiving end of pay policies as a basis for taking action. An example of a reward attitude survey was given in Chapter 29.

Conducting pay reviews

Pay reviews are general or 'across-the-board' reviews in response to movements in the cost of living or market rates, or following pay negotiations with trade unions, or individual reviews that determine the pay progression of individuals in relation to their performance or contribution. They are one of the most visible aspects of reward management (the other is job grading) and are an important means of implementing the organization's reward policies and demonstrating to employees how these policies operate.

Employees expect that general reviews will maintain the purchasing power of their pay by compensating for increases in the cost of living. They will want their levels of pay to be competitive with what they could earn elsewhere. And they will want to be rewarded fairly and equitably for the contribution they make.

General reviews

General reviews take place when employees are given an increase in response to general market rate movements, increases in the cost of living, or union negotiations. They are often combined with individual reviews but employees are usually informed of both the general and individual components of any increase they receive. Alternatively the general review may be conducted separately to enable better control to be achieved over costs and to focus employees' attention on the performance-related aspect of their remuneration.

Some organizations have completely abandoned the use of across-the-board reviews. They argue that the decision on what people should be paid should be an individual matter, taking into account the personal contribution people are making and their market worth – how they as individuals are valued in the marketplace. This enables the organization to adopt a more flexible approach to allocating pay increases in accordance with the perceived value of individuals to the organization.

1 Decide on the budget.

2 Analyse data on pay settlements made by comparable organizations and rates of inflation.

3 Conduct negotiations with trade unions as required.

4 Calculate costs.

5 Adjust the pay structure – either by increasing the pay brackets of each grade by the percentage general increase, or by increasing pay reference points by the overall percentage and applying different increases to the upper or lower limits of the bracket, thus altering the shape of the structure.

6 Inform employees.

Individual reviews

Individual pay reviews determine merit pay increases or bonuses. The e-reward 2009 survey of contingent pay found that the average size of the pay awards made by respondents was 3.5 per cent (it was 3.3 per cent in 2004). Individual awards may be based on ratings; an overall assessment that does not depend on ratings or ranking as discussed below.

Individual pay reviews based on ratings

Managers propose increases on the basis of their performance management ratings within a given pay review budget and in accordance with pay review guidelines. Eighty per cent of the respondents to the e-reward 2009 survey of contingent pay used ratings to inform merit pay decisions.

There is a choice of methods. The simplest way is to have a direct link between the rating and the pay increase; for example:

Rating	Percentage increase
A	6
B	4
C	3
D	2
E	0

This approach was used by 36 per cent of the respondents to the e-reward 2009 survey.

A more sophisticated approach is to use a pay matrix, as illustrated in Figure 17.2 in Chapter 17. This indicates the percentage increase payable for different performance ratings according to the position of the individual's pay in the pay range (the compa-ratio). This approach was used by 41 per cent of the respondents to the e-reward 2009 survey.

Linking pay reviews to performance reviews

Many people argue that linking performance management too explicitly to pay pre-judices the essential developmental nature of performance management. One solution to this problem is to decouple performance management and the pay review by holding them several months apart, and 47 per cent of the respondents to the e-reward 2009 survey did this. There is still a read-across but it is not so immediate. Some try to do without formulaic approaches (ratings and pay matrices) altogether, although it is impossible to dissociate merit pay completely from some form of assessment.

Doing without ratings

Twenty per cent of the respondents to the 2009 e-reward survey of contingent pay did without ratings. One respondent to the e-reward survey explained that in the absence of ratings, the approach used was described as informed subjectivity, which meant considering ongoing performance in the form of overall contribution.

Some companies adopted what might be called a holistic method. Managers proposed where people should be placed in the pay range for their grade, taking into account their contribution and pay relative to others in similar jobs, their potential and the relationship of their current pay to market rates. The decision may be expressed in the form of a statement that an individual is now worth £30,000 rather than £28,000. The increase is 7 per cent, but what counts is the overall view about the value of a person to the organization, not the percentage increase to that person's pay.

Ranking

Ranking is carried out by managers who place staff in a rank order according to an overall assessment of relative contribution or merit and then distribute performance ratings through the rank order. The top 10 per cent could get an A rating, the next 15 per cent a B rating and so on. The ratings determine the size of the reward. A forced ranking or so-called vitality curve system may be used to compel managers to conform to predetermined proportions of staff in each grade. But ranking depends on fair, consistent and equitable assessments, which cannot be guaranteed, and assumes that there is some sort of standard distribution of ability across the organization, which may not be the case.

Guidelines to managers on conducting individual pay reviews

Whichever approach is adopted, guidelines have to be issued to managers on how they should conduct reviews. These guidelines will stipulate that they must keep within their budgets and may indicate the maximum and minimum increases that can be awarded with an indication of how awards could be distributed. For example, when the budget is 4 per cent overall, it might be suggested that a 3 per cent increase should be given to the majority of staff and the others given higher or lower increases as long as the total percentage increase does not exceed the budget. Managers in some companies are instructed that they must follow a forced pattern of distribution (a forced choice system) but only 8 per cent of the respondents to the 2003 CIPD survey (Armstrong and Baron, 2004) used this method. To help them to explore alternatives, managers may be provided with a spreadsheet facility in which the spreadsheets contain details of the existing rates of staff and can be used to model alternative distributions on a 'what if' basis. Managers may also be encouraged to fine-tune their pay recommendations to ensure that individuals are on the right track within their grade according to their level of performance, competence and time in the job compared with their peers. To do this, they need guidelines on typical rates of progression in relation to performance, skill or competence, and specific guidance on what they can and should do. They also need information on the relative positions of their staff in the pay structure in relation to the policy guidelines.

Conducting individual pay reviews

Steps required to conduct individual pay reviews

1 Agree budget.

2 Prepare and issue guidelines on the size, range and distribution of awards and on methods of conducting the review.

3 Provide advice and support.

4 Review proposals against budget and guidelines and agree modifications to them if necessary.

5 Summarize and cost proposals and obtain approval.

6 Update payroll.

7 Inform employees.

A description of how a company makes individual pay decisions is given below.

Making pay decisions in a finance sector company

We look at a number of things when making a decision on an individual's pay. One will be the size of the role as determined by job evaluation, and we also consider market data and location to determine the average salary that you would expect to pay for that role. We then look at how the individual has performed over the last 12 months: Have they contributed what was expected of them? Have they contributed above and beyond their peers? Have they underperformed in respect of what was required of them? These are not ratings, they are just guidelines given to managers as to whether the individual should be given an average, above-average or below-average increase. We have a devolved budget and managers have to make decisions as to what percentage they should give to different people. We suggest that if, for example, a manager has six people carrying out the same roles then, from an equal pay point of view, if they are delivering at the same level and are all competent, they should be getting similar salaries. Individuals paid below the market rate who are performing effectively may get a bigger pay rise to bring them nearer the market rate for the role.

It is essential to provide advice, guidance and training to line managers as required. Some managers will be confident and capable from the start. Others will have a lot to learn.

Reward procedures

Reward procedures deal with grading jobs, fixing rates of pay and handling appeals.

Grading jobs

The procedures for grading jobs set out how job evaluation should be used to grade a new job or regrade an existing one. A point-factor evaluation scheme that has defined grades may be used for all new jobs and to deal with requests for regrading. However, an analytical matching process (see Chapter 14) may be used to compare the role profiles of the jobs to be graded with grade or level profiles or profiles of benchmark jobs.

Fixing rates of pay on appointment

The procedure should indicate how much freedom line managers and HR have to pay above the minimum rate for the job. The freedom may be limited to, say, 10 per cent above the minimum or two or three pay points on an incremental scale. More scope is sometimes allowed to respond to market rate pressures or to attract particularly well-qualified staff by paying up to the reference point or target salary in a pay range, subject to HR approval and bearing in mind the need to provide scope for contingent pay increases. If recruitment supplements or premiums are used the rules for offering them to candidates must be clearly defined.

Promotion increases

The procedure will indicate what is regarded as a meaningful increase on promotion, often 10 per cent or more. To avoid creating anomalies, the level of pay has to take account of what other people are paid who are carrying out work at a similar level, and it is usual to lay down a maximum level that does not take the pay of the promoted employee above the reference point for the new range.

Appeals

It is customary to include the right to appeal against gradings as part of a job evaluation procedure. Appeals against pay decisions are usually made through the organization's grievance procedure.

The use of computers in reward management

The ever-evolving world of IT and electronic communications has changed quite radically the way salary data is reviewed and managed in the last decade. Applications and data can now be accessed and assessed from almost anywhere in the world; organizations are making increasing use of the internet, data on market rates and pay settlements is published on the internet and users can communicate at speed through e-mail. Computers and the software are becoming more and more powerful and sophisticated. HR or reward specialists can analyse the implications of new grade structures, cost pay review matrices and plan salary reviews, and options can rapidly be costed through simple changes on a spreadsheet. Self-serve systems enable line management to carry out a number of reward tasks such as pay reviews. Increasing use is being made of computers to support reward administration and decision making in the areas of:

- providing a reward database;
- job evaluation;
- grade and pay structure modelling;
- pay review modelling;
- equal pay reviews.

The reward database

The reward database stores data on employees' pay, earnings and benefits so that it can be updated, processed and communicated as information to users. It consists of systematically organized and interrelated sets of files (collections of records serving as the basic unit of data storage) and allows for combinations of data to be selected as required by different users. The database contains information imported from the payroll or personnel information system. This information may include personal and job details, job grade, basic pay, position in the pay range (compa-ratio), earnings through variable pay, pay history (progression, and general and individual pay increases), performance management ratings, details of employee benefits, pension contributions, contributions to Save as You Earn schemes and the choices made under a flexible benefits system, including pension contributions.

The database can be used, for example, to:

- Produce listings of employees by job category, job grade, rate of pay, position in range and size in actual or percentage terms of the last increase and, if required, previous individual performance pay increases.

- Generate reports analysing distributions of pay by grade, including compa-ratios for each grade and the organization as a whole. Extracts from these reports can be downloaded to the personal computers of managers responsible for pay decisions to assist them in conducting pay reviews.

- Initiate and print notifications of pay increases and update the payroll database.

- Use electronic mail facilities to transmit data.

In using the database it is necessary that the provisions of the Data Protection Act 1998 are met. Among other things, this requires that personal data held for any purpose should not be used or disclosed in any manner incompatible with that purpose, and appropriate security measures must be taken against unauthorized access to or disclosure of those data. If data is going to be downloaded it will be essential to control who gets what. The importance of data protection will also have to be spelt out to managers.

Computer-aided job evaluation

Computers can be used to help directly with job evaluation processes, as described in Chapter 14.

Software packages

Micro-based software packages have been developed to carry out the various processes referred to above. Proprietary software is usually designed as a standard software shell within which there are a number of functions that allow users to customize the system to meet their own needs.

Grade and pay structure modelling

Software packages use the output from a computerized job evaluation exercise contained in the database to model alternative grade structures by reference to the distribution of points scores against the existing pay rates for the jobs covered by job evaluation. The computer produces a scattergram and a trend line showing the relationship between pay and the job evaluation scores. The programme will then enable a proposed grade structure to be superimposed on the scattergram, identifying those jobs above or below the new grade boundaries. The cost of bringing the pay of those below the new boundaries to the minimum rate for their new grades is then calculated by the computer.

Alternative grade configurations can then be superimposed on the scattergram to find out if the number of jobs below the lower limits of their new grades will be reduced. The computer then calculates the lower costs of bringing the fewer jobs which are now below the minimum up to the minimum. This modelling process can continue until the optimum configuration of grades from the point of view of costs is achieved. A decision can then be made about whether this grade structure or one of the others should be selected. The lowest-cost option would not necessarily be chosen as it might produce an unmanageable grade structure, for example having too few grades with too much scope for pay progression within them.

Pay review modelling

General reviews

The computer can use the database to provide information on the total cost of a proposed general pay review and the effect this will have on other costs, for example pensions. The program can then model alternative levels. Computers can model the effect on costs of alternative increases.

Individual reviews

It is now increasingly typical to manage pay reviews for an organization on a spreadsheet, through which a number of alternative options can be tested. Spreadsheets provide line managers with a worksheet, divided into cells, into which can be inserted text, numbers or formulas. This allows the user to carry out complex 'what if' analyses of the impact on the pay review budget of alternative distributions of awards to staff. Analyses can be saved as a separate file for future recall when the proposals are approved. Spreadsheets can be printed out in report or graphical form. In some organizations, line managers carry out the modelling themselves using a spreadsheet with data provided by HR, and their conclusions can be reviewed and approved and aggregated into an overall cost of the review analysed by departments. In others, HR and reward specialists carry out salary reviews for each function or department with the relevant line managers on site, using a laptop.

The problem with spreadsheets is that they can be quite complex and do not always work well in larger applications. Software such as the pay modellers marketed by a number of consultants may be the answer to these problems.

Equal pay reviews

Software is available to support equal pay reviews and analyses. These range from database tools that enable data to be imported from a range of sources to generate pay gap analyses to more sophisticated tools that allow for a broader range of analysis possibilities using different data cuts.

Communicating to employees

Transparency is important. Employees need to know how reward policies will affect them and how pay and grading decisions have been made. They need to be convinced that the system is fair. They should also be given information on the value of their total reward package. But bear in mind that as Erickson (2004) pointed out: 'Employees won't hear unless they feel they're being listened to – no matter how professionally you handle top-down communications.'

Communicating to employees collectively

Employees and their representatives should be informed about the guiding principles and policies that underpin the reward system and the reward strategies that drive it. They should understand the grade and pay structure, how grading decisions are made, including the job evaluation system, how their pay can progress within the structure, the basis upon which contingent pay increases are determined and policies on the provision of benefits, including details of a flexible benefits scheme if one is available.

Communicating to individual employees

Individual employees should understand how their grade, present rate of pay and pay increases have been determined, and the pay opportunities available to them – the scope for pay progression and how their contribution will be assessed through performance management. They should be informed of the value of the benefits they receive so that they are aware of their total remuneration and, if appropriate, how they can exercise choice over the range or scale of their benefits through a flexible benefits scheme.

As many means as possible should be used to communicate to employees. Possible methods include:

- individual briefings;
- team briefings;
- road shows and open days;
- intranet, including bulletin boards;
- social media;
- newsletters;

- individual letters to employees' home addresses;
- meetings, Q&A sessions, focus groups;
- demonstrations with computer modelling;
- telephone and e-mail helplines;
- one-to-one consultations.

References

Armstrong, M and Baron, A (2004) *Performance Management: Action and impact*, CIPD, London

Equality and Equal Opportunities Commission (2011) Code of Practice on Equal Pay, *Equality and Equal Opportunities Commission* [online] www.equalityhumanrights.com/uploaded_files/EqualityAct/equalpaycode.pdf [accessed 1 January 2012]

e-reward (2004) Survey of Contingent Pay, *e-reward* [online] www.e-reward.co.uk [accessed 20 July 2015]

e-reward (2007) Survey of Grade and Pay Structures, *e-reward* [online] www.e-reward.co.uk [accessed 20 July 2015]

e-reward (2009) Survey of Contingent Pay, *e-reward* [online] www.e-reward.co.uk [accessed 20 July 2015]

Erickson, W (2004) *Connecting Engagement with Reward*, address at the Society for Human Resource Management's Annual Conference, New York

31
Managing reward risk

KEY CONCEPTS AND TERMS

- Moral hazard
- Risk
- Risk management

LEARNING OUTCOMES

On completing this chapter you should be able to define these key concepts. You should also know about:

- Risk management
- Types of risks
- Reward management risks
- The risk management process

Introduction

Risk is inherent in every business activity. Expectations are not realized. Decisions have unintended consequences. Plans go astray. Unforeseen events and costs occur. Reputations suffer.

Activities associated with reward management are not exempt. In fact, they are particularly prone to risk. This chapter starts with a definition of what is involved in risk management generally. It continues with an analysis of the areas of reward management that are subject to risk. Finally the processes that can be used to manage reward risk are explained.

Risk management

Risk has been defined by the Association of Insurance and Risk Managers (2002) as 'the combination of the probability of an event and its consequences'. Risk management is the process of identifying, assessing and managing the uncertainties that impact on an organization's ability to achieve its aims and objectives. It is the basis for informed management. It is about evaluating the risks involved in investments and innovation and in taking steps to prevent things going wrong. It deals with business, financial, marketing and operational risks, the risks involved in developing and implementing new products and systems and the risks related to environmental, compliance and ethical issues.

But as noted by the CIPD (2009):

> Good risk management is not a barrier to risk-taking activity. Risk taking is at the heart of all organizational activity and crucial if organizations are to innovate and develop. The failure to take opportunities that arise from change is a huge risk in itself. Risk management is as much about this as it is about avoiding problems. Effective risk management ensures that this risk taking is carried out as a conscious activity. Judgements need to be made about the appropriateness of the risk taking in line with organizational objectives at that time.

Reward management risks

A survey in 2011 by the CIPD of reward risks as perceived by respondents from 361 UK organizations found that risks connected with reward implementation and change management predominated. The other key reward risks identified by the CIPD research included those concerned with operations, employee behaviour, financial outcomes, legislation and the organization's reputation. The research also revealed that the majority of respondents were concerned about their ability to manage the range of reward risks they identified.

Reward system development risks

The introduction of a new or substantially revised reward system is a risky business. The strategic intent may be clear, the design may be based on what is assumed to be best practice, but things go wrong when it comes to implementation. As Trevor (2011) put it: 'What is desired (approach), and what is intended (design), may not be reflected in what is achieved (operation).'

The main risk is that of spending considerable time, effort and money only to find that the initiative does not achieve objectives such as improving performance, enhancing engagement or helping to attract and retain talented people. The possible reasons for failure are manifold. But the overriding cause is that insufficient attention has been paid to managing the risks involved. These include inappropriate or poor design, resistance to change, the inability or unwillingness of line managers to play their essential part in implementation, the inability of line managers and employees generally to understand the new system, especially, as often happens, if it has been over-engineered, a lack of skill and determination on the part of reward specialists, the costs of implementation compared with the resulting benefits and the absence of adequate supporting processes such as performance management. A further common reason for failure is precipitant implementation, which takes place when the proposed innovation has not been tested properly to identify any problems that might be met.

To deal with development risks it is necessary generally to assess the extent to which the initiative will add value rather than create work. A value-added approach means that processes and schemes will not be introduced or updated without determining the effect they are expected to have on the engagement and performance of people, on the ability of the organization to recruit and keep the right sort of employees and, ultimately, on the results achieved by the organization.

Specifically, the process of developing and implementing reward systems should be evidence-based, realistic about risks, costs and what can be achieved, focused on how it will be put into effect (easier if the watchword is 'keep it simple'), pilot tested, and positive about involving stakeholders and communicating information to them on proposals and plans and how they will be affected by them.

An example of how a large private sector organization addressed reward development risk is set out in Table 31.1.

TABLE 31.1   Analysing and addressing the issues and risks when changing a reward system

Issues and risks	How we address them
Plethora and over-complexity of different reward schemes and practices emerge, damaging cohesion and mobility.	Common principles and frameworks for all aspects of reward. Simple but effective and appropriate design.
Implementation problems.	Design with implementation in mind. Pilot testing. Phased approach to implementation.
New arrangements not communicated or managed as intended.	Extensive preparation. Investment in communications and management training.
Hostile employee/trade union reaction.	Involve in design. Plan and implement a change management programme.
Availability and quality of relevant market data.	Source from a variety of quality providers.
Timing and cost overruns.	Effective project management and phasing.

Operational risks

Operational risks occur when the reward system doesn't deliver. This can happen in a number of ways. It may be because there are faults in the system, which were created when it was developed and were not corrected during implementation. These faults could make it difficult to understand, manage and control reward policies and practices. Poor execution can also arise because line managers are ill-equipped to manage reward or fail to understand reward policies, or because the HR or reward function handles reward matters badly. The effective operation of reward processes is not helped if employees do not understand how their reward package is constructed or resent the fact that they were not involved in its design and feel that it has been imposed upon them. Employees may fail to appreciate the value of the total rewards package they receive.

There are a number of specific risks that can be incurred in running a reward system. The job evaluation scheme may have decayed, leading to unjustified upgradings (grade drift), which create inequities and therefore resentment and also incur unnecessary costs. Benchmark data on market rates may be inaccurate, leading to the establishment of inappropriate pay levels and structures and therefore increasing payroll costs by overpaying people or inhibiting the ability of the organization to attract and retain talent by underpaying them. Performance or variable pay arrangements may have fallen into disrepute and fail to motivate because of perceived lack of fairness in making awards or because rewards are not distributed to people in accordance with their merit. There is the risk that the number of people who are demotivated because they do not get the reward they think they deserve will exceed the number who are motivated.

Behavioural risks

There is a risk that performance pay or bonus schemes will lead to inappropriate behaviours. For example, they can create a moral hazard, ie an incentive to act inappropriately in pursuit of a high-performance pay award or bonus. They can encourage the pursuit of short-term gains or engagement in unduly risky enterprises at the expense of longer-term and sustained success, provide rewards for failure and result in selfish individualism rather than teamwork.

Financial risks

There are three types of financial risks, which singly or in combination can mean that the reward system is unaffordable or that the organization is getting poor value for money. First, the costs of developing and implementing new or substantially revised reward practices may be underestimated. Second, there is the risk that the operation of a reward system will fail to add value because it generates costs which are not justified by the benefits it provides. Third, the procedures for controlling reward budgets and costs may be inadequate.

Development and implementation costs can include the direct cost of consultancy advice, which can all too easily exceed the budget if the project takes longer than anticipated, as it often does. Direct costs may also be incurred if additional reward or HR staff are employed who may have to be paid more than the expected rate. Indirect costs can arise because of the opportunity costs involved in seconding HR staff and other employees to a development team which spends more time on the project than was planned.

There is the risk of underestimating the almost inevitable cost of introducing a new grade and pay structure. This arises because while the pay of those who are overgraded will not be reduced, at least in the short term, the pay of those who are undergraded will have to be increased immediately or phased over two or at most three years. Respondents to the e-reward 2004 survey who had introduced new structures reported that the average proportion of employees who were overpaid was 4.9 per cent and the proportion of those underpaid was 13.2 per cent. Their costs of dealing with underpaid staff averaged just over 2 per cent of payroll and were as high as 8 per cent. It is prudent to assume that there is the risk of an increase to payroll costs of 3–4 per cent unless specific action is taken to control it.

The initial costs of operating a new merit or variable pay scheme can also be underestimated.

Pension and employee benefits schemes provide further sources of financial risk. There is a risk that pension costs are not managed and become unaffordable, involving the possibility of huge deficits in the pension fund. There is a risk that value for money will not be obtained from employee benefits because employees do not appreciate them or because inappropriate or unwanted benefits are provided.

Legal and compliance risks

Legal and compliance risks consist of potential liabilities under employment legislation. This particularly applies to equal pay where in the UK there is a real risk, especially in public sector organizations, that a lot of time may have to be spent in contesting equal pay claims and if they are lost, which they frequently are, the costs are considerable. It is advisable to take steps to minimize equal pay risks by, for example, conducting an equal pay review, ensuring that the job evaluation scheme and base pay management processes are free of bias, and providing equal opportunities for female staff.

Reputational risks

There are risks to the reputation of the company if its reward practices conflict with what is generally accepted as ethical behaviour. This is especially the case with executive bonuses and, to a lesser degree, the amount of dispersion between the pay of the chief executive and the average earnings of employees.

The risk management process

As described by Armstrong and Cummins (2011) the risk management process takes place in the following steps:

1 Develop a framework for managing risk: managing risk is easier if there is clarity about who is involved in risk management decisions, if there is a commonly held understanding about the level of risk that an organization is prepared to tolerate and if a process is set up to integrate risk management into established project and management processes. Risk identification is a subjective process, so it helps to get group input at a sufficient level of seniority to draw on colleagues' combined knowledge and experiences, and to have authority to take actions.

2 Identify risks: establish the nature and extent of significant risks. An evidence-based management approach can be used to obtain information available from research and through benchmarking on the level of risks associated, for example, with the introduction of a new pay structure or a merit pay scheme. Surveys of the views of managers and other employees about reward can reveal risky situations.

3 Assess risks: categorize the risks and then establish the likelihood of those risks turning to reality and what impact they might have.

4 Control risks: decide how to deal with the identified risks.

5 Monitor and review risks: monitor regularly, drawing on what has been learned and feeding this back into the process.

References

Armstrong, M and Cummins, A (2011) *The Reward Management Toolkit*, Kogan Page, London

Association of Insurance and Risk Managers (2002) *A Risk Management Standard*, AIRM, London

CIPD (2009) *Managing Reward Risks: An integrated approach*, CIPD, London

CIPD (2011) *Annual Survey Report: Managing Reward Risks: An integrated approach*, CIPD, London

e-reward (2004) Survey of Grade and Pay Structures, *e-reward* [online] www.e-reward.co.uk [accessed 20 July 2015]

Trevor, J (2011) *Can Pay be Strategic?* Palgrave Macmillan, Basingstoke

32
Responsibility for reward

LEARNING OUTCOMES

On completing this chapter you should know about:

- The role of the reward professional
- The reward role of line managers
- How to use reward consultants

Introduction

Reward strategy is formulated and actioned by people. Top management is in charge and HR professionals, especially reward specialists, are, of course, actively involved. Increasingly, however, it is line managers who have the responsibility for implementing reward policies and practices. This chapter deals with the roles of the reward professional and line managers. The chapter concludes with a brief note on the use of management consultants.

The role of the reward professional

HR and reward specialists develop and implement reward strategies, policies and processes, administer and audit existing systems, and provide advice and guidance to line managers. They deal with employee relations issues such as involvement, communications, negotiations, appeals and grievances.

The key roles for 'high value-adding' reward professionals as described by Brown and Christie (2005) are:

- keeping up with leading-edge thinking and approaches and staying ahead of the game on environmental trends;
- tailoring approaches and arrangements to suit the unique goals, character and culture of the organization, and measuring and demonstrating the value added by them, always in the context of business and organizational knowledge and understanding;
- developing and applying administrative expertise to deliver highly efficient and well-serviced reward processes;
- assessing and influencing the culture of the organization, with responsibility for reward communications;
- operating as an integral part of the HR and business team and providing a reward strategy framework that coordinates all the policies and practices designed to engage and motivate staff to deliver the organization's strategy.

Perhaps the most valuable contribution reward professionals make is to develop reward arrangements that support the business strategy, working with line managers as consultants to assist in this – as one head of reward put it to Brown and Christie: 'shifting our culture to a more performance-oriented business and aligning reward policies accordingly'. Yet research conducted by the CIPD in 2005 found that significant portions of the function's time are still being absorbed in routine administrative activities and responding to immediate queries and crises.

At Citigroup the role of reward specialists is to bring parties together to facilitate and make sustainable and effective decisions, share experiences, transfer successes and encourage a focus on long-term sustainability and future development.

The role of reward in Diageo comprises five key elements:

1 Align the reward approach with the business strategy.
2 Support and enable the talent agenda.
3 Provide clear principles to enable decision making in the business.
4 Enable every employee to understand why they get paid what they get paid.
5 Have a customer service ethic that results in great execution.

Qualities required

Reward specialists need the skills and expertise to design and manage complex systems that meet the needs of users. Strategic thinking is necessary but this is not enough; service delivery is equally important. Reward innovations can affect people deeply and they will resist or at least resent changes that they perceive to be detrimental. It is therefore essential for reward specialists to have change management skills.

The 150 respondents to the 2007 e-reward census of reward professionals stated that the top four qualities required were: (1) business awareness, (2) numeracy and analytical ability, (3) technical reward skills and (4) influencing skills.

The CIPD performance and reward profession map highlights the following competencies required by senior reward professionals:

- understand the organization's strategy, performance goals and drivers;
- speak the language of the business and understand how reward can drive performance;
- know how to translate organization strategy into performance and reward strategies and operating plans;
- consider constituent parts of the reward and recognition package for the organization, ensuring that there is coherence in the overall offer and that it is aligned with and will drive the organization's strategy and plans;
- manage the delivery of planned reward programmes;
- challenge executive leadership to adopt a performance-driven culture underpinned by a strong performance management capability.

Organization of the reward function

The e-reward 2007 census found that 78 per cent of the respondents' organizations had a reward centre of expertise and 40 per cent had a shared service centre.

The role of a reward centre of expertise is to develop and contribute to the implementation of reward strategy, formulate reward policies, provide professional support to business policy for corporate HR, and deal with complex issues raised by the shared service centre if one exists. Its members act as consultants in assessing and designing reward solutions.

The role of a reward shared service centre is to handle some or all day-to-day administrative (transactional) processes. Its activities are centralized into one common unit, often using call centre technology and/or intranet systems for online self-service.

The following are three examples drawn from e-reward 2008 case studies of organizations with centres of expertise and shared service centres:

- Lloyds Banking Group had two centres of expertise, a service delivery function and four dedicated HR sections. The head of pay policy and employee benefits is responsible for external benchmarking, flexible benefits, pay reviews, pay reporting, total reward statements, bonus schemes and reward communications. In addition, there are four reward business partners for each of the main divisions.
- National Australia Bank Group adopted the Ulrich 'three-legged stool' model with a reward centre of expertise and – dealing with all HR matters, including reward – a shared services centre and seven business partners.
- PricewaterhouseCoopers operated a centralized human capital shared services centre alongside a number of centres of expertise, including one dedicated to reward. The role of the three senior managers in the centre is to act as business partners and provide advisory and consultancy services.

Role of line managers

The trend is to devolve more authority to line managers for decisions on pay increases awarded in periodical individual pay reviews and, less commonly, fixing rates of pay on appointment or promotion. This process reflects the general tendency to devolve more decision-making authority to line managers on the grounds that, if managers are to be held accountable for the management of their resources and the performance of their teams, they ought to be given scope within guidelines to determine how their team members should be rewarded. It is also argued that line managers are close to individual employees and are in the best position to know how they should be valued.

The arguments for devolving more authority to line managers for pay decisions are powerful but it is still necessary to ensure that reward policies are followed, pay decisions are consistent and fair, and pay costs are controlled. Policy guidelines as described in Chapter 30 are required to spell out the basis upon which rates of pay are fixed and reviewed. Managers should be expected to keep within their pay budgets.

There is also the issue of the capacity of line managers to carry out their devolved role effectively. As Brown and Purcell (2007) commented: 'How can your reward arrangements ever be effective if your managers can't manage and communicate them?' Their research identified a vicious circle of:

- line managers being given increasing responsibility to manage ever more complex pay processes, with reduced levels of HR function support;
- managers lacking the skills to cope with these increased demands;
- HR therefore not trusting line managers and restricting their discretion in these processes, which leads to managers feeling disempowered and employees not understanding and trusting them either.

Line managers should not be expected to make crucial pay decisions without training in the processes involved and briefing on the policy guidelines. Reward or HR specialists have an important role not only in monitoring the implementation of pay policies but also in providing advice and guidance, always with the aim of developing the skills and confidence of the line managers with whom they are involved. This arrangement should constitute a partnership in which line managers and reward specialists work together on the basis of mutual understanding and trust.

The major difficulties presented by devolving more responsibility to line managers are that:

1 They may not have the knowledge or skills to carry out their responsibilities.

2 They may be unenthusiastic about this aspect of their role, which they would see as a diversion from their real job – 'What's the HR department there for?' they might say.

3 It might be difficult to achieve acceptable standards of fairness, equity and consistency without policing managers so closely that devolution becomes a farce.

The answers to these problems are to develop clear guidelines for managers on the factors they should take into account in making pay decisions, brief and train managers on how to interpret and apply the guidelines, provide continuing but not oppressive support from HR when required and monitor pay decisions to ensure that guidelines are being followed but, again, not oppressively.

Respondents to the 2007 e-reward survey made the following comments on the line manager's role in managing contingent pay schemes:

- ensure managers have bought in to the scheme and are trained in and fully understand its operation;
- make sure managers are willing and able to differentiate high performers from the rest;
- ensure managers can also manage poor performance;
- make certain the messages coming from management and more senior levels are the same and that, overall, decisions made are consistent.

Using reward consultants

Reward consultants are frequently engaged to help with major development projects by providing expertise and additional resources (an extra pair of hands). They can conduct diagnostic reviews and employee attitude surveys, and provide disinterested advice. Effective consultants add credibility and value because they have the knowledge of good practice and project management that may not be available in the organization. The e-reward 2007 survey found that 72 per cent of the respondents had employed them.

To make good use of consultants it is necessary to:

- spell out terms of reference, deliverables and the timetable;
- take great care when selecting them, to ensure that they have the expertise and experience required and will 'fit' into the organization, and that they produce realistic and acceptable indications of the cost of their fees and expenses;
- meet and vet the consultant who is going to carry out the work, not just the senior consultant who presents the proposal;
- agree up front how they will work alongside line management, HR and trade unions, and the basis upon which the project will be monitored and controlled;
- ask for regular reports and hold 'milestone' meetings in order to review progress and costs.

It seems that reward specialists are good at applying these precepts – 97 per cent of the respondents to the e-reward 2007 survey who had used consultants were satisfied with them.

Line managers' responsibility for reward: six tips

1 Devolve as much responsibility for reward decisions to line managers as possible, consistent with the need to ensure that reward policy guidelines are followed and reward decisions are fair and reasonably consistent.

2 Ensure that reward policies and guidelines are clear and unequivocal.

3 Brief managers thoroughly on the policies and guidelines.

4 Train newly appointed managers (and retrain existing managers as necessary) in their reward management responsibilities.

5 Provide guidance and help from HR or reward specialists whenever needed.

6 Monitor reward decisions and advise line managers on alternative approaches as necessary.

References

Brown, D and Christie, P (2005) From Octopus to Sharks: The current and future roles of the rewards professional, *Worldat Work Journal*, second quarter, pp 6–14

Brown, D and Purcell, J (2007) Reward Management: On the line, *Compensation & Benefits Review*, **39**, pp 28–34

CIPD (2005) *Reward Management* Survey, CIPD, London

e-reward (2007) Reward Census, *e-reward* [online] www.e-reward.co.uk [accessed 20 July 2015]

e-reward (2008) Reward Census Case Studies, *e-reward* [online] www.e-reward.co.uk [accessed 20 July 2015]

INDEX

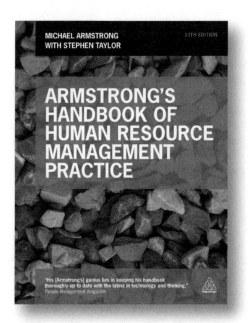

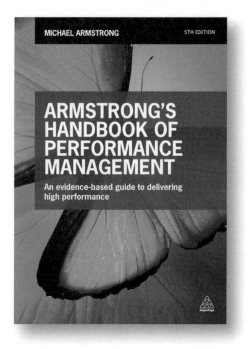